Discover India
by
Rail

REVIEWS – WHAT THEY SAY

- Sandeep Silas, with his experience and his penchant for writing, has done a commendable job. It's a good ready reckoner for foreign as well as domestic tourists.

  THE HINDUSTAN TIMES

- A basic, poetic attempt to introduce each destination. Silas has tried to bring the tourist office home.

  THE TIMES OF INDIA

- Discover India by Rail is a well-researched book, useful for both the backpacker and the comfort traveller. Sandeep Silas takes care of most of your travel anxieties, answering all possible questions that you have.

  INDIAN EXPRESS

- Silas shows the reader just how easy, inexpensive and enriching the discovery of India by rail can be. Silas's book stretches its value beyond the horizon defined by regular travel books.

  THE PIONEER

- It fulfils a great gap in the dedicated traveller's bag. A must for anyone who wishes to discover the country by rail.

  Indiaabroaddaily.com

- Silas is a gifted travel writer. His poetic sensibility and penetrating perception usher in a magical charm into his narration of the places, which he does with unrestrained stream of thoughts, literary and historical details and the haunting secrets behind the places of his depiction.

  INDIAN RAILWAYS

- Exploring India by rail is an experience that one is sure to savour for a long time. And if you are accompanied by a thoroughly informative companion, the pleasure increases manifold. Discover India by rail is such a companion.

  INDIA PERSPECTIVES

- Author Sandeep Silas has captured the essence of what you can do with India's extensive railway network …. Travel wisely and well.

  TODAY'S TRAVELLER

- Discover India by Rail is a view of the country from the windows of a railway carriage.

  LIFE POSITIVE

- The book rekindles the inherent human desire to know one's own land and distant lands in global village. It is a good blend of fact and fiction, combining the hardware of rail transport with the software of travel as a total experience.

  URBAN RAILWAYS

- Discover India by Rail fills a vacuum for the tourist for whom collection of relevant information would be a formidable task.

  DISCOVER INDIA

- This book makes an honest attempt to encapsulate the fascinating geographical diversity of India, the embodiments of its rich cultural legacy and its distinguished historical heritage to the average rail traveller. The book in fact, would revive the romance of rail travel among the psyche of the travel connoisseurs.

  EXPLORE INDIA

Discover India
by
Rail

SANDEEP SILAS

A Sterling Paperback

STERLING PAPERBACKS
An imprint of
Sterling Publishers (P) Ltd.
A-59 Okhla Industrial Area, Phase-II,
New Delhi-110020.
Tel: 6916165, 6916209, 6912677, 6910050
Fax: 91-11-6331241 E-mail: ghai@nde.vsnl.net.in
www.sterlingpublishers.com

Discover India by Rail
©2001, Sandeep Silas (Text)
Satbir Silas (Photographs)
ISBN 81 207 2362 7
First Edition 2001
Revised Edition March 2002

Important Notice
Great care has been taken in the compilation, updating and validation of information and every effort has been made to ensure that all information is as up-to-date as far as possible at the time of going to press. Details like telephone & fax numbers, e-mail addresses, train timings may change. However, the writer and publishers are not responsible for errors if any, and their consequences.

Published by Sterling Publishers Pvt. Ltd., New Delhi-110020.
Printed at Shagun Composer, New Delhi-110029.

DEDICATED

To

My Loving Parents
Dhira & Samuel Silas

CONTENTS

Foreword		xi
Preface		xiii
Tips for Rail Passengers		xv

MOUNTAIN GLORY

1.	Paradise on Earth	Srinagar	3
2.	In the Shadow of Kanchenjunga	Darjeeling	6
3.	Queen of Hills	Mussoorie	9
4.	Snow Queen	Shimla	12
5.	The Bowl of Pleasure	Kullu-Manali	15
6.	Land of Monasteries and Orchids	Sikkim	18
7.	The Jewel Of Kangra	Dharamsala	23
8.	A Starry Retreat	Kodaikanal	25
9.	Trekkers Paradise	Valley of Flowers	27
10.	Switzerland of the East	Imphal	30
11.	Oasis in the Desert	Mount Abu	32
12.	A Diamond in the Blue Hills	Ooty	34
13.	A Clouded Abode	Shillong	37
14.	The Snow Capital	Leh	40
15.	A Virgin Look Hill Station	Dalhousie	43
16.	Moon Country	Kargil	45
17.	In the Shadow of Pirpanjals	Patnitop	47
18.	An Inviting Solitude	Pithoragarh	50
19.	An Orchid by a Waterfall	Aizawl	52
20.	Sunset over the Romantic Woods	Matheran	54
21.	Two Sails and a Yacht	Nainital	56
22.	An Emerald Holiday	Almora	59
23.	Folklore on Muslin	Chamba	62

SEASIDE SOJOURNS

24.	Pearl by the Sea	Goa	66
25.	By the Coral Reefs and Lagoons	Lakshadweep	71
26.	A Fairy Island	Diu	74
27.	The City of Colourful Festivals	Puri	76
28.	India's Biggest Island Lake	Chilika	79
29.	Backwater and Boat Races	Kottayam	81
30.	A Golden Harbour and Fishing Nets	Cochin	84
31.	Sun, Sea and a Lullaby	Trivandrum	88
32.	A Flavour of Portugal	Daman	91
33.	Sea, Rocks and Philosophy	Kanniyakumari	93

ETERNAL CITIES

34.	Eternal City	Delhi	97
35.	Skyscrapers and Silver Screen	Mumbai	102
36.	Imperial City of the Raj	Calcutta	107
37.	Pearl City of India	Hyderabad	111
38.	Home of Dravidian Culture	Chennai	114
39.	Garden City	Bangalore	118
40.	Shan-e-Awadh	Lucknow	122
41.	The City Beautiful	Chandigarh	125
42.	City of Nectar	Madurai	128
43.	City of Victory	Vijayawada	130
44.	Manchester of the East	Kanpur	132
45.	Seat of Ancient Wisdom	Nalanda	134
46.	Home to Mighty Ancient Empires	Patna	136
47.	A Speechless Wonder	Jammu	138
48.	Home of Gandhi	Ahmedabad	141
49.	The Southern Eagle	Tiruchirapalli	144
50.	A Painting on Glass	Thanjavur	146
51.	Gateway to Heaven	Varanasi	149
52.	Buddha's Retreat	Rajgir	152

ROMANCE OF ART

53.	The Land of Erotic Art	Khajuraho	156
54.	The Black Pagoda	Konark	158
55.	Romance of Sculpture and Paintings	Aurangabad, Ajanta and Ellora Caves	160
56.	Epics in Stone	Belur, Shravanabelagola, Halebid	163
57.	Hidden with Sweet Beguile	Tabo	165

JUNGLE SAFARIS

58.	Haven of Tigers	Corbett National Park	169
59.	Wildlife Bonanza	Kanha	171
60.	One-Horned Glory	Kaziranga	174
61.	Elephant Trail	Periyar	176
62.	Tiger Country	Ranthambore	178
63.	Where Birds Sing	Bharatpur	180
64.	Lakes and Tiger Safari	Alwar	182

MYSTICAL EXPERIENCES

65.	The City of Shrines	Amritsar	186
66.	Symbol of Faith	Chitrakoot	189
67.	Spiritual Quest	Puttaparthy	191

68.	In the Lap of Tagore	Shantiniketan	193
69.	Lamp of Enlightenment	Gaya and Bodh Gaya	195
70.	World's First Republic	Vaishali	197
71.	Blessings	Vaishno Devi	199
72.	Temple Towns	Omkareshwar and Maheshwar	202
73.	Pilgrimage Cities	Ajmer and Pushkar	205
74.	Spirituality by the River	Rishikesh	207
75.	Confluence of Mythical and Real Rivers	Allahabad	210
76.	The Home of Kalidasa	Ujjain	213
77.	Ghats and Temples	Mathura	215

FORTS AND PALACES

78.	City of Eternal Love	Agra	220
79.	The Pink City	Jaipur	223
80.	Palaces and Lakes	Udaipur	227
81.	Tales of Grandeur	Jodhpur	230
82.	Golden City of the Desert	Jaisalmer	233
83.	A Silvered Past	Gwalior	235
84.	City of the Nawabs	Bhopal	237
85.	City of Palaces and Birds	Deeg	240
86.	City of Joy	Mandu	242
87.	A Medieval City Frozen in Time	Orchha	244
88.	The Land of Fragrance	Mysore	246
89.	The Unconquerable Fort	Chittorgarh	249

BASKET OF UNUSUALS

90.	A River Island	Majuli	253
91.	In the Neolithic Age	Bhimbetka	255
92.	Romance with a Song	Khandala, Lonavala, Karla	258
93.	Kingdom of Sculpture	Hampi	261
94.	City of the Deccan Dome	Bijapur	263
95.	A Little Bit of France	Pondicherry	265
96.	Nature's Own Habitat	Sunderbans	267
97.	Unfolding a Time Warp	Bhuj (Kutch)	269
98.	Between the Marble Gorge	Jabalpur	272
99.	Seven Days in a Silver Spoon	Royal Orient Express	274
100.	Romance of the Orient	Palace On Wheels	276
	Index		279

FOREWORD

India is one of the most exciting tourism destinations in the world. Perhaps, no other country can give to tourists snow-covered mountains, perennial rivers, a fascinating desert, and golden beaches at the same time in any month of the year. The guest in India has always traditionally been accorded the status of a family member.

India happens to be an exciting blend of tradition and modernity, religion and philosophy, differences and similarities, and a rich culture displaying the best effort of man, be it in the field of painting, sculpture, architecture, literature, or philosophy of life. The Indian Railways criss-cross the sub continent and serve as the arterial system to this great pulsating life force, that is India. Trains bring destinations within one's reach and afford to the visitor a closer look at the beauty that is contained in each region, each destination of India. Responding to the challenge of promoting tourism in India by rail, the Railways have moved consciously towards this dream. Rajdhani and Shatabdi Express trains, which provide comfort to a traveller coupled with speed are a major step in this direction.

I am really very happy that Sandeep Silas, an officer of the Indian Railways, has come out with some suggested itineraries by rail for exploring the beauty and charm that India provides to the tourists. I am sure that "**Discover India by Rail**" would definitely ensure the various Indian tourist destinations coming closer like never before. India would be yours like never before.

Member Traffic
Ministry of Railways
New Delhi

SHANTI NARAIN

PREFACE

Tourism is not just a transitory experience. It is living through the most precious and beautiful moments of life. Tourism is dreams realised. Tourism is the ultimate truth that brings man closer to nature, closer to man, and closer to life.

India undoubtedly is the best tourism experience in the world, as it unfolds before a tourist so many experiences, mystical or real, super-natural, philosophical, religious, artistic, traditional, down-to-earth, and modern. The growth of man right from the times of Indus Valley Civilization to his modern incarnation, as he lived, as he loved, as he celebrated life, is spread on a wide canvas. It was the rich hoary past of kings and sages that has given India astonishingly beautiful buildings, forts, palaces, sculptures, paintings, and streams of religious thought. Hinduism as a way of life grew here, Sikhism as a religious force was born on its soil. Buddhism as a religion originated here from a thought in the mind of a king, and travelled all over the world. Jainism gave India a powerful religious thought. The Christian teachings took root on Indian soil and Christians have contributed admirably to the nation building effort. This huge cauldron of humanity is indeed a unique experience. It has given to the world more than its share.

"Discover India by Rail" is a humble effort to bring to the rail traveller, this strong emotive force that is India. The exotic destinations whether they be in snow-bound territory, by lake side, on the banks of eternal rivers, in lush verdant valleys, by the sea beaches or situated in the thick of jungle extravaganza, are yours for the asking. Care has been taken to describe briefly the destination, capturing its essence, mentioning its places to visit, planning your excursions or treks, choosing the most convenient train journey, and a suitable day of travel in the case of trains which are not running daily, packing days into your tour neither too tight nor too loose, so that you are able to enjoy your trip and your days at the destination. Though the suggested tours take off from major cities, one can travel from anywhere.

I would like to express my sincere thanks to Mr. R. K. Puri, an illustrious senior officer of my service, now placed as Secretary General of the Hotel Association of India, who prompted me to write this book, giving me the confidence that only I could undertake this project. Without his blessings and constant encouragement this book would not have seen the light of day. My wife Dr. Satbir Silas and my sons, Sukrit and Shashwat, have been a source of inspiration to me convincing me that it is the happiness, which is shared that gives one the deepest satisfaction. I would also like to place on record my sincere gratitude to Shri Ashish Trivedi and Shri Ashok Puruthi who toiled in their spare time to put this material on the computer and were of great assistance to me in this endeavour. I am firmly of the view that increased Domestic Tourism is the only solution to many of our problems, the only hope of a strongly united India. Hence, this book underlines my commitment to public service and a happier India.

You only have to decide, flick through the book, choose a destination, board the train, and be there. I do not promise you the moon but definitely an unforgettable experience, some cherished moments, which shall continue to live in your hearts, and in the memory of your young ones, sweetening your lives.

SANDEEP SILAS, IRTS.

Tips for Rail Passengers

The magical railway steam engine has captured the imagination of children and adults alike, and therefore has been celebrated the world over as a symbol of power. Since its invention, travel by train has not only been cost effective but also pleasure giving.

Railway trains became many things to many people as they started criss-crossing the globe– beast of burden for carriage of goods to traders; lifeline of the economy for carriage of essential commodities, food grains, coal, and infrastructure building material like steel to governments; messiah of hope to those afflicted by natural calamities as it brought in water, relief material and medicines; a means to fulfil dreams for pilgrims, relatives; an instrument of pleasure as it brought holiday destinations within easy reach.

To say that railway trains unite a nation's people in a strong social fabric, and serve as the wheels to a nation on the march, would not be exaggeration. **Here are some tips to make your railway journeys pleasurable and most satisfying.**

1. Plan your journey

- You must always plan your journey in advance, as reservation is available 60 days in advance, excluding the date of journey at the train originating station. With computerised reservation on an all India wide network, onward and return reservation for any train from anywhere to anywhere is available at any computer centre.
- If your ticket has an endorsement of RAC, it means that your sitting accommodation is confirmed and berth would be made available on your turn after a cancellation is registered by any other passenger.
- If your ticket is wait listed, you can avail of the Interactive Voice Response System (IVRS) facility for finding out the current status as also the train arrival/departure timings by dialling the IVRS telephone numbers. IVRS numbers for

metropolitan towns are: New Delhi- 1330, 1335: Mumbai–2656565: Calcutta–136, 137, 138: Chennai– 1361, 1362, 1663.

- Tatkal Scheme, which provides a limited number of seats/berths in more than 90 trains at the present, is available at a small premium of Rs. 200/- for AC 2 Tier, Rs. 150/- for AC 3 Tier, Rs. 50/- each for Chair Car and Sleeper Class. Any photo Identity Card like Voter Identity Card, Passport, Driving Licence, Ration Card, and Credit Card is required to be presented at the Tatkal Booking Counter for booking of tickets. Tatkal Booking is available at Reservation Office / Station reservation counter from 8 a.m. onwards one day in advance of the train departure.
- Railways have appointed Railway Tourist Agents, (RTAs) and Rail Traveller's Service Agents (RTSAs) in major cities. You can approach them for getting your tickets booked on payment of prescribed charges. No separate reservation quota has been given to them and they have to send staff to the reservation office for purchasing tickets like any other passenger. They are not supposed to levy any service charge.
- Do not purchase a ticket from a tout or from any person/agency whose credentials are doubtful. Do not travel on confirmed ticket of some other person as this may land you to cough up penalty on train or even face prosecution.
- Some reservation centres also have a credit card booking counter.
- Please fill up a reservation requisition slip with full particulars to avoid last minute realisations. You can book a maximum of six berths for your family on one requisition form.
- Check the break journey rules before booking your tickets as that might be to your advantage (If you hold a journey ticket for more than 500 Kms you can break your journey once for two days at any station en-route. Similarly, if your ticket is for more than 1000 Kms you will be allowed to break your journey twice. Remember to exclude the day of departure and arrival while calculating the number of days eligible for break of

journey. An endorsement on the ticket by the Station Master/ Ticket Collector at the station of break in journey is a must).

- The date of journey on Confirmed/RAC/Wait listed tickets can be advanced or postponed on payment of nominal charges, once only, subject to availability of accommodation. However, for advancement remember to approach up to six hours before scheduled departure, and for postponement up to 24 hours before scheduled departure.
- Should you desire to cover many destinations on one single trip, please avail the facility of Circular Journey Tickets. A maximum of eight break journeys is admissible on these tickets. Some Standard Circular Journey Tickets are also offered for popular tourist circuits.
- For assistance of foreign tourists, International Tourist Bureaus are available which provide personalised service and information to tourists. ITB, New Delhi, Telephone Number 91-11-3734164, 91-11-3346804, FAX: 91-11-3343050.
- Indrail Pass has been specially designed for foreign tourists and is available for a journey of ½ day to 90 days. Indrail passes have to be used within one year of the issue date and the validity begins from the date of the first train journey up to the midnight of the last journey. Indrail passes are also available with GSAs in Bangkok, Dhaka, Durban, Frankfurt, Helsinki, Kuala Lumpur, London, Muscat, New York, Paris, Port Louis, Sharjah, Sydney, Tokyo and Toronto.

2. Feel comfortable on Railway Stations

- The first help you need at a Railway Station is that of a Coolie. These licensed porters are available at station platforms and have fixed rates for carriage of luggage. The rates are usually displayed at prominent places and you must always pay by the notified rates.
- The free allowance of luggage, which a passenger is allowed to carry with him in the compartment, free of cost, is also fixed. If your luggage is in excess of your allowance, please book it at the luggage office.

- Do not carry over size boxes as size is also specified and you may inconvenience co-passengers.
- Catering facilities including refreshment rooms, tea stalls, snack bars, automatic vending machines (beverages) are available at major stations. Rates prescribed by the Railway Administration are supposed to be displayed by each catering unit. Please insist to pay by rate card.
- If you are travelling alone, you can buy a book of your liking from M/s A.H. Wheeler or M/s Higginbotham's bookstall at the railway platform. Newspapers, magazines, comic books for children are also available at these bookstalls.
- In case you have a headache or minor ailment, medicines of common usage, which do not require licence from Drug Controller, are available at the chemist corner of your bookstalls at major stations.
- Indian Railways have standardised signage's for guiding the passengers to the facilities available at each railway station. Please make use of these for avoiding the last minute rush.
- Should you intend to catch a connecting train from the very same station after you have alighted, make use of the waiting room facility, which is separate for ladies and for Upper Classes, and Sleeper Class.
- In case, there is a night halt involved in your break-journey, you can avail of the retiring room facilities at reasonable rates. Booking for these rooms can be availed at the Station Manager's/Janitor/Chief Ticket Inspectors' office.
- The local State Tourist Office might be available in the main concourse of your station for assisting you to a city tour.
- Should you intend to cancel your tickets, you may approach the Booking Office.
- If you have lost your confirmed ticket, please report to the nearest Reservation Office before preparation of the reservation chart. Duplicate ticket will be issued to you on collection of 25% of fare for journey up to 500 Kms, 10% of fare for more than 500 Kms, and 25% of fare for Rajdhani and Shatabdi Trains.

- If you land up with torn/mutilated confirmed / RAC tickets, a duplicate ticket will be issued on collection of the 25% of the fare, after the preparation of reservation chart.
- Should you need some assistance, please feel free to approach the Dy. Station Superintendent/Commercial, to render assistance.
- If you have just remembered something urgent which needs to be conveyed immediately to your office or residence, the Railways have provided STD/ISD/PCO booths at Stations for your convenience.
- Cloak Room facility is provided at each station for keeping your luggage on payment, in case you do not wish to carry it into the city and intend picking it up on your return. Please ensure proper locking.
- In case, a handicapped or ailing relative has to board/alight the train, make use of the wheel chair which is available with the Station Master's office.
- Should you feel harassed at a railway station, record your complaint/suggestion in the complaint book, which is invariably kept in the Station Master's office and the catering refreshment rooms.
- Please make use of the dustbins at a railway platform/premises and do not throw litter on the track or on the platforms.
- Railway Stations have a police outpost manned by Government Railway Police to lodge an FIR and assist you for recovery, in case your baggage has been thieved or your person has been robbed.
- The Railway Protection Force is duty bound to protect Railway property, so please assist them in the discharge of their duties by informing on anything untoward.

3. Enjoy your travel on-board
- In the AC coaches there is an Attendant to supply free of cost bedrolls to passengers around sleeping time. In case, you feel

that the air-conditioning is not proper, please ask the attendant to adjust the AC controls. Should the AC fail, please get a certificate recorded by the Train Superintendent/ Travelling Ticket-Examiner (TTE) to enable you to claim a refund at the destination station on non-provision of this service.

- The AC attendants have a detailed duty list which is available in the coach. It is also their duty to wake up a passenger at his train alighting station in the morning, should it be so requested.
- A first-aid box is available with the Guard/Train Superintendent/Pantry Car Manager for use if so required.
- Should a passenger require immediate Doctor's attention or hospitalisation, please request the Train Superintendent to identify any Doctor travelling in his personal capacity on train and request him to see the patient. Normally the Train Superintendent keeps with him the names of Doctors travelling on train for such emergencies. The train can also be stopped and message conveyed to the next station, which has a Doctor available to attend to the patient.
- Chains are provided below the lower berths to lock your suitcase/attache. You can use this facility and sleep in peace.
- In case water in the toilet or the wash basin is exhausted on a long journey, request the attendant to get it replenished on the next train watering station.
- Smoking is prohibited inside the AC coaches.
- Place your meal preference for vegetarian/non-vegetarian meal in advance with the bearer so that you can enjoy your meal.
- Consumption of liquor on board is an offence.
- You can also request the coach attendant to get the coach or the toilet cleaned, should it be so required.
- Pull the chain only in cases of extreme emergency, example: a companion left on the previous station and train has moved, or noticing any untoward thing on the coach like fire sparks, or attempt to robbery, etc.

- First Information Report (FIR) forms are available with the Guard of the train. Please make use in case of any mishap.
- A complaint/suggestion book is also carried by the Guard/ Train Superintendent/ Pantry Car Manager. You can record your complaint in the book and retain the passenger's copy for record. You can also write to the Additional Divisional Railway Manager of a Railway Division, or Additional General Manager of a Zonal Railway, or Executive Director (Public Grievances), Ministry of Railways, New Delhi.
- Many Shatabdi and Rajdhani trains have also been provided with a pay mobile telephone facility on-board. You can use this facility in an emergency or even before you approach your destination station to call your office/residence for vehicle and any other assistance.
- Shatabdi and Rajdhani trains have the facility of playing music/song cassettes. You can place a request for your choice or desired volume with the attendant.
- Shatabdi trains are being gradually equipped with mini pantry cars in each coach having automatic vending machines for your use.
- The Train timings are as per the latest Indian Railway Time Table enforced from Ist July, 2001. The time table is subject to change.

Wishing you a happy time
at
railway stations and on trains

Mountain Glory

What is there in the quiet presence of Himalayan snow peaks, which draw a person as if magnetised? Is it their magnanimity? Is it their perennial composure? Is it their quality to haunt the human mind and to permeate consciousness levels? Is it their capacity to inspire and bring dreams to the eyes? Is it their colours, which change from dawn to dusk? Or is it the undisturbed disposition and strength of their rugged exterior, perhaps the vision of a godfather, which binds man and mountain. Whatever be the bond, both play the game of smitten and object of desire, day in and day out. There is something so enchanting, and exciting and interesting about a mountain wilderness that it draws you almost like a command. This mysterious call is irresistible to an ordinary human, weakened by a cacophony of city noises.

So if you wish to cleanse your mind of the noises of your own making and let the sweet voices of the wild creep in and soothe the mental waves, come to the mountains. The luxuriant mountains offer an almost unimaginable range of colour through their various folds and creases. Somewhere they glow red with the shrubs and flowers. Somewhere they are virgin white with bushes flowering passionately. The mood is yellow at places where the wild flowers have decided to march up the mountains in congregation. Whether the colours have laid siege to the mountains or the mountains have held the colours captive, the argument is moot, as the effect is devastating.

A morning at mountainside is infinitely enthralling. The senses, dulled by the heavy mountain night open up like a bud on a flowering stalk- tenderly and hesitatingly. The night may have been romantic, but there is no effort to hold it back as the morn is far more captivating. The ears open up before the eyes, to the sweet calls of the wild birds.

Have you ever seen a mountain change its colour? If not, then just sit in the balcony and look at the mountain in front. The rompish rays of the sun falling upon pine bristles seem to robe them in a silvery whiteness. The older pines are a shade of gold, as some of their bristles have aged. This silvery sheen laced with golden hue is so attractive that you want to touch it. Alas, it can't be touched but only seen. Then, there comes a stray cloud before the sun to tell that it is mightier, albeit temporarily. The mountain responds to the cloud and assumes a heart warming green. The soothing effect lasts as long as the cloud so commands.

When your muscles ache to rid themselves of city-bred laziness, take to the mountain trek. Walk amongst the pines on a goat-track, listen to the surprised tweets of winged creatures, watch their flight in amusement, look at slowly crawling snails; discover the dalliance of a family of monkeys, the little ones prancing from branch to branch unmindful of the fall; marvel at how goat and sheep balance their tiny hooves on a precipice, pluck at a tender bush and go to another; sit amongst a host of wildflowers, watch a bird hopping in search of wild strawberries so tiny and attractive; yes, do all that has never been done before. It is assured that the mind will free itself from strain and feel as light as a bird.

With the fast approaching dusk, the mountains are silhouetted against a fading blue of the sky. Lights break forth into a trembling glimmer, in an effort to beat the darkness. Almost each conceivable fold of the mountain sings in a lighted triumph - faint and fairylike. It appears as if a fairy has just flown by, and her veil studded by twinkling stars trails behind. The moon appears hazy, as if a white transparent film is draped upon its shining plate. Its gleam, however, cannot be contained as your joy, which by now has begun oozing like moonshine.

Glory of the Himalayas

1

Paradise on Earth

Cherished by Mughal Kings and Queens, Srinagar was fondly decorated and embellished by them. It is a city, which has grown around the magnificent Dal Lake. By the lake runs the Boulevard road, lights glistening and reflected in the moonlit water. Three exquisite gardens, Chashme Shahi, Nishat, and Shalimar laid by Emperor Jehangir, are the high point in the art of Indian garden laying and its architecture. Terraced, having pavilions, and a water channel flowing along the entire length, running over panels with a cascading effect, spurting through stone fountains, shadowed by stately Chinar trees, these are truly a king's delight. The city has an ancient temple of Shankaracharya, situated on a hill and the modern Hazratbal Shrine. The sight of over a hundred houseboats (guest houses on boats) during the night, reflecting their colours in the softly flowing waves of the lake, is an unparalleled extravaganza.

Places to See: Dal Lake; Char Chinar (floating garden-cum-restaurant on the Dal); Chashme Shahi; Nishat Bagh; Shalimar Bagh; Nehru Guest House; Shankaracharya Temple; Hazratbal Shrine; Lal Chowk bazaar.

Excursions: Wular Lake; Amarnath Caves (140 kms); Pahalgam resort (95 kms); Gulmarg resort and skiing centre; Sonamarg; Avantipur (Stone Temple).

How to Reach: By Air: - Srinagar is an airport.
By Rail / Road:- The nearest railhead is Jammu Tawi where all major mail / express trains come. It is also well connected by road.

Plan your tour by rail

Route: Delhi - 585 kms – Jammu Tawi – 293 kms – Srinagar

Day	Train No./Name	Dep.	Arr.	From	To
One	2403 Jammu Express	2240	-	Delhi	-
Two	Enroute (Travel to Srinagar by bus/taxi/air)	-	0905	-	Jammu
Three/Four/Five	Stay and visit Srinagar and environs. (Travel to Jammu by bus/taxi/air on sixth day)				
Six	2404 Jammu Express	1800	-	Jammu	-
Seven	Enroute	-	0420	-	Delhi

Where to Stay: Tel. Code: 0194
Hotels: 5 Star

Centaur (475631-33) Fax: 471877 Website: www.fhrai.com
Broadway (459001) Fax: 458996 Website: www.fhrai.com
Meena Bazaar Group of Houseboats (474044, 454241)
Fax: 477662 Website: www.fhrai.com, http://travel.vsnl.com/
meena E-mail: aamir33@nde.vsnl.net.in

Budget

Metro (477126)
Ahdoo's (472593) Fax 455251 Website: www.fhrai.com
E-mail: http:/www/kashig.com/ahdoos.htm
Zabarvan (471441, 471442)
Shah Abbas (479334, 479861)
Madhuban (453800)
Welcome (479553)
The Grand Palace (470101, 456701).

Srinagar has many houseboats on the Dal Lake, and other budget hotels. For more information contact J & K Govt. Tourist Reception Centre: 452690-91.

Best Season: March - October

Clothing: Summer-Woollen, Winter-Heavy woollen.

2

In the Shadow of Kanchenjunga

DARJEELING

Ex-Calcutta

*A*n exotic hill station, Darjeeling lies on the spur projecting north-wards from the Ghoom- Senchal Ridge. An enchanting Himalayan hill resort, it gives majestic views of Himalayan peaks, lorded over by Mountain Kanchenjunga. The mountain changes colour from dawn to dusk. At Darjeeling, 6812 feet above sea-level, there is nothing between Kanchenjunga and you. The pale pink slashes and delicate brushes of sunlit gold on the white lofty peak deluge a visitor entirely. By the moonlit night, it becomes a gorgeous silvery white . The pines, ferns, white magnolias and red rhododendrons welcome visitors to Darjeeling. Go, pick wild flowers in the luxurious surroundings or just listen quietly to the coppersmith birds' note. There are around four hundred varieties of butterflies in this region and a tourist can virtually accost colours flying in the air. It also boasts of the Darjeeling Himalayan Railway, which finds mention in Mark Twain's writings and is now a World Heritage Site.

Places to See: Batasia Loop; Tiger Hill; Himalayan Mountaineering Institute; Observatory Hill; Tea estates; Padmaja Naidu Himalayan Zoological Park; Lebong Race Course, (smallest race course in the world); Shanti Stupa; Lloyd Gardens; Samtencholing and Bhutia Basti monasteries.

How to Reach: By Air:- The nearest airport to Darjeeling is Bagdogra.

By Rail / Road:- Darjeeling is well connected to Calcutta. The nearest major railhead is New Jalpaiguri (88 kms) from where a very romantic railway journey begins. The train goes up to Ghoom, 7407 ft. and then comes down to Darjeeling, crossing on its way the Batasia Loop, an engineering marvel. It is also well connected by road.

Plan your tour by rail

Route: Calcutta - 586 kms - New Jalpaiguri - 88 kms - Darjeeling

Day	Train No./Name	Dep.	Arr.	From	To
One	5959 Kamrup Exp.	1525	-	Howrah	-
Two	Enroute	-	0530	-	New Jalpaiguri
	1 D Passenger	0900	1530	New Jalpaiguri	Darjeeling
Three/Four	Stay and visit Darjeeling				
Five	Travel back to New Jalpaiguri and reach before 16.30 hrs by road.				
	5960 Kamrup Exp.	1645	-	New Jalpaiguri	-
Six	Enroute	-	0630	-	Howrah

Where to Stay: Tel. Code- 0354

Hotels: 3 Star

New Elgin (54114), Fax: 544267 Website: www.fhrai.com
E-mail: newellin@cal.vsnl.net.in
Mohit (54723), **Sinclairs** (56431) Fax: 54351, 54706
Website: www.fhrai.com, http://www.fhraindia.com/hotel/darjeeling/mohit E-mail: mohit@dte.vsnl.net.in

2 Star

Garuda (56110), Fax: 56110 Website: www.fhrai.com
Seven Seventeen (55099) Fax: 54717 Website: www.fhrai.com, darjnet.com E-mail: tashi@cal.vsnl.net.in

Budget

Apsara (52983) Fax: 54484 Website: www.fhrai.com
Shambhu (54926) Website: www.fhrai.com, http://fhraindia.com/hotel/darjeeling/shambhu
Lunar (54194) Website: www.fhrai.com
Sun Flower (52052) Fax: 54390 Website: www.fhrai.com
Pineridge (54074) Website: www.fhrai.com
E-mail: pineriga@dte.vsnl.net.ae
Central Executive (56049) Fax: 52647 Website: www.fhrai.com

Heritage Hotels

Windamere (54041/42/44) Fax: 54043, 54211
Website: www.fhrai.com
E-mail: windmere@cal.vsnl.net.in
Fortune Central (56047) Fax: 56048 Website: www.fhrai.com
WBTDC Lodges: Tourist Lodge (54411-2), Maple (54413) and Tiger Hill

Best Season: April to mid-June and mid-Sept. to November.

Clothing: Winter- Heavy woollen, Summer- Light woollen.

3

Queen of Hills

MUSSOORIE
Ex- New Delhi

*M*ussoorie is famous as the Queen of Hills in India. The hill station was discovered and the first house was built in 1823 by Capt. Young and Mr. F.J.Shore. It found popularity amongst Princes of the erstwhile Indian states. Mussoorie still retains most of the old buildings and palaces. The view of the Himalayas from here is gorgeous. The place has been immortalised by Sir George Everest, who as the first Surveyor General of India established his Survey Office here. It retains a thick forest cover and avian life in Landour and Hathipaon area. The walks amidst deodars and mist in a salubrious weather are plentiful. Amongst the young it is popular for its skating rink where one can dance on moving wheels. The environs of Mussoorie closely visited, reveal a passionate saga of love, life, ambition and grandeur. The dancing floors, dressing rooms, yellowed pictures, creeper entwined glass windows, summer benches, fruit-bearing trees, sharp precipices, jungle paths and bowers for lovers— all speak a language understood by a caring visitor.

Places to See: Mussoorie Lake; Municipal Garden; The Rink; LBS National Academy of Administration; Library; Old Churches; Old Palaces and British Buildings; Tibetan Temple; Kempty Falls; Cloud's End; View of snow-covered Himalayas; Gun Hill; Camel's Back; Landour; Lal Tibba.

Excursions:

1. **Dehradun:** Rajaji Sanctuary; Indian Military Academy; Forest Research Institute; Sahastradhara water body.
2. **Dhanolti:** A quiet hamlet near Mussoorie to experience peace and solitude.

How to Reach:

By Rail / Road:- Mussoorie is well connected by both rail and road via Dehradun.

Plan your tour by rail

Route: New Delhi - 399 kms - Dehradun - 36 kms - Mussoorie

Day	Train No./Name	Dep.	Arr.	From	To
One	2017 Shatabdi Exp.	0700	1240	New Delhi	Dehradun
	By bus / taxi to Mussoorie				
Two/Three	Stay and Visit Mussoorie.				
Four	Travel back to Dehradun by bus/taxi				
Four	2018 Shatabdi Exp.	1700	2240	Dehradun	New Delhi

Where to Stay: Tel. Code- 0135
Hotels: 5 Star

Jaypee Residency Manor (631800) Fax: 631022, 631023
Website: www.fhrai.com, http://www.jaypeehotels.com
E-mail: jhl@nde.vsnl.net.in

Heritage
Savoy (632120) Website: www.fhrai.com
Clouds End

3 Star
Solitaire Plaza (632164) Fax: 631930 - 632147
Website: www.fhrai.com

2 Star
Filigree (632380) Fax: 631380 Website: www.fhrai.com,
http://www.mussoorie.com/filigree.html
E-mail: mustimes@nde.vsnl.net.in

Shiva Continental (632174) Fax: 632780
Website: www.fhrai.com

Budget
Dunsvirk Court (631043), Fax: 631669
Website: www.fhrai.com,
Fhraindia.com/hotel/mussoorie/dunsirk
E-mail: ashwanik@ndb.vsnl.net.in
Country Inn (631196), Fax: 631194 Website: www.fhrai.com
Shipra (632494), Fax: 632941 Website: www.fhrai.com
Fort Resort (631611), Fax: 631611 Website: www.fhrai.com,
www.clubmahindra.com E-mail: mustimes@ndse.vsnl.net.in
Padmini Niwas (631093), Fax: 632793 Website: www.fhrai.com
http://www.come.to/padminivas
E-mail: harshada@nde.vsnl.net.in
Classic Heights 632514), Website: www.fhrai.com
E-mail: Classicheights@hotmail.com
Kasmanda Lodge (632424) Fax: 630007
Website: www.fhrai.com E-mail: kasmanda@vsnl.com
Connaught Castle (632210), Fax: 632538
Website: www.fhrai.com
Western (632249), Fax: 632249 Website: www.fhrai.com
Pearl (631045), Fax: 631450 Website: www.fhrai.com
Great Value (631442) Fax: 631442 Website: www.fhrai.com
E-mail: gvhotel@nde.vsnl.net.in

Uttar Pradesh Tourism Development Corporation also provides
good accommodation.

Best Season: March to October.

Clothing: Summer- Light woollen, Winter- Heavy woollen.

Snow Queen

SHIMLA
Ex-New Delhi

Shimla was the summer capital of Imperial India. Today as the capital of Himachal Pradesh, it still retains much of its old charm and colonial buildings in a variety of architectural styles. Set in an English weather, Shimla and its environs retain the best of natural beauty. Lush green forests around the town, apple orchards, and a view of the snow-capped mountains please a visitor like nothing else. Walks in the area of Annadale can be truly inspiring. You establish that wonderful connection with Nature as you trek here. Even in winters, when the blanket of snow covers everything and the pines are laden with snow, Shimla attracts tourists to come and unburden themselves. The town of Shimla forms a well-connected tourist circuit with excellent accommodation facilities developed by HPTDC.

Places to See:
Ridge; Skating Rink; Lakkad Bazaar; Jakhu Hill; Annadale; Imperial Buildings; Christ Church.

Walks:
The Glen; Summer Hill; Prospect Hill; Chadwick Falls.

Excursions:
Wildflower Hall; Fagu; Kufri; Naldehra; Mashobra; Chail.

How to Reach:
By Air:- Shimla is well connected by air. The nearest airport-Chandigarh.
By Rail / Road: - Shimla is well connected by both rail and road.

Plan your tour by rail

Route: New Delhi - 240 kms - Chandigarh - 120 kms - Shimla

Day	Train No./Name	Dep.	Arr.	From	To
One	2011 Shatabdi Exp. By bus/taxi to Shimla.	0740	1100	New Delhi	Chandigarh
Two /Three/Four	Stay and visit Shimla, (Travel back to Kalka by narrow gauge train from Shimla).				
Four	2312 Kalka Mail	2345	-	Kalka	-
Five	Enroute	-	0625	-	Delhi

Where to Stay: Tel. Code- 0177

Hotels: 5 Star

Shilon Resorts (483343-44) Fax: 483362
Website: www.fhrai.com, www.shilonresorts.com
E-mail: shilon@satyam.net.in
The Cecil (204848) Fax: 211024 Website: www.fhrai.com

Heritage

Woodville Palace Resorts (223919) Fax: 223098
Website: www.welcomheritage.com
E-mail: welcome@ndf.vsnl.net.in
Springfields (221297) Fax: 221297, 221298
Website: www.fhrai.com, www.ushashriramhotels.com
E-mail: springfields@vsnl.com

4 Star

The Oberoi Clarkes (251010-15) Fax: 211321
Website: www.fhrai.com E-mail: clarkes@nde.vsnl.net.in
Asia The Dawn (231162-65) Fax: 231007
Website: www.fhrai.com, www.asiadawn.com
E-mail: asiadawn@nde.vsnl.net.in

3 Star

Himland East (222901-904) Fax: 224241
Website: www.fhrai.com, www.himlandeast.com
E-mail: himaland@nde.vsnl.net.in

Honeymoon Inn (224868) Fax: 225880
Website: www.fhrai.com E-mail: honeyinn@nda.vsnl.net.in
Toshali Royal View (483384) Fax: 483301
Website: www.fhrai.com E-mail: toshali@nde.vsnl.net.in

1 Star
Marina (206148) Fax: 25225 Website: www.fhrai.com

Budget
East Bourne Resorts (224975) Fax: 223890
Website: www.fhrai.com, http://www.eastbourneindia.com
E-mail: ebourne@vsnl.com
Gulmarg (253168) Fax: 252380
Website: www.fhrai.com E-mail: gulmarg@nde.vsnl.net.in
Baljees Regency (214054-59) Fax: 252202
Website: www.fhrai.com
E-mail: baljees@nde.vsnl.net.in
Amber (254774) Fax: 258746 Website: www.fhrai.com
E-mail: hotelamber@vsnl.com
Crystal Palace (257588) Fax: 202634
Website: www.fhrai.com, www.hotelcrystalpalace.com
E-mail: hcp@nde.vsnl.net.in
Harsha (258441) Fax: 212868 Website: www.fhrai.com
Daziel (252394) Website: www.fhrai.com
E-mail: dalziel@nde.vsnl.net.in
Surya (201979) Fax: 201979, 258192 Website: www.fhrai.com
E-mail: suryahtl@nde.vsnl.net.in
Sangeet (202506) Fax: 255823
Website: www.fhrai.com
Pineview (257045) Fax: 201427 Website: www.fhrai.com
Shingar (258481), Fax: 252998 Website: www.fhrai.com
E-mail: shingar@nde.vsnl.net.in and many other budget hotels.

Best Season: March to October.

Clothing: Summer- Light woollen, Winter- Heavy woollen.

5

The Bowl of Pleasure

KULLU-MANALI
Ex-New Delhi

The beauty of the Kullu valley is enhanced by its people who delight in song and dance, and celebrate life in its living. Kullu is well known for its colourful Dussehra (in October). The town of Kullu has long been a centre of faith. In the 17th century, Raja Jagat Singh installed here an idol of Lord Raghunathji, which he brought from Ayodhya. The King and his successors regarded themselves as mere regents of Lord Raghunathji, whose temple is of great importance. The lush green valleys of Kullu are a treat to the eye and the soul.

Places to See: Raghunathji Temple; Vaishno Devi Temple; Jagannathi Devi Temple; Bijli Mahadev Temple; Mahadev Temple; Trijugi Narayan Temple.

Other Places: Parashar Lake; Kaisdhara; Raison Meadow; Katrain; Naggar; Malana Valley; Manikaran.

Manali: A jewel in the crown, Manali is an idyllic town north of Kullu at an altitude of 6000 ft. It is a prime tourist destination of Himachal Pradesh and reveals the valley at its best. According to legend, it is believed that when the world was deluged with rain and all that was land was covered by water, Manu first stepped off his celestial boat at Manali (Manu Alya; the home of Manu) and it is here that the human race once again came into being. Close by, between Kullu and Manali is Naggar, the abode of Roerich's. The world famous Roerich Himalayas were painted here. The Roerich house is a silent memorial to the beauty of the mountains and of Roerich's heart.

Places to See: Manikaran Gurudwara, (natural hot water spring inside the Gurudwara premises); Ram Mandir; Hadimba Temple; Manu Maharishi Temple; Vashisht Village; Jagatsukh; Bhrigu Lake; Solang Point; Beas Kund; Pulga and Khirganga; Rahla Falls; Prini.

Adventure activity: Rafting (April to June); Trekking- Several treks are available to trekkers around Manali; Heli-Skiing (month of Feb.); Rock climbing; Mountaineering.

How to Reach: By Air: - The nearest airport is Bhuntar in the Kullu Valley.
By Rail / Road:- The nearest convenient railhead is Chandigarh, and the road is good.

Plan your tour by rail and road

Route: New Delhi - 565 kms - Kullu-Manali (via Chandigarh)

Day	Train No./Name	Dep.	Arr.	From	To
One	2011 Shatabdi Exp. By bus/taxi to Kullu	0740	1100	New Delhi	Chandigarh
Two/Three	Stay and visit Kullu.				
Four/Five/Six	Stay at Manali and Travel back to Chandigarh				
Seven	2006 Shatabdi Exp.	0650	1000	Chandigarh	New Delhi

Where to Stay: Tel. Code- 01902

At Kullu: 4 Star
Apple Valley Resorts (66266-71) Fax: 24116 Website: www.fhrai.com

Budget
Vaishali (4225-26) Fax: 3073 Website: www.fhrai.com
Span Resorts (40138, 40538)

Silver Moon (22488)
Sarvari (22471)
Anglers Bungalow
Amit (65123, 65500)
Sunbeam (65790)
Empire (23397, 22559), and others.

At Manali: 3 Star
Manali Ashok (53103-9), Fax: 53108, 53109
Website: www.fhrai.com
Out Town (52375), Fax: 52131 Website: www.fhrai.com
Holiday Inn.

Budget
Ambassador (52235), Fax: 52173
Conifer (52434), Fax: 52434 Website: www.fhrai.com
Banon Resorts (52490), Fax: 52378 Website: www.fhrai.com
De Vivendi Resorts (52792), Fax: 53117
Website: www.fhrai.com
Manu Deluxe (52893), Fax: 011-3329824 (Delhi)
Website: www.fhrai.com
Manali Inn (53550-54), Fax: 52582 Website: www.fhrai.com
Sagar Resorts (52551), Fax: 5255 Website: www.fhrai.com
Shingar Regency (52251), Fax: 52253 Website: www.fhrai.com
Sterling Himalayan Continental (53011), Fax: 52494
Website: www.fhrai.com
Beas, HPTDC (52832),
Kunzam, HPTDC (53197-98),
Hadimba Cottage, HPTDC (52334),
Rohtang-Manalsu, HPTDC (52332, 53723), and many other
budget hotels. Manikaran Gurudwara also provides
accommodation for night stay.

Best Season: Throughout the year.

Clothing: Summer- Light woollen, Winter- Heavy woollen.

6

Land of Monasteries and Orchids

SIKKIM

Ex- Calcutta

The best kept secret in the Himalayas is nestled between Nepal, China, Bhutan, and West Bengal. Sikkim is a land of extraordinary beauty - soaring mountains, plunging rivers and lush tropical forests, brilliant with a profusion of vivid flowers, birds and butterflies. It is decorated with verdant terraced hillsides, simple stilted villages and colourful monasteries. Sikkim is a land of abundance, beauty and adventure. Whether your passion is long treks or short walks in an ever-changing landscape; white-water rafting, or mountaineering amongst the world's highest peaks, Sikkim is the destination.

Places to See:

West Sikkim:

Pemayangtse Monastery: Is one of the oldest monasteries. Originally, it was established as a high-class monastery for "Pune Monks" Ta Sang.

Rabdentse Ruins: This was the second capital of the erstwhile Kingdom of Sikkim after Yuksom and till the year 1814 AD, the King of Sikkim had ruled the State from this place.

Pelling: Situated at an altitude of 6800 ft., it offers a good view of the entire mountain ranges.

Sangacholing Monastery: Built in 1697 AD, it is considered to be one of the oldest monasteries in the State.

18

Khecheopalri Lake: Khecheopalri Lake is considered to be one of the sacred lakes of this State, both by Buddhists and Hindus.

Yuksom: This was the first capital of Sikkim.

Dubdi Monastery: This was the first monastery established soon after the consecration ceremony of the first Chogyal.

Tashiding Monastery: This monastery is constructed on top of a heart-shaped hill with sacred Mt.Khangchendzonga as a flaming backdrop.

South Sikkim:

Namchi: It is about 78 kms. from Gangtok and 100 kms. from Siliguri. Namchi, meaning sky high, nestles among the hills at an elevation of 5500 ft., commanding a panoramic view of the snow-capped mountains and vast stretches of valley.

Tendong Hill: Historically, this has been a place of recluse for Buddhist Lamas who spent years in meditation amidst the silent scenic grandeur.

Temi Tea Garden: The one and the only Tea Estate existing in the state produces one of the top quality teas for the international market.

Borong: A picturesque village with beautiful landscape and magnificent view is also host to the hot-spring "Borong Tsa-Chu".

Other Places: Ravangla; Manam Hill; Versey.

East Sikkim:

Enchey Monastery: This 200-year-old monastery has in its premises images of gods, goddesses and other religious objects- 3 kms from Gangtok town.

Sikkim Research Institute of Tibetology (SRIT): The most prestigious of its kind in India-this Buddhist Institute is a treasure trove of a vast collection of rare Lepcha, Tibetan and Sanskrit manuscripts, statues and rare *thankas* (tapestries used in Buddhist liturgy) and has over 200 Buddhist icons and other prized objects of art. Today, it is a renowned worldwide centre for study of Buddhist philosophy and religion.

Tsomgo Lake: It is literally known as the "Source of the Lake" in the Bhutia language. The lake is about 1 km long, oval in shape, 15 metres deep, and is considered sacred by the local people. This placid lake remains frozen during the winter months up to mid-May.

Fambong La Wildlife Sanctuary: 25 kms from Gangtok and has an area of 51.76 sq.km. The sanctuary is home to a large number of wild orchids, rhododendrons, etc. The best season is October and April.

Other Places: Do-Drul Chorten (Stupa); Sikkim Time Corporation Ltd.; Saramsa Garden; Rumtek Dharma Chakra Centre; Water Garden; Tashi View Point; Ganesh Tok; Hanuman Tok; Sa-Ngor-Chotshog Centre.

North Sikkim:

Kabi Lungchok: This is where the historic treaty of blood brotherhood between the Lepcha Chief Te-kung Tek and the Bhutia Chief Khey-Bum-Sar was signed ritually.

Phensong Monastery: The place is situated on the gentle slope stretching from Kabi to Phodong with perhaps one of the best landscapes in the region.

Phodong Monastery: One of the six major monasteries in Sikkim.

Singhik: The place offers one of the most spectacular views of Mt.Khangchendzonga and its ranges.

Chungthang: The valley is believed to have been blessed by Guru Rimpoche and one can visit the Holy Guru Lhedo to see the foot and palm prints left behind by the patron saint.

Yumthang: Yumthang, at an elevation of 11,800 ft., and 140 kms. from Gangtok, is a paradise for nature lovers with a fascinating blend of flora and fauna and breathtaking scenic grandeur. It is also home for Shingbha Rhododendron Sanctuary with 24 species of rhododendrons.

How to Reach:
By Air:- The nearest airport is Bagdogra (124 kms) in North Bengal.

By Rail / Road:- The two closest railway stations are Siliguri (114 kms) and New Jalpaiguri (125 kms) connecting Gangtok with Howrah and New Delhi. It is also well connected by road.

Plan your tour by rail

Route: Calcutta - 586 kms - New Jalpaiguri - 125 kms - Sikkim

Day	Train No./Name	Dep.	Arr.	From	To
One	5959 Kamrup Exp.	1525	-	Howrah	-
Two	Enroute	-	0530	-	New Jalpaiguri
	By bus or taxi to Gangtok				
Three/Four /Five	Stay at Gangtok and visit Sikkim				
Six	By bus or taxi to New Jalpaiguri before 16.30 hrs. .				
Six	5960 Kamrup Exp.	1645	-	New Jalpaiguri	-
Seven	Enroute	-	0630	-	Howrah

Where to Stay: Tel. Code- 03592
Hotels: 4 Star
Tashi Delek (22991, 22038)
Central (22105, 22553)

3 Star
Tibet (22523, 23468)

Budget
Denzong Inn (22692)
Mayur, Norkhill (23186, 25639)
Siniolchu Lodge (22074)
Mt. Pandim, Zamden (24997)
Windsor (24286)
Green (23354)
Orchid (23151)
Soyang (22331)

Norbugang (23537, 22237), and many other budget hotels, which provide AC and non-AC accommodation with comfortable facilities.

Best Season: March to late May and Oct. to mid-December.

Clothing: Summer-Light woollen, Winter-Heavy woollen.

7

The Jewel of Kangra

DHARAMSALA
Ex-Delhi

*A*s the name suggests, it is the abode of gods. Situated in Kangra, one of the most charming valleys, it entices with its green meadows and gushing streams. In the backdrop are the sprawling Dhauladhars with their snow-capped granite. The lower town is located on a ridge and is the hubbub. The upper town, McLeodganj, is the headquarters of the Dalai Lama. The spirit of Tibetan people is reflected in fine carvings on metal and wood and motifs woven on cloth. Kangra Valley is home to the Pahari school of painting, which flourished during the reign of Raja Sansar Chand (1774-1823). Dharamsala is a place where the trees speak the language of love and where birds sing the songs of happiness.

Places to See: McLeodganj; Church of St. John in the wilderness (Lord Elgin, former Viceroy of India, is buried in the churchyard); Kangra Museum of Art; Triund; Chinmaya Tapovan; Bhagsunath waterfall; Tatwani Hot Springs; Machhrial waterfall; Norbulingka Tibetan Ashram.

Excursions: Temple of Bajreshwari Devi; Jwalamukhi Temple (56 kms); Nadaun Palace (65 kms); Palampur (52 kms); Andretta (63 kms Museum of Sobha Singh's paintings); Bir and Billing (87 kms Para gliding site); Baijnath (68 kms, ninth century temple, one of the twelve *jyotirlingas*).

How to Reach: By Air:– The nearest airport is Kangra 12 kms. By Rail / Road:- Nearest broad gauge railhead is Pathankot. All major mail and express trains stop at Pathankot. From Pathankot to Dharamsala travel by bus / taxi (90 kms) or take the connecting Kangra Valley narrow gauge train to Palampur railway station.

Plan your tour by rail

Route: Delhi - 484 kms - Pathankot - 90 kms - Dharamsala

Day	Train No./Name	Dep.	Arr.	From	To
One	4033 Jammu Mail .	2110	-	Delhi	-
Two	Enroute	-	0755	-	Pathankot
	By bus/taxi or train to location of choice.				
Three /Four/Five	Stay and visit Dharamsala & environs of Kangra				
	(Travel back to Pathankot before 18.00 hrs.)				
Five	4034 Jammu Mail	1840	-	Pathankot	-
Six	Enroute	-	0555	-	Delhi

Where to Stay: **Tel. Code- 01892**
Hotels: Budget
Dhauladhar, HPTDC (24926-27)
Bhagsu, HPTDC (23191-92)
Kashmir House, Yatri Niwas, HPTDC (23163)
Surya Resorts (21418-20)
Him Queen (21861)
Chinar (21767, 21327)
Tibet (21587, 21426)
Clouds End Villa (22109, 24904), and many other budget hotels in and around the place.

Best Season: March – October

Clothing: Summer- Light woollen, Winter- Woollen.

8

A Starry Retreat

KODAIKANAL

Ex-Chennai

Kodaikanal was first explored by Rev. H.S. Taylor and Rev.C.P. Muzzey in January 1845. The Pallani hills thereafter gained prominence and popularity. A healthy refreshing environment set amidst the Western Ghats and its plateau, streams, shola forests, an unpolluted lake, the unique flora and a cool climate, makes it an enviable retreat. The lake is shaped like a star and melts into the picturesque bank. Boating in the lake, romancing the waves, can become a thrilling experience. The promenade of the lake is 5 kms long and the sight is almost thrilling. There are numerous walks and trekking routes amidst blue gum, wattle pine, pear trees, and coffee plantations. Waterfalls, discovered as you walk are unparalleled in beauty and magnificence.

Places to See: Kodaikanal Lake; Byrant Park; Solar Physical Observatory; Coakers Walk; Kurinji Andavar Temple; Telescope; Pillar Rocks; Bear Shola Falls; Shenbaganur Museum.

Trekking Routes: Periyakulam- Adukkam- Kodaikanal (18 kms, 7 hrs); Periyakulam- Kumbakarai- Shenbaganur- Kodaikanal (27 kms, 7 hrs); Kumbakarai - Vellagavi- Kodaikanal (8 kms, 5 hrs.); Palani- Vilankombai R.E.- Ganguvar Odai Vilpatti – Kodaikanal (16 kms, 7 hrs); Kodaikanal- Berijam (23 kms, 5 hrs).

How to Reach: By Air:– Madurai is the nearest airport (120 kms).

By Rail / Road:– Kodaikanal Road is the railhead and Kodaikanal is well connected by road.

Plan your tour by rail

Route: Chennai - 562 kms – Kodaikanal

Day	Train No./Name	Dep.	Arr.	From	To
One	6717 Pandiyan Express	2100	-	Chennai Egmore	-
Two	Enroute	-	0520	-	Kodaikanal Road
Two /Three/Four	Stay and visit Kodaikanal				
Four	6718 Pandiyan Express	2105	-	Kodaikanal Road	-
Five	Enroute	-	0605	-	Chennai Egmore

Where to Stay: Tel. Code- 04542

Hotels: 5 Star
The Carlton (40056, 40071) Fax: 41170
Website: www.fhrai.com E-mail: carlton@md3.vsnl.net.in

3 Star
Sterling Holiday Resorts (40313-15) Fax: 41065, 40637
Website: www.fhrai.com

2 Star
Kodai Int'l. (40649, 40767) Fax: 40759 Website: www.fhrai.com
E-mail: velu.36@hotmail.com

Budget
Hilltop Towers (40413, 42253) Fax: 40415
Website: www.fhrai.com
Jewel (41029) Fax: 40518 Website: www.fhrai.com
E-mail: glentravels@vsnl.com
J'S Heritage (41323) Fax: 40693 Website: www.fhrai.com
Sornam (40562) Website: www.fhrai.com
Astoria (40524-6)
Tamil Nadu (41336-39), and other budget hotels.

Best Season: Throughout the year.

Clothing: Summer-Light tropical, Winter-Light woollen.

9

Trekkers Paradise

VALLEY OF FLOWERS - HEMKUND SAHIB- BADRINATH-KEDARNATH-GANGOTRI-YAMNOTRI

Ex-Delhi

Valley of Flowers: Sprawling in the lap of the Himalayas is a beautiful valley full of thousands of species of endangered flowers. It is a botanist's delight to roam and collect leaves and petals. A poet or a painter is at his best in such sylvan surroundings.

Hemkund Sahib: A beautiful lake nestling between seven snow-covered peaks, holding bluish –green water was discovered in 1930 by Hawaldar Sohan Singh. The lake is identified with the life of Sikh Guru Gobind Singh who in one of his previous births is reputed to have meditated on the shores of such a lake.

Badrinath: Set amongst rugged mountains, which turn into soft curves with snow, Badrinath is a place of pilgrimage for Hindus. This was established in the 9th century by Shankaracharya.

Kedarnath: Kedarnath is an ancient temple dedicated to Lord Shiva and as per legend, the Pandavas of the epic *Mahabharata* underwent a penance to atone the killing of their kith and kin in the battle of Kurukshetra. This shrine has one of the twelve *jyotirlingas* of Lord Shiva. A beautiful snow peak forms a royal backdrop to the temple.

Gangotri and Yamnotri: Gangotri is the source of the eternal river Ganga. Mythology reveals that the Ganga came down to earth as a result of penance by King Bhagirath. Ganga is worshipped as a river and is believed to wash away the sins of human beings if they take a holy dip. The Yamnotri is the source of the river Yamuna, which flows alongside the Ganga till it merges into the Sangam at Allahabad.

Places to See enroute: Badrinath Temple; Taptkund, Suryakund; Narad Kund; Mata Murti Mandir Temple; Kedarnath Temple, Shankaracharya's Samadhi near Kedarnath Temple; Bhairon Nath Temple; Gandhi Sarovar; Vasuki Tal; Gangotri Temple; Jalmagn Shivlinga; Gauri Kund; Kedarganga Sangam; Deoghat; Temple of Yamuna.

Sightseeing enroute: Narendra Nagar; Tehri; Dharasu; Uttar Kashi; Lanka; Bhairon Ghati; Son Prayag; Garur Ganga; Joshi Math; Chamoli; Chopta; Hanuman Ghati; and many other places.

Festivals: Badrinath-Kedarnath Festival in the month of June, Janamashtmi in July/August, and Festival of Mata Murti in the month of Sept. The opening and closing ceremonies of Pat (doors) of the temples in May and November respectively.

Treks: In the valley of Gangotri and Bhagirathi, many trekking routes are available for the trekkers. One of the known trekking routes is Dodi Tal. It is about 3024 metres above sea level.

Mountaineering: One can enjoy the challenging mountains while mountaineering in these valleys.

Some important distances:
1. Delhi to Badrinath via Haridwar, Rishikesh, Dev Prayag 528 kms.
2. Delhi to Kedarnath via Haridwar, Rishikesh, Dev Prayag, Srinagar- 450 kms or via Rudra Prayag- 438 kms.
3. Delhi to Gangotri via Haridwar, Rishikesh, Chamba, Dharasu- 481 kms.

4. Delhi to Yamnotri via Rishikesh, Narendranagar, Chamba-456 kms.
5. **Straight excursions, FROM Haridwar:**
   a) Haridwar to Yamnotri - 258 kms.
   b) Haridwar to Gangotri - 272 kms.
   c) Haridwar to Badrinath - 324 kms.
   d) Haridwar to Kedarnath - 251 kms.

How to Reach:

According to the religious legend, the journey to the four *dhams* should be started from Haridwar and one should first go to Yamnotri, Gangotri, Kedarnath, and last to Badrinath. But today the tourists and the pilgrims prefer to start their journey direct from Rishikesh to Badrinath and Kedarnath.

Note: The whole journey to four *dhams*, Valley of Flowers and other places enroute is completed in about 12 to 14 days. (Plan your tour accordingly).

Plan your tour by rail

Day	Train No./Name	Dep.	Arr.	From	To
First	2017 Shatabdi Exp.	0700	1240	New Delhi	Dehradun
	By bus / taxi and trekking, plan your tour towards the Valley of Flowers and four *dhams* Travel back to Dehradun by bus/taxi				
Last	2018 Shatabdi Exp.	1700	2240	Dehradun	New Delhi

Where to Stay:

There are Tourist Rest Houses of GMVN and many dharamshalas, lodges available enroute and near the temple sites, providing basic and simple facilities to the pilgrims. For further information contact Garhwal Mandal Vikas Nigam Yatra Office, Muni-ki-Reti, Rishikesh (Ph. 0135- 431793, 431783).

Best Season: From May to June and Sept. to Oct.

Clothing: Summer-Light woollen, Winter-Heavy woollen.

10

Switzerland of the East

IMPHAL
Ex-New Delhi

*M*anipur: An oval shaped virgin valley surrounded by blue green hills, rich in art and tradition. Nestling deep within a lush corner of North-East India is wondrously beautiful little Shangrila called Manipur. Its folklore, myths, and legends, dances, indigenous games and martial arts, exotic handlooms and handicrafts, are invested with the mystique of nature and an indefatigable joie de vivre. The place is as sweet as pure honey made by the bees. The wonders are never ending in Manipur.

Places to See:

Imphal: Capital of Manipur situated at a height of 790 m above sea level is a bustling mini-metropolis: Shri Govindjee Temple, Khwairamband Bazaar or Ima market, (a unique all-women market, having 3000 "Imas" or mothers who run the stalls), War Cemeteries (commemorating the memories of the British Indian soldiers who died during the Second World War) and Khonghampat Orchidarium (12 kms from Imphal which covers 200 acres and houses over 120 rare varieties of orchids, including about a dozen endemic species). Best season is April-May.

Manipur Zoological Gardens: (6 km) To the west of Imphal, see the graceful brow antlered deer (*Sangai*), one of the rarest species in the world.

Keibul Lamjao National Park: The only floating National Park in the world. Loktak Lake is the last natural habitat of *Sangai*, the dancing deer of Manipur.

Other Places: Phubala; Moirang; Shaheed Minar

How to Reach: By Air:- Imphal has an airport.
By Rail / Road:- Dimapur is the nearest railhead 215 kms from Imphal. It is also well connected by road.

Plan your tour by rail

Route: New Delhi - 2296 kms - Dimapur - 215 kms - Imphal

Day	Train No./Name	Dep.	Arr.	From	To
One	2424 Rajdhani Exp. (Tu,W/Sa)	1715	-	New Delhi	-
Two/Three	Enroute By road to Imphal	-	0245	-	Dimapur
Four/Five/Six	Stay and visit Imphal and environs (Travel back to Dimapur)				
Seven	4055 Brahamputra Mail	0545	-	Dimapur	-
Eight/Nine	Enroute		0530	-	Delhi

Where to Stay: Tel. Code- 03852
Hotels: Budget

Hotel Imphal (220459, 223250)
Anand Continental (223433)
Prince (229587)
Excellency (223231)
Pintu (222743)
State Guest House (221212)
White Palace
Maharaja
Nirmala and others.
For more details contact Govt. of India Tourist Office at Imphal: 03852- 221131.

Best Season: Throughout the year.

Clothing: Summer- Light tropical, Winter- Woollen.

11

Oasis in the Desert

MOUNT ABU
Ex-Delhi

$\mathcal{T}$he only hill resort in Rajasthan situated at an altitude of 1220 m above sea-level on the Aravalli hills is a place of impressive grandeur and scenic beauty. The mammoth mountains present sometimes fanciful, sometimes weird sights. There is an interesting legend on the name of Mount Abu- 'Abu' being son of Himalaya, deriving its name from Arbuada, the powerful serpent who rescued Nandi, the sacred bull of Lord Shiva, from a chasm. Another legend associated with the place says that a yagna was performed here and four Agnikula Rajputs or fire-born clans, the Chauhans, Parmars, Pratihars, and Solankis, were created out of the fire. Amidst the Rajasthan desert the hills of Mount Abu are an unusually pleasant sight.

Places to See: Nakki Lake; Toad Rock; Sunset Point; Honeymoon Point; Gaumukh; Mount Abu wildlife sanctuary; Dilwara Jain temples (11th –13th century AD); Museum and Art Gallery; Temple of Raghunathji.

Excursions: Trevor's Tank (5 kms) - it is a delight for bird watchers; Achalgarh (8 kms)-impressive fort with temples (15th-16th century AD); Gurushikhar (15 kms)- highest peak on the Mount.

How to Reach: By Air:– The nearest airport is Udaipur (185 kms).
By Rail / Road: – Mount Abu is well connected by both rail (Abu Road station-28 kms) and road.

Plan your tour by rail

Route: Delhi - 773 kms – Mount Abu

Day	Train No./Name	Dep.	Arr.	From	To
One	2916 Ashram Exp.	1505	-	Delhi	-
Two	Enroute	-	0403	-	Abu Road
Two/Three	Stay and Visit Mount Abu.				
Three	2915 Ashram Exp.	2123	-	Abu Road	-
Four	Enroute	-	1020	-	Delhi

Where to Stay: Tel. Code- 02974

Hotels: Heritage

Palace (43121) Fax: 38674 Website: www.fhrai.com
Lake Palace (3254) Fax: 3354 Website: www.fhrai.com
Savera Palace (3354/38874) Fax: 3354 Website: www.fhrai.com
Connaught House (38560/43439) Fax: 542240
Website: www.fhrai.com, www.welcomheritage.com
E-mail: marwar@del3.vsnl.net.in
Cama Rajputana Club Resort (38205, 38206) Fax: 38412
Website: www.fhrai.com

3 Star

Hotel Hillock (38463-65) Fax: 38467 Website: www.fhrai.com
E-mail: hillock.mtabu@gnahd.globalnet.ems.vsnl.net.in
Hill Tone (38391-94) Fax: 38395 Website: www.fhrai.com
E-mail: hilltone@ad1.vsnl.net.in

Budget

Shikhar, RTDC (38944, 43285)
Sunset Inn (43194, 37094) Fax: 43515 Website: www.fhrai.com
Samrat (43173)
Mount Winds (43187)
Bikaner Palace (43121),
and many others provide comfortable accommodation.

Best Season: Throughout the year.

Clothing: Summer-Light tropical, Winter-Woollen.

12

A Diamond in the Blue Hills

OOTY
Ex-Chennai

*O*oty or Udagamandalam as it is now called, is like a diamond shimmering in the blue mountains of the Nilgiri range. Ooty was discovered in 1819 by Mr. John Sullivan, while he was serving as Collector of Coimbatore District. The lake of Ooty was constructed by bunding a perennial stream flowing through the town. The lake of Ooty is set in serene surroundings in the midst of the hill station and is scene to many a romance. In 1847, the Marquis of Tweeddale established the Botanical Gardens which has a fossil even 20 million years old. There are many lovely trekking routes in the Ooty hills. Ooty abounds in opportunities for trout and carp fishing. Ooty is God's own country. If you are different from the rest, and would prefer to wander in the alleys rising up the mountain, you may come across many buildings caged in a time warp. Being in Ooty is just delightful.

Places to See: Ooty Lake; Botanical Gardens; St. Stephen's Church; Doddabetta Peak; Kalhatti Waterfalls; Wenlock Downs.

Excursions: Coonoor: Sims' Park, Lambs' Rock, Lady Canning's Seat, Dolphin's Nose, Ralliah Dam, Laws' Falls.
Kotagiri: St. Catherine Falls, Rangaswamy Pillar.
Mudumalai Sanctuary: Situated in 321 sq. km. area 67 kms from Ooty, Mudumalai is home to herds of elephants and bison. Other animals like tiger, panther, wild cat, four-horned antelope, mouse deer, giant squirrel and barking deer, are seen in the sanctuary. A variety of birds and vipers also inhabit the sanctuary.

How to Reach: By Air:– Coimbatore is the nearest airport (105 kms).

By Rail / Road:– Ooty is well connected with Mettupalaiyam and Coimbatore by both mountain railway and road.

Plan your tour by rail

Route: Chennai - 530 kms – Mettupalaiyam - 46 kms - Ooty

Day	Train No./Name	Dep.	Arr.	From	To
One	2673 Cheran Exp.	2145	-	Chennai	-
Two	Enroute	-	0610	-	Coimbatore
	By bus / taxi/ mountain rail to Ooty				
Three/Four/Five	Stay and Visit Ooty.				
	By bus/taxi/mountain railway to Coimbatore.				
Six	2674 Cheran Exp.	2310	-	Coimbatore	-
Seven	Enroute	-	0745	-	Chennai

Where to Stay: Tel. Code- 0423

Hotels: Heritage
Savoy (44142,44147) Fax: 43318 Website: www.fhrai.com

3 Star
Holiday Inn Gem Park (42955,41761)
Website: www.fhrai.com, www.holiday-inn.com
E-mail: holiday.ooty@sml.sprintrpg.ems.vsnl.net.in
Nahar (43685) Fax: 52173
Website: www.fhrai.com, http:www.richsoft.com/nahar
E-mail: nahar@giasmdol.vsnl.net.in
Sinclairs Ooty (44308-09) Fax: 44229 Website: www.fhrai.com, http://www.sinclairshotels.com
E-mail: pressman-india@hotmail.com
The Monarch (44420, 44450) Fax: 42455
Website: www.fhrai.com
Welcomgroup Sullivan Court (41416,41418) Fax: 41417
Website: www.fhrai.com

2 Star

The Willow Hill (42686) Fax: 42686 Website: www.fhrai.com,
http://www.leisureplanet.com/a boutus/pressrel.ems.asp
Shiv Sagar (43360) Website: www.fhrai.com
E-mail: bimal@md2vsnl.net.in

Budget

Tamil Nadu, TTDC (44368, 44010-11)
Fernhill Palace (43910-15) Website: www.fhrai.com
Dasaprakash (42434, 43435)
Nilgiri Woodlands (42551,42951) Fax: 42530
Website: www.fhrai.com
Khems (44188)
Lakeview (43904) Fax: 43579 Website: www.fhrai.com
E-mail: lakeview@md3.vsnl.net.in
Regency Villa (42555), Fax: 43097 Website: www.fhrai.com
and many other budget hotels provide comfortable accommodation.

Best Season: April to June and September to October.

Clothing: Summer-Light woollen, Winter-Woollen.

13

A Clouded Abode

SHILLONG
Ex-New Delhi

*W*here hills like a bunch of seven sisters reveal seven moods, where a lake breathes the freshness of dew, where schools of fish frolic beside a thousand lotus blooms, where cascading waterfalls impart a jingle to the wind, where orchid shapes and colours populate the countryside, where golf courses and fish markets cheer up the time space, which can be such a place, but Shillong. Shillong is popular as the Scotland of the East. The climate of Shillong is salubrious and health giving. The hill station displays seven different faces as you traverse in the hills. A gemlike lake is set in the middle of the place and one can boat on this Wards Lake with lotus blossoms flowering on the water sheet. The place has many beautiful waterfalls, and an 18-hole golf course. The hill station has many beautiful buildings and houses, which add to the get-up of the place. Shillong has rich flora and fauna, exotic orchids, and many varieties of butterflies. The place is held by clouds as if it is heaven's own offering.

Places to See: Wards Lake; Lady Hydari Park; Waterfalls-sweet fall, beadon, bishop, elephant and crinoline; Bara Bazaar; Umiam Lake; State Museum ; Shillong Peak.

Excursions:
Cherapunji- Known to have the world's heaviest rainfall (56 kms)
Jakren- A popular health resort with hot springs (64 kms)

Mawsynram- A pre-historic cave of the ancient man (55 kms)
Ranikor- A place of incomparable scenic beauty (140 kms)
Dawki- A picnic spot with silver streams and deep waters (96 kms)

How to Reach: By Air:- Guwahati is the nearest airport.
By Rail / Road:- Guwahati is the nearest railhead from where it takes two hours road journey to Shillong.

Plan your tour by rail

Route: New Delhi - 2046 kms - Guwahati - 104 kms - Shillong

Day	Train No./Name	Dep.	Arr.	From	To
One	2424 Rajdhani Exp. (Tu, W/Sat)	1715	-	New Delhi	-
Two	Enroute **By bus / taxi to Shillong**	-	2100	-	Guwahati
Three/Four/Five	**Stay and Visit Shillong**				
Six	2423 Rajdhani Exp. (Mon, Thur, Fri.)	0600	-	Guwahati	-
Seven	Enroute	-	1010	-	New Delhi

Where to Stay: Tel. Code- 0364
Hotels: 3 Star
Alpine Continental (220991, 223617) Fax: 220996
Website: www.fhrai.com E-mail: alpine@dte.vsnl.net.in
Polo Towers (222341-42) Fax: 220090
Website: www.fhrai.com E-mail: deval@cal.vsnl.net.in

Budget
Orchid (224933, 222052)
Pinewood Ashok (223146, 223116)
Orchid Lake Resort, Meghalaya Tourism (64258 / 96)
Magnum
Pine Borough
Centre Point (225210, 220480)
Pegasus Crown (220667, 220669)

Shillong Club (225497), and many others provide comfortable accommodation. For more information contact Govt. of India Tourist Booking Office, Shillong. Tel.: 0364- 225632.

Best Season: September to May.

Clothing: Summer-Light woollen, Winter-Woollen.

14

The Snow Capital

LEH

Ex-Delhi

*U*nfolding a unique culture, a distinctive lifestyle, and the indomitable struggle of man against inclement weather is the town of Leh. The landscape is ruled by Sengge Namgyal's nine-storey palace, a building in the true tradition of Ladakh architecture, known to have been inspired by the famous Potala in Lhasa. The ruins of the erstwhile royal residence, dating to the 16th century are above on Namgyal Tsemo, the mountain peak. Jokhang, a modern Buddhist temple, unravels a particularly spiritual experience. The Chang Gali behind the main bazaar has intriguing artefacts on sale. The labyrinthine alleys of the old city at the foot of the palace, and clustered around the hill are an experience of being in moon country. The religious philosophy of Buddhism runs through the region and the city – represented in clothing, headgear, dance forms, decorative items, masks, lifestyle, festivals, paintings and food. Close to the original man, archery and polo are both sport and obsession. The region is an out of the world experience.

Places to See: Zangsti; Moravian Church; Ladakh Ecological Centre; Sankar Gompa; Changspa Village; Ladakh Shanti Stupa; Skara Suburb; Choglamsar; Spituk Gompa; Jo-khang; Palace; Fort Ruins; Chang Gali.

Excursions: Nubra Valley; Pangong Lake Circuit; Tso-moriri Lake Circuit; Biama; Drok-pa Circuit.

40

How to Reach: By Air:- Leh is an airport well connected to New Delhi.

By Rail / Road:- Jammu is the nearest railhead and Leh is also approachable by road from Srinagar and Manali.

Plan your tour by rail

Route: Delhi - 585 kms - Jammu - 293 kms - Srinagar - 434 kms - Leh

Day	Train No./Name	Dep.	Arr.	From	To
One	2403 Jammu Express	2240	-	Delhi	-
Two	Enroute (Travel from Jammu to Leh by air)	-	0905	-	Jammu
Three/Four/ Five/Six	Stay at LEH and Visit Environs (Travel to Jammu by air)				
Seven	2404 Jammu Express	1800	-	Jammu	-
Eight	Enroute	-	0420	-	Delhi

Where to Stay: Tel. Code- 01982

Hotels: 3 Star
Shambha-la (62100) Website: www.fhrai.com

Budget
Bijoo (52131)
Caravan Centre (52282)
Snow View Changspa (52136)
Himalaya (52104)
Sun-N-Sand (52468)
Rockland (52589)
Bimla (52754)
Khangri (52051)
Lasermo (53349)
Ladakh Sarai (52777)
Lharino (52101)
Choskor (52746)

Shambha-la (62100) Website: www.fhrai.com
For more information contact J & K Govt. Tourist Reception
Centre, Srinagar: 0194 (452690-91).

Best Season: April to October.

Clothing: Summer – Woollen, Winter – Heavy woollen.

A Virgin Look Hill Station

DALHOUSIE
Ex-Delhi

*T*here is a strange sweetness in the bond of a shared secret between two beings. And the bond is established between man and honeyed mountains, once you visit Dalhousie. Dalhousie is still a virgin hill station (2039 m above sea-level), retaining the flavours, sights, sounds, and smells of a bygone past. Sometimes you feel strange as to how the rolling wheels of time have yet not overrun it. The five hills, on which Dalhousie is spread, never give an impression of a cluster. The city hubbub is around the central hill, called *Moti Tibba*, which is encircled by the *thandi* and the *garam sadak* (cold and warm lanes). The British Governor General, Lord Dalhousie, so liked and admired the untouched quality of the place, that in 1854 he established it as a hill station. The most beautiful and enchanting aspect about the place is that the Dhauladhar mountain range at Dalhousie runs almost parallel to the Pirpanjal range. The place has been host to legendary people like Rabindranath Tagore and Subhas Chandra Bose.

Places to See: Gandhi Chowk; Subhash Chowk; Moti Tibba; Jandhrighat; Karelnu; Kalatope Sanctuary; Panjpulla; St. John's Church.

Excursion: Khajjiar: (a beautiful meadow of vast proportions, 22 kms popularly called India's Switzerland.)

How to Reach: By Air:- Kangra is the nearest airport (180 kms). By Rail / Road:- Chakkibank / Pathankot are the nearest railheads and Dalhousie is also easily approachable by road (90 kms).

Plan your tour by rail

Route: Delhi – 574 kms - Dalhousie

Day	Train No./Name	Dep.	Arr.	From	To
One	2403 Jammu Exp.	2240	-	Delhi	-
Two	Enroute	-	0655	-	Chakkibank
Two	By bus/taxi to Dalhousie				
Two /Three/ Four /Five	Stay and Visit Dalhousie				
Five	By bus/taxi back to Chakkibank		.		
Five	2404 Jammu Exp.	2005	-	Chakkibank	-
Six	Enroute	-	0420	-	Delhi

Where to Stay: Tel. Code- 01899

Hotels: 2 Star

Grand View (40760,42823) Fax: 40609 Website: www.fhrai.com

Budget

Mount View (42120) Fax: 40741
Website: www.fhrai.com,www.mountviewindia.com
E-mail: mchadha@mountviewindia.com
Taj Palace (42406) Fax: 0186-33609 Website: www.fhrai.com
Emporium Apartments (42674) Fax: 42674
Website: www.fhrai.com
Alps Holiday Resort (40775) Fax: 40721
Website: www.fhrai.com, http://www.vacationvalue.com/alps
E-mail: valvalue.dhl/sml
Geetanjali, HPTDC (42155)
Shangri-La (42314)
Surya Resorts (42158, 42316)
Silverton (42329), and many others.
Hotel Devdar, HPTDC at Khajjiar (36333).

Best Season: April to October.

Clothing: Summer - Light woollen, Winter –Woollen.

16

Moon Country

KARGIL
Ex-Delhi

*K*argil was an important trade and transit route in the pan-Asian trade network. Caravans carrying silk, brocade carpets, tea, ivory, etc., used to traverse through this moon country. Kargil town lies along the rising hills of the lower Suru basin. Two tributaries of the Suru river that meet here are Drass and Wakha. Thick plantations of poplars and willows besides apricot, apple and mulberry trees beautify Kargil. The town is like an oasis against a lunar mountainscape. Come the month of May, and the entire area blooms with white apricot blossoms, which fill the vale with a sweet fragrance. Those interested in adventure tourism-trekking, mountaineering, camping, river rafting, etc - are welcome to sink their heels at Kargil and bloom with joy like a mountain flower.

Excursions:

Mulbek: Mulbek is 45 kms from Kargil at an altitude of 3230 m. Mulbek Chamba is a 9 m rock sculpture in deep relief of Maitreya, the future Buddha. At Mulbek Gompa, the Buddhist monastery with its frescoes and statues, adorns the valley.

Shergol: A picturesque village 40 kms from Kargil is a base for an exciting four-day trek into the charming Suru Valley. This village in the Wakha river valley boasts of a cave monastery in a vertically rising ochre hill.

Urgyan Dzong: Tucked away in the Zanskar range a little away from Shergol is this monastic establishment. There are several caves tucked in the hills where Buddhist saints meditated in seclusion.

Wakha Rgyal: Upstream of Mulbek, Rgyal appears like a medieval settlement of cave dwellings with modern extensions. The neatly stacked houses, dug into the sheer face of a cliff, make it appear like a colony of beehives.

How to Reach: By Air:- Srinagar is the nearest airport (204 kms). By Rail / Road:- Jammu Tawi is the nearest railhead. The road is closed during winters.

Plan your tour by rail

Route: Delhi - 585 kms – Jammu Tawi - 293 kms - Srinagar - 204 kms - Kargil.

Day	Train No./Name	Dep.	Arr.	From	To
One	2403 Jammu Express	2240	-	Delhi	-
Two	Enroute (Travel to Srinagar by bus/taxi/air)	-	0905	-	Jammu
Three	Travel to Kargil by bus/taxi.				
Four/Five/ Six/Seven	Stay and visit Kargil and environs. (Travel to Srinagar by bus/taxi on eighth day)				
Nine	Travel to Jammu Tawi by bus/taxi/air.				
Ten	2404 Jammu Express	1800	-	Jammu	-
Eleven	Enroute	-	0420	-	Delhi

Where to Stay:

There are several hotels classified as A, B, C and Economy: **Broadway Suru View, D'Zojila, Siachen, Greenland and Caravan Sarai.** Chinese, Continental and Indian cuisine is served by the A&B class hotels. The tourist bungalows at Kargil can also be booked. For more information contact J & K Govt. Tourist Reception Centre, Srinagar: 0194 (452690-91).

Best Season: May to September.

Clothing: Summer- Woollen, Winter –Heavy woollen.

17

In the Shadow of Pirpanjals

PATNITOP
Ex-Delhi

Situated right before the majestic Pirpanjal mountains is the thick forest of Patnitop. On one side, one can view the mountain-scape and there is also to the view the basin of the river Chenab. Peaceful walks and sprawling meadows afford many picnic opportunities to a family outing. The trees bordering the meadows are like sentinels guarding the green offering. Wild flowers seem to be engaged in singing a chorus to the beauty of the place. During the winters, the area is covered with a thick layer of snow and various snow games including skiing are available for fun. Clouds merge with the pine bristles and seem to waft through a person. Closeby are many attractions, which boast of a rich cultural and historical heritage.

Excursions:

Sanasar (17 kms) The cup-shaped meadow has been developed as a golf course.

Sudh Mahadev: The Shiva shrine is visited by pilgrims on a full moon night in *Sawan*.

Kud: Kud is a popular hill resort near Patnitop at an altitude of 738 mtrs.

Batote: The hill resort straddles the forest slopes overlooking the spectacular Chenab gorge.

Attractions:

i) **Trekking:** A range of trekking options are available in the region.

ii) **Skiing:** Ski courses are conducted during January and February. Madha Top (5-6 kms from Patnitop) has excellent possibilities for all levels of skiing.

iii) **Aero-Sport:** J& K Tourism has introduced paragliding at Sanasar, equipment can be hired from the Tourist Office in Jammu. (May –June and September –October are suitable months for paragliding at Sanasar.)

How to Reach: By Air:- Jammu is the nearest airport.
By Rail / Road:- Jammu is the nearest railhead, and Patnitop is also easily approachable by road.

Plan your tour by rail

Route: Delhi - 585 kms – Jammu Tawi - 112 kms - Patnitop

Day	Train No./Name	Dep.	Arr.	From	To
One	2403 Jammu Express	2240	-	Delhi	-
Two	Enroute	-	0905	-	Jammu
	(Travel to Patnitop by bus/taxi)				
Three/Four/Five	Stay and visit Patnitop				
	(Travel to Jammu by bus/taxi on sixth day)				
Six	2404 Jammu Express	1800	-	Jammu	-
Seven	Enroute	-	0420	-	Delhi

Where to Stay: Tel. Code- 019928

Budget
Tourist Bungalow, JKTDC (87511)
Patni Enclave, JKTDC (87511)
Pandova Enclave, JKTDC (87511)
Green Top (87519, 87529)
Dogra Residency (87508)
Patnitop (87509, 87534)

Mount Shivalik (87507)
Vardhan (87525-26) provide comfortable accommodation. For more information contact J & K Tourist Office, Jammu: 0191-544527, 548172.

Best Season: March to October.

Clothing: Summer- Tropical, Winter -Woollen.

An Inviting Solitude

PITHORAGARH

Ex-Delhi

Pithoragarh is located in a valley which is immensely charming and full of picturesque locations. One can discover oneself in these surroundings of solitude. The district borders Tibet in the north, and across the river Sharda is Nepal. The pilgrim route to Kailash-Mansarover passes through this district and there are visible many ruins of ancient forts and temples. The area is a trekkers paradise and trekking is the best way to imbibe and experience the beauty of Kumaon. There are many caves of religious significance in the area, the most celebrated being the cave-city of Patal Bhuwaneshwar. Seasonal festivals like Hariyala (July/August), before harvesting, Uttaraini (January), and Nandashtami (August/September) in honour of goddesses Nanda and Sunanda are held every year.

Places to See: Rai Gufa (Caves); Ulka Devi (Temple)

Excursions: Jauljibi (68 kms); Lohaghat 62 kms (1706 m); Abbot Mount (2001 m) 56 kms; Berinag (2134 m) 96 kms; Champawat (1615 m) 76 kms; Chaukori (2010 m) 115 kms.; Devidhura (2500 m) 58 kms.; Didihat 54 kms; Gangolihat 77 kms.; Purnagiri (3000 m) 171 kms.; Patal Bhuwaneshwar cave city 90 kms.

How to Reach: By Air:-The nearest airport is Pantnagar. By Rail / Road:- Tanakpur is the nearest railhead and Pithoragarh is easily approachable by road.

Plan your tour by rail

Route: Delhi - 490 Kms - Pithoragarh

Day	Train No./Name	Dep.	Arr.	From	To
One	5013 Ranikhet Exp.	2245	-	Delhi	-
Two	Enroute By bus/taxi to Pithoragarh	-	0615	-	Kathgodam
Three/Four/Five	Stay and Visit Pithoragarh By bus/taxi to Kathgodam				
Six	5014 Ranikhet Exp.	2045	-	Kathgodam	-
Seven	Enroute	-	0445	-	Delhi

Where to Stay:

Kumaon Mandal Vikas Nigam tourist bungalows at Pithoragarh (05964-25434), Champawat (059652-2030), Chaukori, Lohaghat and Purnagiri. Bookings can also be availed at Kumaon Mandal Vikas Nigam Office, Nainital: 05942-36209.

Best Season: May to June and mid-September to early-November.

Clothing: Summer-Light woollen, Winter- Woollen.

An Orchid by a Waterfall

AIZAWL
Ex-Guwahati

Aizawl is the capital of Mizoram and is set in thick forests rich in flora and fauna. The ridge of Aizawl town is surrounded by a deep green valley of the river Tuirial on the east, and by another verdant valley of the river Tlawng on the west. The craggy hills of Durtlang, on the north found a citadellike protection of Aizawl. The people are hospitable and love music. In the evenings, out come the guitars on the streets and many young voices merge with the evening. The silhouette shapes, the wafting music and the flutter of young hearts have to be seen to be felt. Nearby lakes, waterfalls and orchids make the place attractive. Aizawl is truly an experience of a highlanders life.

Places to See: Museum at Macdonal's Hill; Zoological Garden; Bethlehem Vengthlang; Durtlang Hills; Bung Picnic Sport.

Excursions: Tamdil Lake (85 kms); Vantawng Waterfalls (137 kms); Champhai (192 kms); Lunglei (235 kms).

How to Reach: By Air:- Aizawl is an airport connected to Calcutta, Guwahati, and Silchar.
By Rail / Road:- Guwahati is the nearest railhead and Aizawl is easily approachable by road.

Plan your tour by rail

Route: Guwahati - 500 kms - Aizawl

Day	Train No./Name	Dep.	Arr.	From	To
One	5959 Kamrup Exp.	1630	2015	Guwahati	Lumding
One	5801 Cachar Exp.	2115	-	Lumding	-
Two	Enroute	-	0800	-	Silchar
Two	By bus/taxi to Aizawl				
Three/Four/Five	Stay and Visit Aizawl				
Six	By bus/taxi to Silchar				
Six	5802 Cachar Exp.	1800	-	Silchar	-
Seven	Enroute	-	0415	-	Lumding
Seven	4055 Brahamputra Mail	0745	1200	Lumding	Guwahati

Where to Stay: **Tel.Code- 0389**

Hotels: Budget
Ritz (2385)
Embassy (2570)
Tourist Lodge Chaltlang (3526)
Moonlight (2647)
Raji Int'l (2532)
Yatri Niwas
Ahimsa
Sangchia
Chawlhna
Tourists Home
Luangmual
For more information contact Govt. of India Tourist Office at Guwahati: 0361- 547407.

Best Season: October to April.

Clothing: Summer-Light woollen, Winter- Woollen.

20

Sunset over the Romantic Woods

MATHERAN

Ex-Mumbai

*I*f you wish to reap honey with a sickle in moonlit splendour, though quite unusual it may sound, it is possible if you are at Matheran. Close to the tinsel town of Mumbai, there is located this most romantic hill station wrapped in mist and clothed by dense forest. Eight square miles of woods, silent jungle pathways, and occasional mists, is what Matheran is all about. Situated on top of the Western Ghats near Mumbai, it holds a navel-shaped beautiful lake on its bellylike structure called Charlotte Lake. There are no roads here but pathways amidst the forests. The circular path runs for about 20 kms on the top of the plateau traversing through many viewpoints. The walks are pleasant and bring about the much sought-after stress release. In the midst of the woods you stumble across quaint bungalows with tiled roofs and long verandahs. Most of the Bollywood film songs are shot at this picturesque location. The place was extremely popular as a health sanitarium. The weather and surroundings are ideal for a quiet get-away.

Attractions at Matheran: Honeymoon Point; Panorama Point; Porcupine Point; Louise Point; One tree hill; Sunset Point; Charlotte Lake; Panthers Cave; Paymaster Park.

How to Reach: By Air:- Mumbai is the nearest airport.
By Rail / Road:- Matheran is connected by narrow gauge toy train to Neral (21 kms). Neral is the railhead on broad gauge connected to Mumbai. It is directly approachable by road from Mumbai.

Plan your tour by rail

Route: Mumbai - 108 kms – Matheran

Day	Train No./Name	Dep.	Arr.	From	To
One	1007 Deccan Exp.	0635	0817	Mumbai CST	Neral
One	601 Pass.	0840	1040	Neral	Matheran
One /Two	Stay and Visit Matheran				
Three	By bus /taxi to Mumbai				

Where to Stay: Tel. Code- 02148
Hotels: 3 Star
Brightlands Resorts(30417-18) Fax: 6451930
Website: www.fhrai.com, www.brightlands.com
E-mail: brightlands@vsnl.com
The Byke A Hotel (30365) Fax: 30316 Website: www.fhrai.com
E-mail: byke@bom5.vsnl.net.in
Usha Ascot (30360-61) Fax: 30213 Website: www.fhrai.com
E-mail: ushaascot@bol.net.in

2 Star
Regal (30243) Fax: 30243 Website: www.fhrai.com
E-mail: regal@regalmatheran.com

Budget
Panorama (30241, 30254) Fax: 30381 Website: www.fhrai.com
Rugby Limited (30291) Fax: 30252 Website: www.fhrai.com
Rangoli (30272) Website: www.fhrai.com
and many others.

Best Season: October to May.

Clothing: Summer-Light Tropical, Winter-Tropical.

21

Two Sails and a Yacht

NAINITAL
Ex-Delhi

A perfect gem popularly called the land of lakes, having its origin from the dropped left eye of goddess Sati, consort of Shiva, the Naini Lake waters are considered to be holy. The lake of Nainital gives fantastic opportunities to yatching and boating enthusiasts. The sun shining on the emerald green mountains surrounding the lake; the lake shimmering with reflections; the reflections dancing upon the waves, attract a tourist magically. The luxuriant pine forests give excellent trekking opportunities. A bird's eye view of Nainital from the Naina Peak can surely be uplifting.

Places to See: Bhimtal; Sat Tal; Naukuchia Tal; Nainital; Khurpa Tal; Naini Devi Temple; Flat; Bazaar; Hanumangarhi; State Observatory (a Centre for Astronomical Studies); Kilbury; Mahesh Khan.

Several peaks surrounding the opaline Naini Lake: Naina Peak (2611 m. the highest); Laria Kanta (2481 m. the next highest peak); Snow View (2270 m.); Dorothy's Seat (2292 m. offering a sectional view of the town); Land's End (2118 m. presenting a sweeping view of the gem-like Khurpa Tal).

Excursions: Bhimtal (22 kms); Bhowali (11 kms); Corbett National Park (115 kms); Jeolikote (26 kms); Ramgarh (25 kms); Sat Tal (21 kms).

How to Reach: By Air:-The nearest airport is Pantnagar.
By Rail / Road:- Kathgodam is the nearest railhead (35 kms).
Nainital is also easily approachable by road from Haldwani /
Kathgodam.

Plan your tour by rail

Route: Delhi – 318 kms - Nainital

Day	Train No./Name	Dep.	Arr.	From	To
One	5013 Ranikhet Exp.	2245	-	Delhi	-
Two	Enroute	-	0615	-	Kathgodam
	By bus/taxi to Nainital				
Two/Three/Four	Stay and Visit Nainital				
	By bus/taxi to Kathgodam				
Four	5014 Ranikhet Exp.	2045	-	Kathgodam	-
Five	Enroute	-	0445	-	Delhi

Where to Stay: Tel. Code- 05942

Hotels: 4 Star
Vikram Vintage Inn (36177) Fax: 36177, 36179
Website: www.fhrai.com

Heritage
Belvedere Palace (35082) Fax: 35082 Website: www.fhrai.com
Royal (35357) Fax: 35357 Website: www.fhrai.com,
http://www.fhraindia.com/hotel/nainital/royal
Fairhavens (36057) Fax: 36604 Website: www.fhrai.com
E-mail: hotels@bol.net.in

3 Star
Arif Castles (35801-03) Fax: 36231 Website: www.fhrai.com
E-mail: manager@nde.vsnl.net.in
Shervani Hilltop Inn (36128) Fax: 36304
Website: www.fhrai.com E-mail: star@del3.vsnl.net.in

2 Star
Metropole (35589) Fax: 36379 Website: www.fhrai.com
Swiss (36013) Fax: 35493 Website: www.fhrai.com

Budget

Manu Maharani (37341-48) Fax: 37350
Website: www.fhrai.com
Claridges Naini Retreat (35105-08) Fax: 35103
Website: www.fhrai.com
Pratap Regency (35865) Website: www.fhrai.com
Lakeside Inn (35777) Website: www.fhrai.com
Classic The Mall (37704) Fax: 35173 Website: www.fhrai.com
Grand (35406) Fax: 37057 Website: www.fhrai.com
Radha Continental (36267) Website: www.fhrai.com
Silverton (35249) Fax: 35493, 35007 Website: www.fhrai.com
and the tourist bungalows/log cabins of Kumaon Mandal Vikas
Nigam (36209) ensure a comfortable stay at reasonable rates.

Best Season: May to June and mid-September to early-
·November.

Clothing: Summer- (up to April) Cotton for day and Light
woollen for night and for hill trekking, Winter- Heavy woollen.

22

An Emerald Holiday

ALMORA
Ex-Delhi

$\mathcal{I}$t is the mountain air and tranquillity at Almora. A blue sky and passing clouds over the undulating mountains leave a tourist besotted. Almora lies along a saddle–ridge amidst a lush amphitheatre of terraced slopes, where one can enjoy without jostling against milling holiday -makers. Excursions from Almora to nearby lakes, temples displaying a rich cultural tradition are an exercise in learning and pleasure. The folk music of Kumaon, the sounds of local percussion instruments like Hurka, and a flute of reed, to local dances of Jhora, Chholia, and Chhapeli enthrall a visitor.

Places to See: Mohan Joshi Park; Bright End Corner; Deer Park; Simtola; Kalimath; Kasar Devi Temple.

Excursions: Bageshwar (77 kms - a pilgrim town at the confluence of the Gomti and Saryu rivers, is also base for treks to Pindari and Kafni glaciers); Baijnath (71 kms - a picturesque temple town); Binsar (30 kms - a summer retreat of erstwhile rulers); Chitai (8 km - a temple with hundreds of brass bells); Gananath (47 kms - caves and scenery); Gwalakot (26 kms - an enticing river bend); Jageshwar (34 kms - ancient Deodars and *jyotirlinga* Shiva temple); Katarmal (17 kms - 800-year-old sun temple); Kausani (53 kms - hill station with spectacular views of snow hills); Lakhu-Udyar (16 kms - pre- historic wall paintings in caves); Ranikhet (49 kms - a quiet hill station with dense pine forests and orchards).

How to Reach: By Air:-The nearest airport is Pantnagar.
By Rail / Road:- Kathgodam is the nearest railhead (90 kms).
Almora is also easily approachable by road.

Plan your tour by rail

Route: Delhi – 384 kms - Almora

Day	Train No./Name	Dep.	Arr.	From	To
One	5013 Ranikhet Exp.	2245	-	Delhi	-
Two	Enroute	-	0615	-	Kathgodam
	By bus/taxi to Almora				
Two/Three/ Four/Five	Stay and Visit Almora By bus/taxi to Kathgodam				
Five	5014 Ranikhet Exp.	2045	-	Kathgodam	-
Six		-	0445	-	Delhi

Where to Stay: Tel. Code- 05962
Hotels: 2 Star
Corrett Rataganga Resort (33650) Fax: 33007 Website:
www.fhrai.com, www.corbettramganga.com
E-mail: abc@ajaybahlco.com

Budget
Snow View Resort (33508) Fax: 33007 Website: www.fhrai.com
E-mail: sychem@ndf.vsnl.net.in
Holiday Home (22250)
Ambassador (30118)
Ashoka (30066 / 22066)
Aparna (30192)
Kailash (30624)
Konark (31217)
Pawan (30252, 22288)
Ranjana (30301)
Shikhar (30253)

Kumaon Mandal Vikas Nigam Tourist Bungalows- Almora (05962-30250), Bageshwar (05963-22034), Binsar, Dhakuri, Dwali, Jageshwar, Kausani (05962-45006), Khati, Loharkhet, Phurkiya, Ranikhet (05966-20893, 20588), Sitalakhet (05966-44005).

Best Season: May to June and mid-September to early-November.

Clothing: Summer-Light woollen, Winter-Woollen.

23

Folklore on Muslin

CHAMBA
Ex-Delhi

Like the beauty of a Chamba *rumal* is the mountain city itself-richly embroidered on fine muslin. The town of Chamba, on the east bank of the river Ravi owes its name to Champavati, daughter of Raja Sahil Varman, the founder king. The ancient town came to life in 920 AD and since then has been fondly endowed by the royal dynasties. The numerous plateaus in the valley, the green contoured fields and the romancing river Ravi create a perfect picture of beauty. The erstwhile palace is the signature building in front of the Chaugan: the open flat space venue to seasonal fairs and festive celebrations. The Lakshmi Narayan group of temples, dating back to the 10th and 11th century AD, have delightful statues. The valley speaks highly of the cultural attainments of the people of Chamba. The Chamba *rumal*, the miniature paintings and the fountain slabs are unique to the place. Beyond are the attractive Pirpanjals, which invite you for a climb.

Places to See: Chaugan (Minjar Fair is celebrated in July/ August); Group of Temples- Lakshmi Narayan, Radha Krishna, Chandragupta, Gauri Shankar, Trimukeshwara, Lakshmi Damodara; Hari Rai Temple; Chamunda Devi Temple; Jhamwar; Rani Sui Temple; Sarol; Bhuri Singh Musuem.

Excursions: Saloni and Bhandal Valleys; Khajjiar Meadow; Bharmaur (Trek to Mount Mani Mahesh Kailash in August / September).

How to Reach: By Air: -Kangra is the nearest airport (180 kms).

By Rail / Road:- Chakkibank / Pathankot are the nearest railheads and Chamba is easily approachable by road (116 kms).

Plan your tour by rail

Route: Delhi - 520 kms – Chamba

Day	Train No./Name	Dep.	Arr.	From	To
One	2403 Jammu Exp.	2240	-	Delhi	-
Two	Enroute	-	0655	-	Chakkibank
Two	By bus/taxi to Chamba				
Two /Three/ Four /Five	Stay and Visit Chamba (By bus/taxi back to Chakkibank).				
Five	2404 Jammu Exp.	2005	-	Chakkibank	-
Six	Enroute	-	0420	-	Delhi

Where to Stay: Tel. Code- 01899

Hotels: Budget
Iravati, HPTDC (22671)
Champak, HPTDC (22774)
Akhand Chandi (22371) Website: www.fhrai.com
Mount View (24067)
Chamunda View (24067)
River View (25175, 24067).

Best Season: Throughout the year.

Clothing: Summer- Tropical, Winter –Woollen.

Seaside Sojourns

The sea is playful. It plays upon your mood like none other. The blue waves as they rush to embrace the sand, call out to you in a strange music. The call is irresistible. You cannot sleep through the morn and start walking towards the source. The sun is early at the sea, and five' o 'clock is just the right light to walk barefoot on the sand. At this time the sky is different shades of gold—coloured by the dawn. Puffs of cloud scattered in the sky assume hues of orange gold and flaming red. The patch of sand visited by a wave remains wet awhile. The reflections of the rising sun on this piece are pure and elemental. It appears as if you have struck gold. But, there is a difference. This gold is not for greed and can only be feasted upon by the eyes. Fill them with what nature has momentarily offered, as the sun in its stride will spread more warmth later, than colour.

A little away, a group of fishermen can be seen involved in the motions of their profession. A blue net on the sand is being readied. Here it stands out in sharp contrast, but in the bosom of sea it will melt into its colour. Boats are being cleaned, wiped and equipped. Lo, there a fisherman is already pushing his boat up a wave. Those who ride the waves, rule them. The fishermen carry aspirations of their families along with as they embark upon a voyage. The sight of a hundred fishing boats upon the sea, sails lustily filled with breeze, under a golden sky is heart warming. Their position keeps shifting with the prancing waves. They gain prominence as a wave rises, and diminish in size as a wave falls. How golden is my morn — is the only thought that remains.

Miles to go before I sleep

Seaside Chimes

The sea first invites and then entices you. Jumping on the waves is wholesome fun. Frolic runs unrestrained as the strong waves first push you towards the beach, then pull you in a suck motion on their return to sea. Tired, lie down on the beach and let the waves roll over you. A masseur may be waiting up there, to massage weary limbs. It is a right royal treatment under the warming sun.

The air beside the sea draws you to an indulgent rest each day on your return from an excursion. Strangely, it brings sleep like never before. There is another golden morn at the end of dreams, there is another day to live and love. Seaside cities are like pearls washed ashore by the sea, shining lustrously with splendid colours. Come, explore the magic of the sea and the city, together, at these wonderful places.

24

Pearl by the Sea

GOA

Ex- Mumbai / New Delhi

Goa is like a treasure trove. It is in Goa that the East and West meet falsifying Rudyard Kipling. The confluence of cultures is reflected vividly in the music of church and the hymns of temples. The history of Goa could be traced to Lord Parshurama (sixth incarnation of Lord Vishnu), who is believed to have created the land by shooting an arrow (Pashupatastra) from the Sahyadris into the Arabian Sea and ordering the sea to retreat. The arrow fell at Banahalli (present Benaulim). Then came human habitation and their gods and goddesses. Today Goa is a perfect picture of the past and present. The golden beaches of Goa cast a magic spell upon a visitor. Goa just keeps you forever.

Places to Visit: Towns: Panaji; Margao(33 kms); Vasco (30 kms); Mapusa(13 kms); Mormugao Harbour (34 kms).; Pilar (11 kms).

Beaches: Calangute (16 kms); Colva Beach 6 kms. from Margao; Dona Paula 7 kms; Miramar 3 kms; Anjuna 18 kms; Vagator 22 kms; Arambol Beach 50 kms; Aguada 37 kms; Palolem 70 kms.

Churches: i) Basilica of Bom Jesus, built in the 16th century, is the most popular and famous of all churches in Goa; ii) Se Cathedral, biggest church in Goa, iii) Church of St. Francis of Assissi, the only miracle of its kind in the East, iv) St.Cajetan Church, v) Church of Our Lady of Rosary, one of the earliest built in Goa; vi) Nunnery of Santa Monica: built like a fortress; vii) Ruins of Church of St.Augustine; close to the Nunnery is a lofty tower defying the torrential rains; viii) Viceroy's Arch; one of the gates of Adil Shah's fort, ix) Reis Magos Church constructed in 1555 AD (dedicated to the three magi-kings), x) Church of Mae de Deus at Saligao (Bardez); this beautiful church is the finest in Gothic style, xi) The Church of St.Alex at Curtorim; it is one of the oldest churches in Goa built in 1597, xii) The Church of St.Ana at Talaulim, Ilhas, the unique feature of this church is that it has a hollow wall through which people can walk in secrecy to confess; xiii) Rachol Seminary, built in 1521; it is in this seminary that the Museum of Christian Art is housed.

Temples: Shri Bhagwati Temple, Rudreshwar Temple, Shri Mahadeo Bhumika; Morjaee Temple; Brahma Temple, (There are more than 25 temples in Goa, which can be seen and admired).

Other places: Aguada Fort, Dudhsagar Water Falls, Bondhla Forest and Zoo, Kesarval Spring; Mayem Lake; the Big Foot-Loutulim, Gardens, Museum; and Nyara Art Gallery-Loutulim.

How to Reach: By Air:- Goa is well connected by air.
By Rail / Road:- Goa is well connected by both rail and road from Mumbai and New Delhi.

Plan your tour by rail

Route: **(A) Mumbai - 588 kms - via Konkan Rly. - Goa**
(B) New Delhi - 1870 kms - Madgaon

A) From Mumbai CST

Day	Train No./Name	Dep.	Arr.	From	To
One	0111 Konkan Kanya Exp.	2250	-	MumbaiCST	-
Two	Enroute	-	1045	-	Madgaon
Three/Four/Five	Stay and visit Goa				
Five	0112 Konkan Kanya Exp.	1800	-	Madgaon	
Six	Enroute	-	0605	-	Mumbai CST

B) From New Delhi (Nizamuddin)

Day	Train No./Name	Dep.	Arr.	From	To
One	2432 TVC Rajdhani (Sun, Tue.)	1100	-	NZM	-
Two	Enroute	-	1250	-	Madgaon
Three/Four/Five	Stay and Visit Goa				
Six	2431 TVC Rajdhani (Fri.)	1145	-	Madgaon	-
Seven	Enroute	-	1350	-	NZM

Where to Stay: Tel. Code- 0832
Hotels: 5 Star
Fort Aguada Beach Resort (276201-10) Fax: 276044
Website: www.fhrai.com
Leela Beach Resort (746363) Fax: 746352
Website: www.fhrai.com,
www.theleela.com E-mail: leela@goa1.dot.net.in
Majorda (754871-80) Fax: 755382, 754342
Website: www.fhrai.com
Cidade De Goa Beach Resort (221133) Fax: 223303
Website: www.fhrai.com, http://www.cidadedegoa.com
E-mail: hotelcdg@goa1.dot.net.in
Renaissance Goa Resort (745200-16) Fax: 745225
Website: www.fhrai.com, http://renaissancehotels.com/goirn
E-mail: grresort@goa1.dot.net.in
Bogmalo Beach Park (513311) Website: www.fhrai.com
Holiday Inn Resort (746303-09) Fax: 74333
Website: www.fhrai.com
E-mail: hi.goa@sma.sprintrpg.ems.vsnl.net.in

4 Star
Dona Sylvia Beach Resort (746321-27) Fax: 746320
Website: www.fhrai.com, www.donasylvia.com
E-mail: donasylvia@gnpun.globalnet.ems.vsnl.net.in
Taj Holiday Village (276201-09) Fax: 276045
Website: www.fhrai.com E-mail: thvresv.goa@taj

3 Star

De Souza Resort (279409-14) Fax: 279415
Website: www.fhrai.com, www.sun-village.com
E-mail: sunvil@goa1.dot.net.in
Heritage Village Club (754311-12) Fax: 754324
Website: www.fhrai.com
Delmon (420075 / 76) Fax: 223527 Website: www.fhrai.com
Nova Goa (226231) Fax: 224958 Website: www.fhrai.com
E-mail: novagao@bom2vsnl.net.in
Mandovi (224405-09) Fax: 225451
Website: www.fhrai.com E-mail: mandovi@goa1.dot.net.in
Nanu Resort (734950-53) Fax: 734428, 733175
Website: www.fhrai.com, nanuindia.com
E-mail: nanuresort@nanuindia.com

2 Star

Baia Do Sol (276084) Fax: 731415
Website: www.fhrai.com, http://fhraindia.com/hotel/goa/
baiadosol
E-mail: ndnaik@goal.dot.net.in
Prainha Cottages (227221) Fax: 229959
Website: www.fhrai.com,
www.prainha.com E-mail: prainha@goal.dot.net.in

Budget

Concha Beach Resort (276056) Fax: 276056
Website: www.fhrai.com
Seema (234172) Fax: 224155
Website: www.fhrai.com
Aroma (228310) Fax: 224330
Website: www.fhrai.com E-mail: butterchicken@hotmail.com
Park Plaza (422601) Fax: 225635
Website: www.fhrai.com E-mail: parkplaz@goal.dot.net.in
Vista Do Rio (212939) Fax: 212939
Website: www.fhrai.com, www.vistadorio.com,
vista@goa1.dot.net.in E-mail: vista@goal.dot.net.in

Paradise Village Beach Resort (276475) Fax: 276155
Website: www.fhrai.com E-mail: bombay.prince@axcess.net.in
Sea Queen Beach Resort (720499, 734256)
Website: www.fhrai.com www.clubmahindra.com
E-mail: goa@clubmahindra.com
Goa Woodlands (705121-23, 712838) Fax: 738732
Website: www.fhrai.com, E-mail: woodland@goa1.dot.net.in
Varma Beach Resort (276077, 279734) Fax: 276022
Website: www.fhrai.com E-mail: varmabeach@hotmail.com
The Goa Tourism Development Corporation also operates a
chain of resorts at beaches and tourist spots (224132, 226515).

Best Season: October to June.

Clothing: Summer- Cotton, Winter- Tropical.

By the Coral Reefs and Lagoons

LAKSHADWEEP
Ex-Mumbai

Lakshadweep has a precious heritage in its ecology and culture. The tiniest Union Territory and the country's only coral island is formed from coral rocks, (the beautiful formations can be seen all over the lagoons). Approximately 400 kms west to the coast of Kerala, the history of Lakshadweep is not much known. However, enough evidence exists to piece together a history of these islands. The people converted to Islam under the influence of Hazrat Ubaidullah who set off from Mecca after Prophet Muhammad appeared to him in a dream, commanding him to leave for distant shores to propagate Islam. The ship on which Hazrat Ubaidullah was sailing was wrecked and after drifting on a plank of wood he reached the island of Amini, from where his mission succeeded. Lakshadweep has thirtysix islands covering a land area of 36 sq kms and ten islands are still virgin.

Island Attractions:

Agatti: One of the most beautiful lagoons in Lakshadweep.

Bangaram: Indescribably romantic, uninhabited island.

Kavaratti: Spread with 52 mosques and a beautiful people. View marine life through glass bottom boats.

Kalpeni: Bays and lagoon, a sparkling island. Good coral life.

Kadmath: A haven of solitude, perfect for swimming, water sport facilities.

Minicoy: Light house, coconut greens, and a distinctive culture.

Water Sport: Water sports facilities like Kayaking, sailing, paddle boats, inflatable motorboats, glass-bottom boats and skiing are available in the islands of Kavaratti, Kalpeni, Kadmath, and Minicoy.

How to Reach: By Air:- Agatti is an airport in the group of islands.

By Rail / Road:- Cochin (Ernakulam) is the nearest railhead and the most convenient road connection.

Plan your tour by rail

Route: Mumbai – 1249 kms - Ernakulam - by ship / air - Lakshadweep

Day	Train No./Name	Dep.	Arr.	From	To
One	2618 Mangala Exp..	1120	-	Panvel	-
Two	Enroute	-	1250	-	Ernakulam Jn.
Two/Three	By air/ship to Agatti Island				
Four/Five/Six/Seven	Stay and Visit Lakshadweep				
Seven	By air/ship to Ernakulam				
Eight	2617 Mangala Exp.	1155	-	Ernakulam Jn.	-
Nine		-	1350	-	Panvel

Where to Stay: Tel. Code- 04896
Heritage
Society for Promotion of Nature Tourism
Website: www.fhrai.com E-mail: lkdmin@400.nicgw.nic.in

Resorts at
Kadmat, Kavarathi (62255, 74203) Fax: 62356

Bangaram Island Resorts (Contact Casino Hotel, Cochin: Ph. 0484- 666821, 668221)
Paradise Island Huts, and other tourist huts at islands.

Best Season: Throughout the year (during monsoon ship service is not in operation, helicopter is available).

Clothing: Summer- Tropical, Winter-Tropical. (In Oct-Nov. a water-proof coat is useful).

26

A Fairy Island

DIU

Ex-Ahmedabad

Diu is a celebrated island on the western coast of India. The island is almost private, measuring just 39 sq kms. The 21-km coastline appears to be forever in frolic with sea waves. They are separated by an altitude of only 29 metres. The story of King Jalandhar who ruled Diu in ancient times is plastered to the ruins of his temple. The rule of Chanda and Vaghela Rajputs was abolished by Mohammedan rulers in 1380 AD. Diu during these times was one of the best seaports and naval bases. An Italian traveller, Ludoviko de Vartherma who visited it in 1504 AD called Diu a Bander Atturk, as trade with Turkey was prominent. The Mughal King of Delhi had attacked Bahadurshah, Sultan of Gujarat, who then held sway over Diu. The Sultan entered into a pact with the Portuguese to evade the northerner's threat. Diu slowly drifted into Portuguese hands. Now, Diu is an exciting Indian island holiday.

Places to See: Diu Fort, Fortem Du Mar (Panikotha), Nagoa Beach, Chakratirath Beach, Vanakbara, Bucharwada, Gangeshwar temple, Fudam village, St. Paul's Church, Diu Museum, Bird Sanctuary, Diu City.

How to Reach: By Air:–Diu is an airport connected to Mumbai.
By Rail / Road:- Veraval is the nearest railhead connected to Ahmedabad. Diu is also easily approachable by road.

Plan your tour by rail

Route: Ahmedabad - 431 kms – Veraval - 60 kms - Diu

Day	Train No./Name	Dep.	Arr.	From	To
One	9946 Girnar Exp.	2145	-	Ahmedabad	-
Two	Enroute	-	0820	-	Veraval
	By bus/taxi to Diu (Approx. one and half hours)				
Two/Three/Four	Stay and Visit Diu.				
Four	9945 Girnar Exp.	1925	-	Veraval	-
Five	Enroute	-	0620	-	Ahmedabad

Where to Stay: Tel. Code- 02875
Hotels: Budget
Alishan (52340)
Ankur (52388)
Apna (52112)
Ashiana (52260)
Ganga Sagar (52249)
Hemal (52227)
Mozambique (52223)
Nilesh (52319)
Samrat (52354)
Sea View (52371), and others.

Best Season: Throughout the year.

Clothing: Summer-Light tropical, Winter-Light tropical.

27

The City of Colourful Festivals

PURI

Ex-New Delhi

*P*uri is one of the holy *dhams* placed in India. Located on the shores of the Bay of Bengal, it has one of the finest beaches in the world. Jagannath Temple at Puri has a clear-cut embossed presence on city life. Never would you have witnessed a city so dependent upon a temple. The motions of different prayers, *darshans* and *prasada* (temple offering) at various times of the day dictate city life. It serves as a fulcrum around which the city moves. The waves are playful and it is sheer pleasure to learn the art of jumping the waves. Alternatively one can just lie on the wet sand and let waves roll over. Puri is just the place to witness and participate in colourful festivals round the year. Puri is famous for its annual festival of chariots, the *Rathyatra*. The pilgrimage town is also the abode of artisans and craftsmen who produce a wide range of unique handicrafts. Puri serves as a pivot to stay and discover the culture of the river Mahanadi belt.

Places to See: Sri Jagannath Temple, The Beach, Bada Danda; Swarg Dwar.

Excursions: Balighai (8 kms), Baliharachandi (27 kms), Beleshwar (15 kms), Raghurajpur (14 kms), Konark (36kms).

How to Reach: By Air:- The nearest airport is Bhubaneswar-61 kms.

By Rail / Road:- Puri is well connected by both rail and road.

Plan your tour by rail

Route: New Delhi – 1321 kms - Puri

Day	Train No./Name	Dep.	Arr.	From	To
One	2802 Purshottam Express	2235	–	New Delhi	–
Two/Three	Enroute	–	0645	–	Puri
Three/Four/Five	Stay and Visit Puri				
Five	2801 Purshottam Express	2015	–	Puri	–
Six/Seven	Enroute	–	0440	–	New Delhi

Where to Stay: Tel. Code- 06752

Hotels: 4 Star

Toshali Sands Resort (22888) Fax: 23899
Website: www.fhrai.com

Heritage

South Eastern Railway Hotel (erstwhile BNR, 22063, 23006)

3 Star

Vijoy International (22702, 24371) Fax: 22881
Website: www.fhrai.com
Mayfair Beach Resort (27800, 24041) Fax: 24242
Website: www.fhrai.com

2 Star

Holiday Resort (24370-71) Fax: 23968 Website: www.fhrai.com
E-mail: holidayresortpuri@vsnl.net

Budget

Panthaniwas (22740, 22562)
Samudra (22705) Fax: 033-3583346 Website: www.fhrai.com
Hans Coco Palms (30038) Fax: 30165 Website: www.fhrai.com
Sonali (23545) Fax: 22877 Website: www.fhrai.com

Neelachal Ashok (23639-51) Fax: 23676
Website: www.fhrai.com
E-mail: purashok@indiatourism.com
Puri (22114, 22744)
and many others in and around Puri.

Best Season: Throughout the year. Mid-April heralds the summer and is the season for famous Chandanyatra, and June-July for the Rathyatra of Lord Jagannath.

Clothing: Summer- Light tropical, Winter- Tropical.

28

India's Biggest Island Lake

CHILIKA
Ex-Calcutta

India's biggest island lake nestles in the heart of coastal Orissa. The lake is spread over 1100 square kilometres, stretching across the length of three districts of Puri, Khurda and Ganjam. It joins up with the Bay of Bengal through a narrow mouth, forming an enormous lagoon of brackish water. Encircled by hills all along its arched shape, Chilika Lake's colour changes with passing clouds overhead and the shifting sun. The water ripples languidly, occasionally moved by a gentle breeze from across the Bay of Bengal. By the night the sky merges into the silent waters of Chilika, the birds fall silent and only the creatures of the night rule the lake.

Places to See: Attractions within the lake: Nalabana; Birds Island; Kalijai; Satapada; Brahmapura; Parikud and Malud.

Excursions: Nirmala Jhar (11 kms): place of worship.
Narayani (10 kms): temple, natural spring.
Banpur (13 kms): shrine of goddess Bhagabati.
Gopalpur-on-sea (75 kms): ancient port.

How to Reach: By Air:- Bhubaneswar is the nearest airport.
By Rail / Road:- Chilika is well connected by both rail and road.

Plan your tour by rail

Route: Calcutta - 590 kms - Chilika

Day	Train No./Name	Dep.	Arr.	From	To
One	7479 Tirupati Exp.	2330	-	Howrah	-
Two Enroute		-	1258	-	Chilika
Two/Three	Stay and Visit Chilika				
Four	7480 Tirupati Exp.	1226	-	Chilika	-
Five Enroute		-	0400	-	Howrah

Where to Stay:

Hotels: Budget

Panthniwas, OTDC at Rambha (06810-57346)

Barkul (06756-20488)

Ashoka Hotel at Balugaon (06756- 20408/09)

Yatri Niwas at Satpada

Tel.- For booking contact Govt. of India Tourist Office at Bhubaneswar: 0674- 432203.

Best Season: Throughout the year.

Clothing: Summer- Light tropical, Winter- Woollen.

29

Backwater and Boat Races

KOTTAYAM
Ex-Chennai

Situated in the foothills of the Western Ghats is Kottayam - noted for its trade in rubber, pepper, etc. The delightful place is punctuated by scenic backwater along the limpid palm fringed banks. Kottayam is one of the main centres of Syrian Christian faith and has some beautiful churches. Traditional Kerala style tourist resorts offer a close interaction with Kerala. The famous boat races held in August on the backwater are a real royal attraction. The spirit of gaiety, competitiveness and celebration of life is most evident during the boat races. The churning of the river by determined men wielding oars is an unforgettable sight. One can stay on house boats, sailing on the backwater, imbibing a lot of Kerala.

Places to See: Valiapalli Church, Cheriapalli Church, Kumarakom Lake, Shiva Temple, Ettumanoor, Backwater between Kollam, Kottayam and Alappuzha.

Backwater Races: Nehru Trophy at Alappuzha, Indira Gandhi Boat Race at Kochi; Rajiv Gandhi Boat Race at Pulinkunnu, Champakulam Boat Race, Kottayam Mannar Boat Race; Payippad; Jalotsavam at Haripad; Aranmula Boat Race at Pathanamthitta (in the month of August).

How to Reach: By Air:– The nearest airport is Cochin.
By Rail / Road:- Kottayam is well connected by both rail and road.

Plan your tour by rail

Route: Chennai - 760 kms - Kottayam

Day	Train No./Name	Dep.	Arr.	From	To
One	6619 Chennai-Trivandrum Mail	1900	-	Chennai	-
Two	Enroute	-	0800	-	Kottayam
Two/Three	Stay and Visit Kottayam				
Four	6620 Chennai-Trivandrum Mail	1720	-	Kottayam	-
Five	Enroute	-	0725	-	Chennai

Where to Stay: Tel. Code- 0481

Hotels: Heritage

Coconut Lagoon (525834) Fax: 524495 Website: www.fhrai.com
E-mail: casino@giasmd01.vsnl.net.in

3 Star

Anjali (563661) Fax: 563669 Website: www.fhrai.com

2 Star

Aida (568391) Fax: 568399 Website: www.fhrai.com
E-mail: aida@md3.vsnl.net.in
Vembanad Lake Resort (564298) Fax: 564298
Website: www.fhrai.com, url.vembanadlakeresort.com
E-mail: kurianpj@md3.vsnl.net.in

1 Star

Ambassador (563293) Fax: 563755 Website: www.fhrai.com

Budget

Green Park (563311) Fax: 563312 Website: www.fhrai.com
Homestead (562346) Fax: 560740 Website: www.fhrai.com
Prince (578809) Fax: 573138 Website: www.fhrai.com
Tipsy (535541) Fax: 536708 Website: www.fhrai.com
Taj Garden Retreat (524377) Fax: 524371
Website: www.fhrai.com
E-mail: tgrgm.kmr.@tajgroup.sprintrpg.ems.vsnl.net.in

Aiswarya, KTDC (581256, 581440)
Kodimath
Nisha Continental and many others offer comfortable accommodation.

Best Season: Throughout the year.

Clothing: Summer-Light tropical, Winter-Light tropical.

A Golden Harbour and Fishing Nets

COCHIN
Ex-New Delhi

The continuity of the Jewish tradition is visible in this seaside town over 4000 years of its historical evolution. Though it is assimilated into the social systems, yet an unbroken link with ethnic and religious traditions of Judaism has been maintained. The place has two indigenous Jewish communities, viz the Malayalam-speaking Jews of Cochin and the Marathi-speaking Ben Israel (children of Israel). Religious diversity in India is at its best and is placed into a historical time warp. Kerala was connected by way of trade with the Jews since the times of the legendary Kings Solomon and Nebuchadnezar. The harbour is still the focal point of the city. Pepper, seafood, rubber and coir are exported from here. The serene backwater, golden sunsets and lagoons form a picture perfect amidst coconut trees that is unsurpassable.

Places to See: Jew Town; Paradesi Synagogue; Mattancherry; Cochin Harbour Terminus; Fishing Nets; Public Gardens; High Court Building; Broadway Shopping Centre; Bolghatty Palace; St.Francis Church; Museum of Kerala History; Islands of Vypeen, Willingdon, Ramanthuruth, Vallarpadam and Bolghatty.

How to Reach: By Air:– Cochin is an airport.
By Rail / Road:– Cochin / Ernakulam is well connected by both rail and road.

Plan your tour by rail
Route: New Delhi - 2579 kms – Ernakulam - 8 kms - Cochin

Day	Train No./Name	Dep.	Arr.	From	To
One	2432 Rajdhani Exp. (Sun,Tue.)	1100	-	Nizamuddin	-
Two/Three	Enroute	-	0145(night)	-	Ernakulam
Three/Four/Five	Stay and Visit Cochin				
Six	2625 Kerala Exp.	1550	-	Ernakulam	-
Seven/Eight	Enroute	-	1545	-	New Delhi

Where to Stay: Tel. Code- 0484
Hotels: 5 Star
Taj Malabar (666811) Fax: 668297 Website: www.fhrai.com
E-mail: malabar.cochin@tajhotels.com
Taj Residency (371471) Fax: 371481 Website: www.fhrai.com
E-mail: trhgm.enk@tajgroupspringrpg.ems.vsnl.net.in

Heritage
Fort Heritage (225333) Website: www.fhrai.com

4 Star
Mercy (367372) Fax: 351504 Website: www.fhrai.com
Quality Inn Presidency (394300) Fax: 393222
Website: www.fhrai.com E-mail: presid@md2.vsnl.net.in
The Avenue Regent (372660) Fax: 370129
Website: www.fhrai.com, http://www.avenuergent.com
E-mail: avenue@md2.vsnl.net.in
The Renaissance Cochin (344463) Fax: 331561
Website: www.fhrai.com, www.renaissancecochin.com
E-mail: enquiry@renaissance-cochin.com

3 Star
Abad Plaza (38112) Fax: 370729 Website: www.fhrai.com,
E-mail: abad@giasmd01.vsnl.net.in
Hilltop Resorts (348198) Fax: 348223 Website: www.fhrai.com,
www.fhraindia.com/hotel/cochin/hilltop
E-mail: intlclub@md3.vsnl.net.in

Cochin Tower (401910) Fax: 401922 Website: www.fhrai.com,
http://www.ypindia.com/cochintower
E-mail: cochintower@ypindia.com
Sealord (382472) Fax: 370135 Website: www.fhrai.com,
www.indiamart.com/sealordhotel
E-mail: sealord@giasmd01.vsnl.net.in
International (382091) Fax: 373929 Website: www.fhrai.com,
http://www.kerala-interactive.com/international
E-mail: international@kerala-interactive.com
Metropolitan (352412) Fax: 382227 Website: www.fhrai.com,
www.metropolitancochin.com
E-mail: metropol@md3.vsnl.net.in
The Trident (669595) Fax: 669393 Website: www.fhrai.com
E-mail: resvn@tridentcochin.com

2 Star
ATS Willingdon (667643) Fax: 667043 Website: www.fhrai.com
Bolghatty Palace KTDC (355003) Fax: 354879
Website: www.fhrai.com
Excellency (374001-8) Fax: 374009 Website: www.fhrai.com,
http://www.richsoft.com/excellency
Sangeetha (368487) Fax: 354261 Website: www.fhrai.com,
www.gaanam@md.3 E-mail: gaanam@md3.vsnl.net.in

1 Star
Lucia (381177) Fax: 361524 Website: www.fhrai.com
Paulson Park (382170-79) Fax: 370072 Website: www.fhrai.com,
E-mail: paulson@kelnet07.xlweb.com

Budget
Blue Diamond Aiswarya (364454, 371640)
Woodlands (382051) Fax: 382080 Website: www.fhrai.com
E-mail: woodlandl@vsnl.com
Bharat (353501) Fax: 370502 Website: www.fhrai.com,
http://www.bharathotel.com E-mail: bthekm@md2.vsnl.net.in
Crystal Palace
Grand (382061) Fax: 382066 Website: www.fhrai.com

Blue Nile (355277) Fax: 367838 Website: www.fhrai.com
Casino (668221) Fax: 668001 Website: www.fhrai.com
E-mail: casino@giasmdol.vsnl.net.in
Alapatt Regency (344413) Fax: 381701 Website: www.fhrai.com
and many others offer comfortable accommodation.

Best Season: Throughout the year.

Clothing: Summer-Light tropical, Winter-Tropical.

Sun, Sea and a Lullaby

TRIVANDRUM
Ex-New Delhi

Trivandrum city is a unique blend of ancient and modern Indian architecture. It features temples as old as 1733 AD. celebrating the Hindu pantheon. The mythology and art of the place are caged in splendid museums. The place has musical waterfalls, gurgling streams, exotic botanical gardens, hill resorts and a roaring sea. At Trivandrum, one can take time out on boats, hiking, sea-surfing and visiting lagoons. The Kovalam beach is unique in the world having a sheltered bay and an undying beauty. The swaying coconut trees by the golden Kovalam beach, the roaring waves of the Indian Ocean and the excited bird calls present to the mind's eye a picture of perfect solitude.

Places to See: Padmanabhaswami Temple (1733 A.D.), Priyadarshani Planetarium, Science and Technology Museum, Napier Museum, Observatory, Aruvikkara picnic spot (temple, waterfall, stream); Kovalam Beach (16 kms.); Veli lagoon, East Fort, St. Joseph's Church, Palayam, Kanakakunnu Palace.

Excursions: Ponmudi hill station (61 kms.), Akkulam Boat Club (lake), Palaruvi Waterfalls.

How to Reach: By Air:– Trivandrum is an airport.
By Rail / Road:– Trivandrum is well connected by both rail and road.

Plan your tour by rail
Route: New Delhi - 3054 kms – Trivandrum

Day	Train No./Name	Dep.	Arr.	From	To
One	2626Kerala Exp.	1130	-	New Delhi	-
Two/Three	Enroute	-	1545	-	Trivandrum
Four/Five /Six	Stay and Visit Trivandrum				
Seven	2625 Kerala Exp.	1110	-	Trivandrum	-
Eight/Nine	Enroute	-	1545	-	New Delhi

Where to Stay: Tel. Code- 0471

Hotels: 4 Star
The South Park (333333) Fax: 331861 Website: www.fhrai.com,
http://www.thesouthpark.com E-mail: southpark@vsnl.com
Lucia Continental (463443) Fax: 463347
Website: www.fhrai.com,
http://fhraindia.com.hotels/thiruvananthapuram/lucia
E-mail: sajlucia@md2.vsnl.net.in

Heritage
Surya Samudra (480413) Fax: 481124 Website: www.fhrai.com

3 Star
Pankaj (464645) Website: www.fhrai.com
Horizon (326888) Fax: 324444 Website: www.fhrai.com
E-mail: horizon@md3.vsnl.net.in
Mascot (318990) Fax: 317745 Website: www.fhrai.com,
http://www.kerala tourism.com E-mail: ktdc@giasmdovspl
Manaltheeram Beach Resorts (481610) Fax: 481611
Website: www.fhrai.com, www.richsoft.com/soma.htm
E-mail: soma@richsoft.com

Budget
Madison Fort Manor (462222, Fax: 460560)
Chaithram, KTDC (330977)
Navaratna (331784)

Jas (324881) Website: www.fhrai.com
E-mail: jas@md2.vsnl.net.in
Regency (330377, 331541)
Residency Tower (331661) Fax: 331311 Website: www.fhrai.com
E-mail: tower@md2vsnl.net.in
Geeth (471987)
Safa International
Shalimar Inn
Amritha (323091) Fax: 324977 Website: www.fhrai.com
Silver Sand (460318, 460942)
YMCA Int'l (477308)
and many others provide comfortable accommodation.

Best Season: Throughout the year.

Clothing: Summer-Light tropical, Winter- Tropical.

A Flavour of Portugal

DAMAN
Ex-New Delhi

On the western coast of India is a little bit of Portugal, cradled by the Kolak and Kalai rivers. The Daman Ganga river, originating from the Sahyadri range, parts the territory into two and bestows it with fertility. The strategic importance of Daman dates back to ancient times. The Abyssinian chief, Siddu Bapita, held control over this fiefdom. The Portuguese, who then ruled the waves, captured the territory and ruled it for four and a half centuries. The forts of Moti Daman and Nani Daman and the many ornate churches which the Portuguese built are a treat to the visitor. The lighthouse at the fort of Moti Daman still sends out its beams to fishermen on the sea. The three beaches of Daman are distinct in character. One at Nani Daman showcases the local fishermen and their lifestyle. The Devka is rocky and is thronged by picnickers. The Jampore is quiet and you have for company the trees, the crabs and the waves.

Places to See: Fort of Moti Daman, Fort of Nani Daman, Lighthouse, Devka Beach, Jampore Beach, Nani Daman Beach, Church of Bom Jesus, Salt Pans, Kachigam Park.

How to Reach: By Air:– Mumbai is the nearest airport. By Rail / Road:– Vapi is the nearest railhead (11 kms) and Daman is on the Mumbai - Baroda Road.

Plan your tour by rail

Route: New Delhi - 1221 kms - Vapi - 11 kms - Daman

Day	Train No./Name	Dep.	Arr.	From	To
One	2926 Paschim Exp.	1700	-	New Delhi	-
Two	Enroute (By bus or taxi to Daman)	-	1217	-	Vapi
Three/Four	Stay and Visit Daman				
Five	2925 Paschim Exp.	1403	-	Vapi	-
Six	Enroute	-	1035	-	New Delhi

Where to Stay: Tel. Code- 0260
Hotels: Budget
Miramar (254471, 254971)
Sandy Resort (254751, 254844)
Shilton (254558)
Dariya Darshan (254476) Fax: 54286 Website: www.fhrai.com
Sun-N-Sea (254506)
Ratnakar
Ashoka Palace
Marina (254420)
Gurukripa (255046) Fax: 55631 Website: www.fhrai.com
E-mail: gurukripa@vapi.wbbs.net
Kohinoor (252209) Fax: 52613, 52372 Website: www.fhrai.com
Brighton
Gokul
Diamond (254235, 255153)
Paradise (254404)
China Town (254416, 254920)
and many others provide comfortable accommodation.

Best Season: Throughout the year.

Clothing: Summer-Light tropical, Winter- Tropical.

Sea, Rocks and Philosophy

KANNIYAKUMARI
Ex-Chennai

The tip of peninsular India was coloured by the philosophy of Swami Vivekananda. At this point the oceans met and so did the lofty thought of the Swami. According to legend, it is here that goddess Parvati undertook penance to gain the hand of Lord Shiva in marriage. The beautifully adorned deity has a sparkling diamond nose ring which is supposed to be visible even from the sea. On the rocky island here, one can also see Shri Pada Parai- the footprints of the virgin goddess. It is here on this rocky island that the memorial to Swami Vivekananda stands in mute testimony to his rich thought. The Gandhi Memorial at Kanniyakumari has been erected at the place where his ashes were kept before immersion. Sunset at the point where three oceans meet is unparalleled, and as you can see the setting sun, you also can sight the rising moon in another part of the same sky.

Places to See: Temple of Virgin Goddess, Vivekananda Rock Memorial, Vattakottai, Gandhi Memorial, Sunrise and Sunset.

Excursions: Nagaraja Temple (20 kms), Suchindram (13 kms), Udayagiri Fort (34 kms), Padmanabhapuram Palace (45 kms); Tiruchendur, Courtallam Falls (137 kms).

How to Reach: By Air:- Thiruvananthapuram (90 kms) is the nearest airport.
By Rail / Road:- Kanniyakumari is a railhead, and is also easily approachable by road.

Plan your tour by rail

Route: Chennai - 738 kms - Kanniyakumari

Day	Train No./Name	Dep.	Arr.	From	To
One	6121 Kanniyakumari Exp.	1900	-	Chennai Egmore	-
Two	Enroute	-	0955	-	Kanniyakumari
Two/Three/Four	Stay and Visit **Kanniyakumari**				
Four	6122 Kanniyakumari Exp.	1600	-	Kanniyakumari	-
Five	Enroute	-	0715	-	Chennai Egmore

Where to Stay: Tel. Code- 04653

Hotels: Budget

Cape Tamilnadu (71424-28, 71258)
Vivekanandpuram (71250-1)
Township Lodge (71279)
and many others provide comfortable accommodation. For more information contact Govt. of India Tourist Office, Chennai: 044-8524295, 8510459.

Best Season: Throughout the year.

Clothing: Summer-Light tropical, Winter -Tropical.

Eternal Cities

Sometimes the very mention of the name of a city conjures up more than what the cup of imagination can hold. It has a life beyond life, a character beyond comprehension, an excitement beyond expectation, a sense ahead of sensibility, a discipline beneath the chaos, a desire to excel, and an ambition surpassing the ordinary to realize goals and be recognized as simply the best. Come to think of cities in the Indian milieu and instantly some names would come to the lips.

It is always that cities play a leading role in an individual's life; cradling him in infancy, watching the toddler in amusement; its lanes and bowers participating in his adolescent pranks; its lakes and gardens playing home to his courtship; its streets making him toil; its ruins bringing him closer to finality, till one day the rainbow coloured sky turns pale and dark. Discover cities through their sons or daughters, who by their heroic acts of valour have brought it an envious placement in history.

There are many cities in India where successively fortunes have been made; where gems as precious as the irresistible *Kohinoor* have passed hands; which have remained the cynosure of kings for many centuries; where lofty buildings as high as ambitions themselves have been erected; cities which have ruled the hearts and minds of people; erstwhile capitals which defined the borders of a State; places where love blossomed in the hearts of kings; a sky under which dreams have been realised. Come, discover the undying quality of many Indian cities, live history as you walk in their lanes, marvel at human ingenuity and hear of those glorious days.

Times may have changed but the character of Indian cities has not, and it is this flame of honour, which has kept the city glowing. Come, feel for yourself the pulse of the place.

A Celebration of Creativity

The Spirit lives on

34

Eternal City

DELHI
Ex-Mumbai

Delhi is perhaps the only metropolis, which has a vibrant undying quality. It has a heart which has withstood onslaughts by plunderers, mass slaughter, rapine greed and loot, scores of times. Names do not matter. Almost anyone who thought he was powerful militarily had Delhi as his target for proving his might. Yes, Delhi has since time immemorial been the ultimate ambition, the absolute possession of which was recognition in the Orient. It still continues to be the most powerful symbol of power and glory. The main gateway to Northern India welcomes you in more than a million ways. India's capital, a bustling metropolis, Delhi has been a perfect blend of history and modernity. Delhi has witnessed great civilisations. Many dynasties and rulers have risen to power on its regal soil. Delhi was laid seven times and of all the seven cities of Delhi, Shahjahanabad is today most alive. Many architectural wonders have been erected by the Sultans and Kings of Delhi. The forts of Delhi and the bazaars of Chandni Chowk are an interesting study of humanity. These, today form its proud heritage. Delhi, where the past meets the present, boldly and aesthetically welcomes every traveller.

Places to See:
Historical and modern buildings / places: Red Fort; Chandni Chowk; Purana Quila; Jama Masjid; India Gate; Rashtrapati Bhawan; Parliament House; Rajiv Gandhi Chowk (Connaught

Place); Jantar Mantar; Hauz Khas; Baha'i House; Safdarjung Tomb; Qutub Minar; Humayun's Tomb.

Temples, gardens and museums: Lakshmi Narayan Temple; Sis Ganj Gurdwara; Bangla Sahib Gurdwara; Lodhi Gardens; Air Force Museum; National Rail Museum; Shankar's International Dolls Museum; National Gallery of Modern Art; National Science Centre Museum; Nehru Memorial Museum and Planetarium; Buddha Garden; Rose Garden; Lotus Temple.

Samadhis: Rajghat; Shanti Van; Vijaya Ghat; Shakti Sthal; Veer Bhumi; Samta Sthal.

How to Reach: By Air:- Delhi is well connected by air. By Rail / Road:- Delhi is well connected by both rail and road.

Plan your tour by rail

Route: Mumbai - 1384 kms – New Delhi

Day	Train No./Name	Dep.	Arr.	From	To
One	2951/2953 Rajdhani Exp.	1655/1740	-	Mumbai	-
Two	Enroute	-	0955/1055	-	New Delhi/NZM
Two/Three/ Four	Stay and Visit Delhi				
Five	2952/2954 Rajdhani Exp	1600/1655	-	New Delhi/NZM	-
Six	Enroute	-	0835/1015	-	Mumbai

Where to Stay: **Tel. Code- 011**

Hotels: 5 Star

Ashoka (6110101) Fax: 6873216, 6876060
Website: www.fhrai.com, http://www.ashokgroup.com
E-mail: ashoknd@ndb.vsnl.net.in
Le Meridien (3710101) Fax: 3714545 Website: www.fhrai.com, http://www.lemeridien-newdelhi.com
E-mail: info@lemeridien-new delhi.com
Best Western Surya (6835070) Fax: 6837758
Website: www.fhrai.com E-mail: cosmohtl@2vsnl.net.in

Hyatt Regency (6791234) Fax: 6791024
Website: www.hyatt.com
E-mail: info@hyattdelhi.com
Taj Mahal (3026162) Fax: 3026070 Website: www.fhrai.com,
tajgroup@tata.com
E-mail: tajmahal@giasdel01.vsnl.net.in
Taj Palace (6110202) Fax: 6110808
Website: www.fhrai.com, tajhotels.com
E-mail: bctpd@tajgroup.sprintrpg.ems.vsnl.net.in
Maurya Sheraton (6112233) Fax: 6113333
Website: www.fhrai.com, http://www/cyber.club.com
E-mail: maurya@welcomgroup.com
Claridges (3010211) Fax: 3010625 Website: www.fhrai.com
E-mail: claridge@del2.vsnl.net.in
Imperial (3341234) Fax: 3342255, 8149 Website: www.fhrai.com,
gminp@gaisdl.01.vsnl.net
E-mail: gminp@giasdl.01.vsnl.net.in
Centaur (5652223) Fax: 5652256, 5652239
Website: www.fhrai.com, www.centaurhotel.com
E-mail: centaur@ndf.vsnl.net.in
The Oberoi (4363030) Fax: 4360484, 4304084
Website: www.fhrai.com, www.oberoihotels.com
E-mail: oberoi2@giasde101.vsnl.net.in
Radisson (6129191)
The Park (3743737) Fax: 3742055 Website: www.fhrai.com,
www.theparkhotels.com
E-mail: resv.del@park.sprintrpg.ems.vsnl.net.in
Park Royal (6223344) Fax: 6224288
Website: www.fhrai.com, www.parkroyal.com.au
E-mail: sales@parkroyal.co.in, admin@parkroyal.co.in
Inter-Continental (3411001) Fax: 3412233, 3709123
Website: www.fhrai.com, http://www.interconti.com
E-mail: newdelhi@interconti.com
Vasant Continental (6148800) Fax: 6145959
Website: www.fhrai.com, http://www.jaypeehotels.com
E-mail: hvc@del3.vsnl.net.in

Grand Hyatt (6121234) Fax: 6895891 Website: www.hyatt.com
E-mail: info@hyattdelhi.com
Samrat (6110606) Fax: 4679056, 6887047
Website: www.fhrai.com
Ambassador (4632600) Fax: 4632252/8219, 4697232
Website: www.fhrai.com
E-mail: ambassadorhotel@vsnl.com

4 Star
Kanishka (3344422) Fax: 3368242 Website: www.fhrai.com,
http://www.ashokgroup.com & http://www.indiatourism.com
E-mail: kanishka@ndf.vsnl.in
Marina (3324658) Fax: 3328609 Website: www.fhrai.com
E-mail: marina@nde.vsnl.net.in
Rajdoot (4316666) Fax: 4317442 Website: www.fhrai.com
Alka (3344328) Fax: 3732796 Website: www.fhrai.com
Diplomat (3010204) Fax: 3018605 Website: www.fhrai.com
E-mail: diplomat@nda.vsnl.net.in
Janpath (3340070) Fax: 3347083, 3368618
Website: www.fhrai.com
E-mail: janpath@ndf.vsnl.net.in
Oberoi Maidens (3914841) Fax: 3980771
Website: www.fhrai.com, http://www.oberoihotels.com
E-mail: bsparmar@tomdel.com

3 Star
Lodhi (4362422) Fax: 4360883, 4362082
Website: www.fhrai.com
York (3323769) Fax: 3352419 Website: www.fhrai.com
Broadway (3273821) Fax: 3269966 Website: www.fhrai.com
E-mail: owhpl@nda.vsnl.net.in

Budget
Ranjit (3231256) Fax: 3233166, 3239499
Website: www.fhrai.com
E-mail: reservation@indiatourism.com
Bright (3329145) Fax: 3736049 Website: www.fhrai.com

Natraj (3522699) Website: www.fhrai.com
E-mail: asses@del3.vsnl.net.in
Centre Point (3354304) Fax: 3329138 Website: www.fhrai.com
E-mail: cpoint@del2.vsnl.net.in
Satkar (6567811) Website: www.fhrai.com
Tourist (7510334) Fax: 3559418 Website: www.fhrai.com
E-mail: tourist@s.chad.com
South Indian (5717126) Fax: 5780130, 5752579
Website: www.fhrai.com
Jukaso Inn (3324451–53) Fax: 3324448
http://www.hoteljukasoinn.com
E-mail: jukaso@vsnl.com
Vivek (3324451) Fax: 7537103 Website: www.fhrai.com
E-mail: vivekhotel@mailcity.com
Rail Yatri Niwas (3233484)
Tourist Camps run by DTTDC and many other budget hotels.

Best Season: September to March.

Clothing: Summer- Light tropical, Winter- Woollen.

35

Skyscrapers and Silver Screen

MUMBAI

Ex-New Delhi

$\mathcal{M}$umbai, the new name of Bombay, is derived from Mumba Devi, a local deity, but the Portuguese, predecessors of the British, preferred to think of it as Bom Baim or the Good Bay (originally a set of seven marshy islands). Cosmopolitan in nature, Mumbai is a cultural melting pot where people of various religions live happily under a common designation - the Bombayite. Mumbai, better known as India's fashion capital, has some of the best up-market shops and boutiques. The beautiful Himroo Shawls, the silk and cotton saris of Paithan, Pune and Nagpur and the *chappals* (leather slippers) of Kolhapur are famous all over the country. Mumbai is also the Bollywood of India - film city par excellence. It has a life beyond life, a character beyond comprehension, an excitement beyond expectation, and an ambition to be recognised as simply the best.

Places to See: The Afghan Memorial Church; the Gateway of India; the Victoria Terminus; Prince of Wales Museum; Marine Drive or the Queen's Necklace is a beautiful sight at night; Essel World.

Beaches: Surrounded on three sides by sea, Mumbai has some popular beaches, namely Chowpatty in Central Bombay, Juhu, Versova, Madh Island, Marva, Monori and Gorai. Further away, a ride by motor launch takes visitors to the island of Elephanta Caves, which is the site of magnificent 7th and 8th century rock-cut cave temples.

Excursion: Pune: 170 kms from Mumbai, once the capital of the Maratha empire.

Places to See: The Raja Kelkar Museum; Agha Khan Palace, (an unlikely prison for Mahatma Gandhi and his wife Kasturba, who died while here); Forts of Shivaji (a 17th century Maratha warrior whose brave and clever anti-imperialist tactics are retold in ballads).

How to Reach: By Air:-Mumbai is well connected by air.
By Rail / Road:- Mumbai is well connected by both rail and road.

Plan your tour by rail

Route: New Delhi - 1384 kms - Mumbai

Day	Train No./Name	Dep.	Arr.	From	To
One	2952/2954 Rajdhani Exp.	1600/1655 -		New Delhi/NZM -	
Two	Enroute	-	0835/1015 -		Mumbai
Three/Four/Five	Stay and Visit Mumbai				
Five	2951/2953 Rajdhani Exp.	1655/1740 -		Mumbai	-
Six	Enroute	-	0955/1055 -		New Delhi

Where to Stay: Tel. Code- 022
Hotels: 5 Star
Taj Mahal (2023366) Fax: 2872711
Website: www.fhrai.com, www.tajhotels.com
E-mail: business.centre@vsnl.com
Taj President (2150808) Fax: 2151202 Website: www.fhrai.com
E-mail: tphbcbom@giasbm01.vsnl.net.in
Oberoi (2025757) Fax: 2043282 Website: www.fhrai.com,
http://www.oberoihotels.com
E-mail: reservation@oberoi.mumbai.com
Oberoi Towers (2024343) Fax: 2043282
Website: www.fhrai.com, http://www.oberoihotels.com
E-mail: reservation@oberoi.mumbai.com

Leela Kempinski (8363636) Fax: 8360606
Website: www.fhrai.com, www.theleela.com
E-mail: leela.bom@leela.sprintrpg.ems.vsnl.net.in
Centaur Juhu (6113040) Fax: 6116343 Website: www.fhrai.com
E-mail: centaur@bom3.vsnl.net.in
Holiday Inn (6704444) Fax: 6204452, 6701710
Website: www.fhrai.com, http://www.holidayinbombay.com
E-mail: reserve@holidayinnbombay.com
Centaur Airport (6156660) Fax: 6156535
Website: www.fhrai.com
E-mail: canthot@bom5.vsnl.net.in
Marine Plaza (2851212) Fax: 2828585 Website: www.fhrai.com,
planetindia.net/sparkplaza
E-mail: marplaza@bom3.vsnl.net.in
The Resort (8823331) Fax: 8820738, 8818641
Website: www.fhrai.com,
E-mail: resbom@bom5.vsnl.net.in
The Retreat (8825335) Fax: 8825171 Website: www.fhrai.com,
http://www.hotelretreat.com
The Orchid (6164040) Fax: 6164141 Website: www.fhrai.com,
www.orchidhotel.com
E-mail: ohmu@orchidhotel.com
Ramada Palm Grove (6112323) Fax: 6113682, 6110641
Website: www.fhrai.com, http://fhraindia.com/hotel/mumbai/
ramada
E-mail: palmgrov@giasbm01.vsnl.net.in
Sun-n-Sand (6201811) Fax: 6202170 Website: www.fhrai.com,
http://www.sun-n-sand@bom2.com
E-mail: sunnsand@bom.2
Sea Princess (6117600) Fax: 6113973 Website: www.fhrai.com,
http://www.seaprincess.com
E-mail: seaprinc@bom4.vsnl.net.in

4 Star
Ambassador (2041131) Fax: 2040004 Website: www.fhrai.com
E-mail: ambassador@vsnl.com

Ritz (2850500) Fax: 2850494 Website: www.fhrai.com
West End (2039121) Fax: 2057506 Website: www.fhrai.com
E-mail: west.hotel@gems.vsnl.net.in
Horizon (6117979) Fax: 6116715 Website: www.fhrai.com

3 Star

Air Link (6183595) Fax: 6105186 Website: www.fhrai.com
E-mail: universal@bom5.vsnl.net.in
Citizen (6117273) Fax: 6117170 Website: www.fhrai.com,
http://www.optimal-india.com/citizen E-mail: citizen@vsnl.com
Godwin (2872050) Fax: 2871592 Website: www.fhrai.com,
www.cybersols.com\godwin
E-mail: hgodwin@bom5.vsnl.net.in
Atlantic (6184263) Fax: 6104838 Website: www.fhrai.com,
http://www.indialog.com/atlantic
E-mail: pelican@bom3.vsnl.net.in

2 Star

Chateau Windsor (2043376) Fax: 2026459 Website:
www.fhrai.com
Garden (2841476) Fax: 2044290 Website: www.fhrai.com, http:/
/www.cybersols.com/godwin
E-mail: gardenht@bom5.vsnl.net.in
Balwas (3863613) Website: www.fhrai.com
Diplomat (20216610) Fax: 2830000 Website: www.fhrai.com
E-mail: diplomat@bom3.vsnl.net.in

1 Star

Silver Inn (8506392) Fax: 8505498 Website: www.fhrai.com
Rupam (2618302) Fax: 4950325 Website: www.fhrai.com,
http://www.leisureholidays.com
E-mail: buddha@giasbm01.vsnl.net.in
Park Lane (4114741) Fax: 4112389, 2044290
Website: www.fhrai.com
E-mail: goradiagebom5.vsnl.net.in
Sea Green South (2822294) Fax: 2836158
Website: www.fhrai.com

Budget

Fariyas (2042911) Fax: 2834992 Website: www.fhrai.com
E-mail: fariyas@bom3.vsnl.net.in
Natraj (2044161) Fax: 2043864 Website: www.fhrai.com
Sahil (3081421) Fax: 3079244 Website: www.fhrai.com
E-mail: hsahil@bom5.vsnl.net.in
Juhu (6184012) Fax: 6192578 Website: www.fhrai.com
Classic (6491456) Fax: 6494001 Website: www.fhrai.com
E-mail: hclassic@satyam.net.in, hclassic@yahoo.com
Grant (3871491) Fax: 3870215 Website: www.fhrai.com
E-mail: hotelgrant@vsnl.com
Heritage (3714891) Fax: 3738884 Website: www.fhrai.com
Pearl (52840) Fax: 5284027 Website: www.fhrai.com
Shelleys (2840229) Fax: 2840385 Website: www.fhrai.com
Strand (2882222) Fax: 2841624 Website: www.fhrai.com
E-mail: strandh@bom5.vsnl.net.in
MTDC also has many resorts and motels all over the city.

Best Season: Throughout the year.

Clothing: Summer- Light tropical, Winter- Tropical.

Imperial City of the Raj

CALCUTTA
Ex-New Delhi

Calcutta till 1911 was the capital of British India. Discovered by Job Charnock in August 1690, it has grown not by chance but by a definite direction, given to it by the Britishers. The Indian Renaissance started here and Calcutta has given more to the world than its due. It retains the romance of the Raj in its many buildings and fascinating names. The Victoria building floodlit by night, grandiose and majestic, symbolises Calcutta. It is also famous as an intellectual city having produced Nobel laureates. The people of Calcutta live by soccer, which is the passion of every child. Rabindra Sangeet at Calcutta has the unique quality of inspiring noble thoughts, motivating men to achieve great things in life.

Places to See: Shahid Minar (built in honour of Sir David Octerlony who fought the Nepalese war 1812-1814 to victory); Indian Museum; Victoria Memorial Hall and Museum; Academy of Fine Arts; Nandan (cultural and multiple film theatre complex); Birla Planetarium; Netaji Museum; Zoological Gardens; Rabindra Sarovar (Dhakuria lake); Marble Palace; Belur Math.

Excursions: Bakkhali Sea resort (132 kms); Barrackpore (24 kms); Digha Beach resort (187 kms,); Murshidabad (220 kms, the medieval capital of Bengal); Sunderbans (biggest estuarine forest in the world, and Delta); Vishnupur (152 kms, rich historical relics and temples with exquisite terracotta craftsmanship).

How to Reach: By Air:– Calcutta is an airport.
By Rail / Road:- Calcutta is an important railhead and is well connected by both rail and road.

Plan your tour by rail

Route: New Delhi - 1441 kms - Calcutta

Day	Train No./Name	Dep.	Arr.	From	To
One	2302/2306 Rajdhani Exp.	1700/1700 -		New Delhi	-
Two	Enroute	-	0955/1245 -		Howrah
Three/Four/Five	Stay and visit Calcutta and environs.				
Six	2301/2305 Rajdhani Exp.	1700/1345 -		Howrah	-
Seven	Enroute	-	0950/0950 -		New Delhi

Where to Stay: Tel. Code- 033

Hotels: 5 Star

Taj Bengal (2233939) Fax: 2231766/8805
Website: www.fhrai.com
E-mail: tajbeer@cal.vsnl.net.in
The Oberoi Grand (2492323) Fax: 2491217/2453229
Website: www.fhrai.com, www.oberoihotels.com
E-mail: grand@giasd01.vsnl.net.in
Hindusthan International (2802323) Fax: 280011
Website: www.fhrai.com, www.hindusthan.com
E-mail: reservation@hindusthan.com
Airport Ashok (5119111) Fax: 5119137 Website: www.fhrai.com
E-mail: airpotel@cal.vsnl.net.in
The Park (2497336) Fax: 2499457 Website: www.fhrai.com,
http://www.theparkhotels.com
E-mail: resv.cal@park.sprintrpg.ems.vsnl.net.in

4 Star

Peerless Inn (2280301) Fax: 2287883, 2286650, 2281270
Website: www.fhrai.com, peerlessinn.com
E-mail: peerin@giascl01.vsnl.net.in

Kenilworth (2828394) Fax: 2825136/381
Website: www.fhrai.com, www.bestwesternkenilworth.com
E-mail: calctta@nkli.wipri.vsnl.net.in

3 Star

Rutt Deen (2475240) Fax: 2475210 Website: www.fhrai.com,
www.fhraindia.com/hotel/calcutta/ruttdeen
E-mail: ruttdeen@vsnl.com
Lytton (2491872) Fax: 2491747 Website: www.fhrai.com,
www.lyttonhotel.com E-mail: lytton@giasd01.vsnl.com

2 Star

Fairlawn (2451510) Fax: 2441835 Website: www.fhrai.com
E-mail: fairlawn@cal.vsnl.net.in
North Star (5514171) Fax: 5514339 Website: www.fhrai.com
Shalimar (2285030) Fax: 2280616 Website: www.fhrai.com

1 Star

Lindsay (2452237) Fax: 2450310 Website: www.fhrai.com
E-mail: lindsay@giaschl01.vsnl.net.in
Larica Sagar Vihar (40226-27) Fax: 2404358
Website: www.fhrai.com

Budget

Astoria (2449679) Fax: 2448589 Website: www.fhrai.com,
http://www.theglobaledge.com/astoria
E-mail: astoria@hotmail.com
Green Inn (2440957) Fax: 2448396 Website: www.fhrai.com
Hollywood (4709372) Fax: 2359234 Website: www.fhrai.com
Dolphin (2442248) Fax: 2442248 Website: www.fhrai.com
Gulshan International (2290566) Fax: 2290566/2602
Website: www.fhrai.com, http://epages.webindia.com
E-mail: hotel-gulshan@epages.webindia.com
Harry (3215096) Fax: 3217376 Website: www.fhrai.com
Shilton (2451512) Website: www.fhrai.com
Rituraj (2321603) Fax: 2312052 Website: www.fhrai.com,
http:www.alwaysindia.com/rituraj
E-mail: rituraj@ca12.vsnl.net.in

Samilton (4748805) Fax: 4748809 Website: www.fhrai.com
Circular (2841533) Fax: 2842263 Website: www.fhrai.com
E-mail: circular@cal2.vsnl.net.in
Airlines (2364167) Website: www.fhrai.com
Avenue Club (2257337) Fax: 2360609 Website: www.fhrai.com
Executive Tower (2451338) Fax: 2490254
Website: www.fhrai.com
Astor (2829957) Fax: 2827430 Website: www.fhrai.com
Bliss (4404637) Website: www.fhrai.com
Plaza (2446411) Website: www.fhrai.com
Swagath (4756150) Fax: 4758324 Website: www.fhrai.com
Wellesley (2449114) Fax: 2445147 Website: www.fhrai.com
E-mail: lakshmi@cal.vsnl.net.in
Himalaya (2381961) Fax: 231-0774 Website: www.fhrai.com
E-mail: himalay@ca12.vsnl.net.in

Best Season: Throughout the year.

Clothing: Summer- Light tropical, Winter-Tropical.

37

Pearl City of India

HYDERABAD
Ex-New Delhi

Hyderabad is a city, which was fondly embellished by the erstwhile Nawabs. Mohammed Quli Qutub Shah, fifth Sultan of Golconda, founded Hyderabad in 1591 AD. Hyderabad is named after Hyder Mahal, originally Bhagamathi, a beautiful lady, who joined the Royal House of Quli Qutub Shah. The stories of the Nawabs and their immense wealth are known the world over. Hyderabad was decorated by them with numerous magnificent palaces and buildings. They were connoisseurs of art and collected original paintings, sculpture, ancient clocks, and many delicate and rare items. The city boasts of the magnificent Golconda Fort, which is a marvel in strategic planning. It can be witnessed at the gate of this fort how the slight sound of a clap can be heard resounding in the king's topmost chamber. The city is famous for Golconda wine, bangles, and the delicious Mughal *biryani*. Hyderabad is also known as the pearl city of India and one can buy the most charming pearls and ornaments from here.

Places to See: Golconda Fort; Salarjung Museum; Charminar; Hussain Sagar; Falaknuma Palace; Mecca Masjid; Qutub Shahi Tombs; Sri Venkateswara Temple; Nehru Zoological Parks; Budh Purnima Project; Tank Bund; Osmania University; Shilpa Gram; Hi-tech City; Public Gardens; Ramaji Film City.

Excursions: Nagarjunasagar (150 kms.)-relics of Buddhist civilisation dating back to 3rd century AD, and Tallest Masonry Dam in the world, Museum; Osman Sagar (20 kms.)-a Picnic Spot; Ethipothala Waterfalls (161 kms).

How to Reach: By Air:– Hyderabad is an important airport. By Rail / Road:– Hyderabad is well connected by both rail and road.

Plan your tour by rail

Route: New Delhi - 1671 kms – Hyderabad

Day	Train No./Name	Dep.	Arr.	From	To
One	2430 Rajdhani Exp. (Mon,Tue,Fri,Sat.)	2050	-	Nizamuddin	-
Two	Enroute	-	1855	-	Secunderabad
Three/Four/Five	Stay and Visit Hyderabad				
Six	2429 Rajdhani Exp. (Tue,Thur, Fri, Mon)	0645	-	Secunderabad	-
Seven	Enroute	-	0505	-	Nizamuddin

Where to Stay: Tel. Code- 040

Hotels: 5 Star

The Krishna Oberoi (3392323) Fax: 3393079 Website: www.fhrai.com

Holiday Inn Krishna (3393939) Fax: 3392684
Website: www.fhrai.com,
http://www.holidayinn.com/hyderabadind
E-mail: hik@hyd@rml.sprintrpg.ems.vsnl.net.in

Taj Residency (3399999) Fax: 3392218
Website: www.fhrai.com, www.travelweb.com
E-mail: trhbc-hya@tajgroup.sprintrpg.ems.vsnl.net.in

Welcomgroup Grand Kakatiya (3310132)
Fax: 3311045 Website: www.fhrai.com
E-mail: gn.kakatiya@welcomemail.wiprobt.ems.vsnl.net.in

4 Star

Bhaskar Palace (3301523) Fax: 3304036
Website: www.fhrai.com
Ramada Monohar (819917) Fax: 819801, 818836
Website: www.fhrai.com

3 Star

Green Park (3757575) Fax: 3757677 Website: www.fhrai.com
E-mail: greenpark.hyd@rml.sprintrpg.ems.vsnl.net.in
Ashoka (230105) Fax: 230105 Website: www.fhrai.com
Golkonda (3320202) Fax: 3320404 Website: www.fhrai.com,
www.icpl.com/golkonda
E-mail: golkonda@hd2.dot.net.in
Ohri's Cuisine Court (236504) E-mail: baseraa@hd2.vsnl.net.in
Central Court (3233262) Fax: 3232737
Website: www.fhrai.com, http://www.thecentralcourt.com
E-mail: cencourt@hd2.dot.net.in
The Residency (3204060) Fax: 3204040 Website: www.fhrai.com
E-mail:tres.hot@gmyd.tres.globalet.ems.vsnl.net.in
Minerva (3220448) Fax: 040-3222068 Website: www.fhrai.com

2 Star

Nagarjuna (3220201) Fax: 7714911 Website: www.fhrai.com
E-mail: afl.hyd.neehyd.xeemail
Jaya Intl. (4752929) Fax: 4753919 Website: www.fhrai.com

Budget

Krystal (3229874) Fax: 3227877 Website: www.fhrai.com
Sarovar (237299) Website: www.fhrai.com
Rajmata (3201000) Fax: 3204133 Website: www.fhrai.com
E-mail: celebra.t.shoppe@axcess.n.net
Blue Moon (3312815) Fax: 3321700 Website: www.fhrai.com
Rajdhani (590650) Website: www.fhrai.com
Royal (3202998) Website: www.fhrai.com
Viceroy (7538383) Fax: 7538797 Website: www.fhrai.com
E-mail: viceroy@hdl.vsnl.net.in
Shree Venkateswara Lodge (236871) Fax: 235914
Website: www.fhrai.com
and others.

Best Season: Throughout the year.

Clothing: Summer-Light tropical, Winter-Tropical

38

Home of Dravidian Culture

CHENNAI
Ex-New Delhi

Chennai still exudes the charm of traditional Dravidian culture. The city provides a fascinating vignette of its varied heritage. The ancient traditions, festivals, fine crafts, classical music, and dance are a treat to a visitor. The Kapaleeswarar Temple, a magnificent example of Dravidian architecture, has inscriptions dating back to 1250 AD. Another temple dedicated to Lord Vishnu, the Parthasarathy Temple, built by Pallava kings in the eighth century, is a star attraction. The British added magnificently to the city as they built Fort St. George in 1640 AD. – the first bastion of British power. St. Thomas Mount where the Apostle was martyred in 72 AD adds to the city heritage. The Chennai music and dance festival from mid-December to mid–January is a month-long extravaganza. The exotic silk dresses, brass and wood pieces, Thanjavur glass paintings and plates and ceramic pottery reaffirm the faith of its people in beauty.

Places to See: Fort St.George; St. Mary's Church; St.George's Church; St. Andrew's Church; San Thome Basilica; Parthasarathy Temple; Kapaleeswarar Temple; Valluvar Kottam; Guindy Zoo and Snake Park; Kalashetra; Marina Beach; Elliots Beach.

How to Reach: By Air:– Chennai is an important airport. By Rail/Road:– Chennai is well connected by both rail and road.

Plan your tour by rail

Route: New Delhi - 2190 kms – Chennai

Day	Train No./Name	Dep.	Arr.	From	To
One	2434 Rajdhani Exp. (Wed & Fri)	1530	-	Nizamuddin	-
Two	Enroute	-	2005	-	Chennai
Three/Four	Stay and Visit Chennai				
Five	2433 Rajdhani Exp. (Fri & Sun)	0620	-	Chennai	-
Six	Enroute	-	1125	-	Nizamuddin

Where to Stay: Tel. Code- 044

Hotels: 5 Star

Taj Coromandel (8272827) Fax: 8257104
Website: www.fhrai.com
E-mail: tajcorom@md3.vsnl.net.in
Taj Connemara (8250123) Fax: 8523361
Website: www.fhrai.com
E-mail: tajcon@giasmd01.vsnl.net.in
Welcomgroup Chola Sheraton (8278779) Fax: 8280101
Website: www.fhrai.com
E-mail: chola@md2.vsnl.net.in
Welcomgroup Park Sheraton (4994101) Fax: 4997101
Website: www.fhrai.com
E-mail: parksheraton@writeme.com
Fisherman's Cove (74301) Fax: 74303 Website: www.fhrai.com
E-mail: fishco@mds.vsnl.net.in

4 Star

Ambassador Pallava (8554476) Fax: 8554492
Website: www.fhrai.com
E-mail: pallava@vsnl.com
Buena Vista Resorts (4925624) Fax: 4928301
Website: www.fhrai.com

GRT Grand Days (8220500) Fax: 8230778
Website: www.fhrai.com,
www.grtgranddays.com E-mail: grtgranddays@vsnl.net.in
President (8532211) Fax: 8532299, 8533336 Website:
www.fhrai.com,
www.presiden.com E-mail: reserve@presiden.com
Savera (8274700) Fax: 8273475 Website: www.fhrai.com,
http://www.saverahotels.com E-mail: hotsavel@md2.vsnl.net.in
Grand Orient (8524111) Fax: 8523412 Website: www.fhrai.com
E-mail: empee.grand@orient.wiprobt.ems.vsnl.net.in

3 Star

Ambica Empire Best Western (3721818) Fax: 4817708
Website: www.fhrai.com E-mail: ambica@md4.vsnl.net.in
Ganga Int'l (8231340) Fax: 8235193 Website: www.fhrai.com
Breeze (6413334) Fax: 6413301 Website: www.fhrai.com
http://www.fhraindia.com/hotel/chennai/breeze
E-mail: breeze@giasmd0.1vsnl.net.in

2 Star

Atlantic (8553914) Fax: 8553239 Website: www.fhrai.com
Premier (583311) Fax: 832299 Website: www.fhrai.com
Peninsula (8254826) Fax: 8254745 Website: www.fhrai.com
Pandian (8252901) Fax: 8258459 Website: www.fhrai.com
E-mail: hotelpandian@vsnl.com
Shevaroys (2383-22385) Fax: 22387 Website: www.fhrai.com

Budget

Arunachala (8213312) Fax: 8213319 Website: www.fhrai.com
E-mail: arunacha@md3.vsnl.net.in
Aadithya (4880488) Fax: 4844303 Website: www.fhrai.com
Ganpat (8271889) Fax: 8260096 Website: www.fhrai.com
Karpakam (4942987) Fax: 4942991 Website: www.fhrai.com
Vaigai (8534959) Fax: 8535774 Website: www.fhrai.com
Ranjith (8270521) Fax: 8277688 Website: www.fhrai.com
Abu Palace (6412222) Fax: 6428091 Website: www.fhrai.com
E-mail: abuin@giasmd01.vsnl.net.in

Radisson (2310101) Fax: 2310202 Website: www.fhrai.com
E-mail: macnur@vsnl.com
Swagath (8268466) Website: www.fhrai.com
Sree Krishna (8525147) Fax: 8525037 Website: www.fhrai.com
MGM Grand (4980320), and many others offer comfortable
accommodation.

Best Season: Throughout the year (festival from mid-
December to mid-January).

Clothing: Summer-Light tropical, Winter-Light tropical.

39

Garden City

BANGALORE

Ex-New Delhi

*B*angalore ranks amongst the fastest growing cities in South Asia. Bangalore is one of India's most attractive and enjoyable cities. It is located 1000 m above sea-level. This bustling capital city of Karnataka has a perpetual holiday atmosphere. It is known as the garden city and Silicon Valley of India. Bangalore is fast emerging as the science capital of India and is known for its software park. The shopping centres of Bangalore offer you a fine selection of silks, sandalwood, souvenirs, handicrafts, and fragrant incense sticks. Bangalore was also home to the Roerichs who established the Tattagani estate. A cosmopolitan spirit pervades Bangalore and humanity is at its best in the city.

Places to See: Vidhan Sabha; Attara Kacheri; Cubbon Park; Bangalore Palace; Bull Temple; Tipu's Palace; Ulsoor Lake; Nanjangod; Muthyalamaduvu; Shivaganga; Channapatna; Mekedatu.

How to Reach: By Air:- Bangalore is well connected by air. By Rail / Road:- Bangalore is well connected by both rail and road.

Plan your tour by rail

Route: New Delhi - 2444 kms - Bangalore

Day	Train No./Name	Dep.	Arr.	From	To
One	2430 Bangalore Rajdhani (Mon,Tue, Fri, Sat.)	2050	-	Nizamuddin (New Delhi)	-
Two/Three	Enroute	-	0655	-	Bangalore
Three/Four/Five	Stay and Visit Bangalore				
Five	2627 Karnataka Exp.	1825	-	Bangalore	-
Six/Seven	Enroute	-	1205	-	New Delhi

Where to Stay: Tel. Code- 080
Hotels: 5 Star

The Oberoi (5585858) Fax: 5585960 Website: www.fhrai.com,
www.oberoihotels.com E-mail: rkeswani@oberoiblr.com
Ashok (2269462) Fax: 2250033 Website: www.fhrai.com,
http://www.indiatourism.com & http://www.indiahotels.com
E-mail: htlashok@blr.vsnl.net.in
Taj West End (2255055) Fax: 2200010
Website: www.fhrai.com, http://www.mondao.com/hotel/india
E-mail: twebcl@giasbgol.vsnl.net.in
Golden Waters (5595031) Fax: 5586473
Website: www.fhrai.com, www.holidaysindia.com
E-mail: alexebir.vsnl.net.in
Taj Residency (5584444) Fax: 558474 Website: www.fhrai.com
E-mail: cferns@giasbg01.vsnl.net.in
Windsor Manor Sheraton (2269898) Fax: 2264941
Website: www.fhrai.com, www.welcomegroup.com
Le Meridien (2262233) Fax: 2267676 Website: www.fhrai.com
E-mail: leme@bir.vsnl.net.in

4 Star

Gateway (5584545) Fax: 5584030 Website: www.fhrai.com
E-mail: gateway.banglore@tajhotels.com
The Park Kensington (5594666) Fax: 5594029
Website: www.fhrai.com, www.theparkhotels.com
E-mail: admin.ban@park.sprintrpg.ems.vsnl.net.in

St. Mark's (2279090) Fax: 2275700 Website: www.fhrai.com
E-mail: stmarks@vsnl.com

3 Star

Smart Residency (3360822) Fax: 3465657
Website: www.fhrai.com
E-mail: samrat@bg1.vsnl.net.in
Museum Inn (5594001) Fax: 5581313 Website: www.fhrai.com
Nahar's Heritage (2278731) Fax: 2278737
Website: www.fhrai.com
Central Park (5584242) Fax: 5588594 Website: www.fhrai.com
E-mail: centpark@bir.vsnl.net.in
Ramanashree California Resort (8461250-53) Fax: 8461254
Website: www.fhrai.com

2 Star

Abhishek (2262713) Fax: 2268953 Website: www.fhrai.com,
www.hotelabhishek.com E-mail: satram@bom07.vsnl.net.in
Broadway Annex (2266374) Fax: 2203661
Website: www.fhrai.com
Indraprasta (2202622) Fax: 2202636 Website: www.fhrai.com
Kamat Yatri Niwas (2260088) Fax: 2281070
Website: www.fhrai.com, http://www.kamatyarinivas.com
E-mail: kamat@bir.vsnl.net.in
Woodlands (2225111) Fax: 2236963 Website: www.fhrai.com

Budget

Airlines (2273783) Fax: 2218776 Website: www.fhrai.com
Highgates (5597172) Fax: 5597799 Website: www.fhrai.com
E-mail: highgates@bg1.com
Chalukya (2265055) Fax: 2256576 Website: www.fhrai.com
Kanishka (2265544) Fax: 2204186 Website: www.fhrai.com
Maurya (2254111) Fax: 2256682 - 2256409
Website: www.fhrai.com
Rama (2273381) Fax: 2214857 Website: www.fhrai.com
E-mail: ramabgir@bgl.vsnl.net.in

Swagath (2877200) Fax: 2259837 Website: www.fhrai.com, indiahotels.net E-mail: swinn@bir.vsnl.net.in
Ivory Tower (5589333) Fax: 5588697 Website: www.fhrai.com, http://www.bangalorenet.com E-mail: ivorytower@vsnl.com
Berrys (5587211) Fax: 5586931 Website: www.fhrai.com
Curzon Court (5582997) Fax: 5550631, 5582278
Website: www.fhrai.com E-mail: curzoncourt@iname.com
and many others in the city.

Best Season: Throughout the year.

Clothing: Summer- Light tropical, Winter- Light woollen.

Shan-e-Awadh

LUCKNOW
Ex-New Delhi

*L*ucknow found a permanent place in Indian history as the capital of Nawabs of Awadh. It flourished as a centre for culture in the late Mughal period and came to be known for its grace in mannerism and poise. Retains its old world charm and as the capital of Uttar Pradesh Lucknow is politically important. The alleys of Bara Imambara are a test to a visitors sense of direction. One can be lucky to find his way out of the alleys, once inside. Royalty probably had use for these alleys as a security system to effectively safeguard them from treachery and guile. During the freedom struggle, the people of Lucknow played an important role. Lucknow *chikan* work (embroidery on fine muslin and cotton) is popular amongst apparel manufacturers and lovers. The city indulges in a royal pastime of kite flying once every year by the banks of the river Gomti. Lucknow boasts of the most famous mouth-watering *kababs*, which are famous all over the country.

Places to See: Bara Imambara; Chota Imambara; Mausoleums of Nawabs of Awadh; Lucknow Residency; Picture Gallery; Hazratganj Shopping Centre; many other old buildings and gardens built by erstwhile Nawabs; Nawabganj Bird Sanctuary.

How to Reach: By Air:-Lucknow is well connected by air.
By Rail / Road:- Lucknow is well connected by both rail and road.

Plan your tour by rail

Route: New Delhi - 487 kms - Lucknow

Day	Train No./Name	Departure	Arrival	From	To
One	2004 Shatabdi Exp.	0620	1220	New Delhi	Lucknow
Two/Three	Stay and Visit Lucknow				
Four	2003 Shatabdi Exp.	1535	2145	Lucknow	New Delhi

Where to Stay: Tel. Code- 0522

Hotels: 5 Star

Taj Residency (393939) Fax: 392282
Website: www.fhrai.com, www.tajgroup.com
E-mail: tmhgm.luc@tajgroup.sprintrpg.ems.vsnl.net.in
Clarks Avadh (216500-09) Fax: 216507 Website: www.fhrai.com
E-mail: clark@1w1.vsnl.net.in

4 Star

Deep Palace (237247) Fax: 216507 Website: www.fhrai.com
E-mail: clark@1w1.vsnl.net.in

3 Star

Carlton (224021-04) Fax: 231886 Website: www.fhrai.com
Gomti, UPSTDC (220624) Fax: 212659
Website: www.fhrai.com,
http://www.up-tourism.com E-mail: upstdc@1w1.vsnl.net.in

Budget

Arif Castle (211313-17)
Kohinoor (217693) Website: www.fhrai.com
Deep Avadh (216521-24) Fax: 228832 Website: www.fhrai.com
Charans International (212516) Fax: 220411
Website: www.fhrai.com
Capoor's (227262) Fax: 222601 & 210376
Website: www.fhrai.com
Mohan
Tulsi

Presidency Inn (211070) Fax: 211082
Website: www.fhrai.com
and many others provide comfortable accommodation.

Best Season: Throughout the year.

Clothing: Summer- Light tropical, Winter- Woollen.

The City Beautiful

CHANDIGARH
Ex-New Delhi

Chandigarh was laid as the first modern planned city of independent India. The architect was Le Corbusier. The city is known for its Rock Garden the world over, designed by Shri Nek Chand, an internationally acclaimed artist. The artist has used broken bangles, cups and saucers, twisted wires, throwaway electric fuse pieces and broken sanitaryware to piece together a most beautifully conceptualised garden complex. The use of waste material to create a most charming presentation is an effort worth a visit. It serves as a capital to the States of Punjab and Haryana. One can boat at leisure on the Sukhna Lake, reflecting upon the beauty of life. The spirited people of Chandigarh take a lot of pride in maintaining harmony and gaiety in the city.

Places to See: Rock Garden; Zoo; Rose Garden; Sukhna Lake; Modern commercial complexes.

Excursion: Pinjore Garden: Located 12 kms from Chandigarh this garden was laid by Fidai Khan, a Governor of Mughal Emperor Aurangzeb in the 17th century. The garden is laid in seven terraces each holding a beautiful building or arch formation. A rippling waterway runs underneath the entire length of the garden.

How to Reach: By Air:- Chandigarh is well connected by air. By Rail /Road:- Chandigarh is well connected by both rail and road.

Plan your tour by rail

Route: New Delhi - 244 kms - Chandigarh

Day	Train No./Name	Dep.	Arr.	From	To
One	2011 Shatabdi Exp.	0740	1100	New Delhi	Chandigarh
Two/Three	Stay and Visit Chandigarh & Pinjore Garden.				
Three	4096 Himalayan Queen	1738	2210	Chandigarh	New Delhi

Where to Stay: Tel. Code- 0172
Hotels: 5 Star
Mount View (740544) Fax: 742220, 742565
Website: www.fhrai.com,
www.fhraindia.com/hotel/chandigarh/mountview
E-mail: citcol0@ch1.dot.net.in

4 Star
Sunbeam (708100-07) Fax: 708900 Website: www.fhrai.com
E-mail: sunbeam@ch1.dot.net.in
Piccadily (707521) Fax: 705692 Website: www.fhrai.com
E-mail: picadily@ch1.vsnl.net.in

3 Star
Park Inn (660111) Fax: 660110 Website: www.fhrai.com
President (771731) Fax: 549054 Website: www.fhrai.com,
http://fhraindia.com.hotel/chandigarh/president
Maya Palace (600547) Fax: 660555 Website: www.fhrai.com
E-mail: maya@ch1.vsnl.net.in
Aroma (700045) Fax: 700051
Website: www.fhrai.com, hotelaroma.com
E-mail: hotelaromawelcom@sml.sprint.pg.ems.vsnl.net.in

2 Star
Himanis Residency (661070) Fax: 661429
Website: www.fhrai.com
Pankaj (709891) Fax: 706480 Website: www.fhrai.com,
http://www.web.weavers.india.com/hotel/chanool.htm#pankaj
E-mail: colharsharan@hotmail.com

Classic (606092) Fax: 663275 Website: www.fhrai.com
Heritage (602479) Fax: 601221 Website: www.fhrai.com

Budget

Shivalik View (700001) Fax: 701094 Website: www.fhrai.com,
http//www.leisureplan.com E-mail: citcd@ch1.vsnl.net.in
Chandigarh Yatri Niwas (706038) Fax: 714061
Website: www.fhrai.com
Regency (604972) Fax: 604971 Website: www.fhrai.com
Kapil (603366, 603163)
Rikhy's International, and many others in the city.
Haryana Tourism also offers tourist bungalows and rest houses at
Pinjore and Chandigarh.

Best Season: Throughout the year.

Clothing: Summer- Light tropical, Winter- Woollen.

42

City of Nectar

MADURAI
Ex-Chennai

The ancient capital of Pandyan kings, on the banks of the Vaigai river, Madurai is reputed to be a sacred place. As per legend, the divine nectar falling from Lord Shiva's locks gave the town its earlier name – Madhurapuri. In the heart of the town stands the grandiose Meenakshi Sundareswarar temple, with immense *gopurams* towering over the city skyline. The most important festival celebrates the sacred wedding ceremony of goddess Meenakshi with Lord Sundareswarar during March–April. A chariot carrying the images of the couple is taken round the city amidst drumbeats and festive spirit. The Float Festival, when images of the sacred couple are floated on the Mariamman Tank on an illuminated raft bedecked with flowers, is also a strong attraction. The city revolves round the temple.

Places to See: Vaigai River; Meenakshi Sundareswarar Temple; Tirumalai Nayak Palace; Vandiyur Mariamman Tank.

How to Reach: By Air:- Madurai is an airport linked to Chennai, Mumbai, Bangalore, Calicut, and Tiruchirapalli.
By Rail / Road:- Madurai is well connected by both rail and road.

Plan your tour by rail
Route: Chennai - 492 kms – Madurai

Day	Train No./Name	Dep.	Arr.	From	To
One	2635 Vaigai Express	1225	2015	Chennai (Egmore)	Madurai
Two/Three	Stay and Visit Madurai				
Four	2636 Vaigai Express	0645	1430	Madurai	Chennai (Egmore)

Where to Stay: Tel. Code- 0452
Hotels: Heritage
Taj Garden Retreat (601020) Fax: 604004
Website: www.fhrai.com
E-mail: tgrgm.madu@tajgroup.sprintrpg.ems.vsnl.net.in

3 Star
Madurai Ashok (ITDC, 537531) Fax: 537530
Website: www.fhrai.com, http://www.ashokgroup.com
E-mail: reservation@indiatourism.com
Supreme (743151) Fax: 742637 Website: www.fhrai.com,
www.supremehotels.com
E-mail: supreme@md3.vsnl.net.in

Budget
International (741552) Fax: 740372 Website: www.fhrai.com
Pandyan (537090) Fax: 533424 Website: www.fhrai.com,
www.pandyan hotel.com E-mail: bhasker@md3.vsnl.net.in
and many others offer comfortable accommodation.

Best Season: Throughout the year (festivals in March-April).

Clothing: Summer-Light tropical, Winter-Tropical.

City of Victory

VIJAYAWADA
Ex-Hyderabad

Vijayawada, where the purest form of Telugu is spoken, is the heart of Andhra Pradesh. It is a cultural, political and educational centre located between the Krishna river and its tributary, Budameru. Legend has it that Arjuna, of the epic *Mahabharata*, prayed on top of Indrakila Hill and won the blessings of Lord Shiva. The name of Vijayawada is thus derived from *Vijaya* or Victory. The goddess of power, riches and benevolence is considered the presiding deity of Vijayawada. Three cave temples, dating back to the 5th century AD provoke the interest of a serious traveller. An experience of the temple tradition is not only educative but also interesting. The architectural style, the elaborate ritual of worship, and the chant of *mantras* create a holy atmosphere amidst the ringing of temple bells.

Places to See: Konaka Durga Temple; Lord Maleswara Temple; the Gandhi Stupa; Gandhi Memorial Planetarium; the Mogalarajapuram Cave; Temple of Lord Narasimha; Hazrat Bal Mosque; St.Mary's Church.

How to Reach: By Air:- Vijayawada is well connected by air. By Rail /Road:- Vijayawada is well connected by both rail and road.

Plan your tour by rail

Route: Hyderabad - 361 kms – Vijayawada

Day	Train No./Name	Dep.	Arr.	From	To
One	2714 Satavahana Exp.	1635	2150	Secunderabad	Vijayawada
Two/Three	Stay and Visit Vijayawada.				
Three	7007 Godavari Exp.	2355	-	Vijayawada	-
Four	Enroute	-	0600	-	Secunderabad

Where to Stay: Tel. Code- 0866

Hotels: 3 Star

Ilapuram (571282) Fax: 575251 Website: www.fhrai.com
E-mail: hotelilapuram.@com
Kandhari International (471310) Website: www.fhrai.com
Manorama (572626) Fax: 575619 Website: www.fhrai.com
Mamata (571251) Fax: 574373 Website: www.fhrai.com
Raj Towers (571311) Fax: 571317 Website: www.fhrai.com
Quality Inn Dv Manor (474455) Fax: 483170
Website: www.fhrai.com
E-mail: dvmanor@hotmail.com

Budget

Sree Lakshmi Vilas (572525) Website: www.fhrai.com
Krishnaveni Motel, AP Tourism (426382)
Sitanagram
Tilothama
Anupama
Chaya
and many others within the city.

Best Season: Throughout the year.

Clothing: Summer- Light tropical, Winter- Light woollen.

Manchester of the East

KANPUR

Ex-New Delhi

The city has been instrumental in making an unforgettable contribution to the Indian freedom struggle. It was a prominent centre of activities of stalwarts like Nanarao Peshwa, Tantya Tope, Sardar Bhagat Singh and Chandrashekhar Azad. The propagation and popularisation of Hindi also owes much to this city, with great Hindi litterateurs like Acharya Mahavir Prasad Diwedi, Ganesh Shankar Vidyarthi, Acharya Gaya Prasad Shukla, and many others having hailed from here. Nestling on the banks of the eternal river Ganga, Kanpur stands as one of North India's major industrial centres. It is believed that Kanpur was founded by King Hindu Singh of the erstwhile State of Sachendi. Historically, Jajmau on the eastern outskirts of present-day Kanpur is regarded as one of the most archaic townships of Kanpur district.

Places to See: Jajmau; Shri Radhakrishna Temple; Jain Glass Temple; Allen Forest Zoo; Kamla Retreat; Phool Bagh; Nana Rao Park; Bithoor 27 kms.; Moti Jheel; Tulsi Upvan; Tapeshwari Devi Temple; Prayag Narain Temple (*shivala*).

Excursions: Bhitargaon (59 kms); Musanagar (55 kms); Kannauj (80 kms.); Nawabganj Bird Sanctuary.

How to Reach: By Air:- There is no airlink to Kanpur. The nearest airport is Lucknow (90 kms.)
By Rail / Road:- Kanpur is well connected by both rail and road.

Plan your tour by rail

Route: New Delhi – 435 kms – Kanpur

Day	Train No./Name	Dep.	Arr.	From	To
One	2004 Shatabdi Exp.	0620	1105	New Delhi	Kanpur
Two/Three	Stay and Visit Kanpur.				
Four	2003 Shatabdi Exp.	1650	2145	Kanpur	New Delhi

Where to Stay: Tel. Code- 0512

Hotels: 5 Star
The Landmark (317601-05) Fax: 315291, 312247
Website: www.fhrai.com E-mail: landmark@lwi.vsnl.net.in

3 Star
Gaurav (318531-35) Fax: 314776 Website: www.fhrai.com

1 Star
Swagat (541923) Fax: 542100 Website: www.fhrai.com

Budget
Meghdoot (311999) Fax: 310209 Website: www.fhrai.com
Pandit (318413) Fax: 313492 Website: www.fhrai.com
Deep Mayur (547114) Website: www.fhrai.com
Ganges (352853) Website: www.fhrai.com
Park Royal (217126) Fax: 217126 Website: www.fhrai.com
Geet (311024, 311042)
Sarvodaya Plaza (217126-28)
Prithviraj (317807-08)
Saurabh and many others.

Best Season: Throughout the year.

Clothing: Summer- Light tropical, Winter- Woollen.

Seat of Ancient Wisdom

NALANDA

Ex-New Delhi

*N*alanda has a very ancient history. Hieun Tsang, the renowned Chinese traveller of the seventh century, records that according to tradition the place owed its name to a Naga of the same name which resided in a local tank, but he thought it more probable that Lord Buddha, in one of his previous births as Bodhisattva, became a king with his capital at this place, and that his liberality won for him and his capital, the name Nalanda or "Charity without intermission." It is also supposed to be the birthplace of Sariputra, one of the Chief Disciples of Lord Buddha. The University of Nalanda was founded in the 5th century by Gupta emperors. There were thousands of students and teachers. The university received royal patronage of the Great Emperor Harshavardhana of Kannauj and also Pala kings. Nalanda acquired a celebrity status all over the East as a centre of Buddhist theology and educational activities. Today Nalanda gives to its tourists a glimpse of the past glory that once was Nalanda.

Places to See: Nalanda University Archaeological complex; Nalanda Archaeological Museum; Hieun Tsang Memorial Hall; Surajpur Baragaon.

Excursions: Rajgir; Pawapuri.

Other attractions: Rajgir Dance Festival (from Oct. 24th to 26th every year); Chath Puja (in Vaishakha April-May) and Kartika (October-November).

Arts and Crafts: The places around Nalanda are famous for stone sculptures.

How to Reach: By Air:- Patna is the nearest airport.
By Rail / Road:- Nalanda is well connected by both rail and road.

Plan your tour by rail

Route: New Delhi - 992 kms - Patna - 103 kms – Nalanda

Day	Train No./Name	Dep.	Arr.	From	To
One	2310/2306 Patna/Howrah Rajdhani Exp.	1715/1700	-	New Delhi	-
Two	Enroute	-	0545/0535	-	Patna
Two /Three	Stay and Visit Nalanda				
Three	2309/2305 Patna/Howrah Rajdhani Exp.	2115/2115	-	Patna	-
Four	Enroute	-	1010/0950	-	New Delhi

Where to Stay: Tel. Code- 06119
Hotels at Rajgir

Budget
Centaur Hokke (5245)
Gautam Vihar, BSTDC (25273)
Tathagat Vihar, BSTDC (25176)
Ajatshatru Vihar, BSTDC (25027)
Rajgir (25266, 25322)
Mamta (25044)
For more information contact Govt. of India Tourist Office at Patna, Ph: 0612-345776.

Best Season: Throughout the year.

Clothing: Summer- Light tropical, Winter- Light woollen.

135

Home to Mighty Ancient Empires

PATNA
Ex-New Delhi

The capital of Bihar State, in past history, Patna has been crowned by new names in its evolution -Kusumpur, Pushpapur, Patliputra and Azeemabad. Its period of glory spanned a thousand years, from 6th century BC to 6th century AD. Ajatshatru, second in the line of Magadha kings, built a small fort at Patliputra (Patna). Patna was then ruled by Chandragupta Maurya (a contemporary of Alexander the Great), and his grandson, Ashoka, is acclaimed for the spread of Buddhism. Today Patna is an important business centre of eastern India. More significantly, it is a gateway to the Buddhist and Jain pilgrim centres of Vaishali, Rajgir, Nalanda, Bodhgaya and Pawapuri. Patna is also of great religious significance to the Sikh community.

Places to See: Golghar; Harmandir (this shrine consecrates the birth place of the tenth religious Guru of the Sikh faith, Guru Gobind Singh); Jalan Museum; Martyrs' Memorial; Kumrahar; Pathar-ki-Masjid; Patna Museum; Khuda Baksh Oriental Library; Agam Kaun.

How to Reach: By Air:- Patna is an important airport.
By Rail / Road:- Vaishali is well connected by rail. Hajipur is the nearest railhead (35 kms) but one can also go from Patna to Vaishali (56 kms) by road.

Plan your tour by rail

Route: New Delhi - 992 kms - Patna

Day	Train No./Name	Dep.	Arr.	From	To
One	2310/2306 Patna/Howrah Rajdhani Exp.	1715/1700	-	New Delhi	-
Two/Three	Enroute	-	0545/0535	-	Patna
Two/Three	Stay and Visit Patna				
Three	2309/2305 Patna/Howrah Rajdhani Exp.	2115/2115	-	Patna	-
Four	Enroute	-	1010/0950	-	New Delhi

Where to Stay: Tel. Code-0612

Hotels: 5 Star
Maurya (222061) Fax: 222069 Website: www.fhrai.com
E-mail: maurya@cal2.vsnl.net.in

3 Star
Patliputra Ashok (226270-75) Fax: 223467, 224207
Website: www.fhrai.com, http://www.indiatourism.com
E-mail: patashok@bih.nic.in
Chanakya (220590-96) Fax: 220598 Website: www.fhrai.com
E-mail: chanakya@giasd01.vsnl.net.in
Republic (655021-24) Website: www.fhrai.com
Samrat Int'l (220560-67) Fax: 226386 Website: www.fhrai.com,
www.zyworld.com/samrat2 E-mail: samratin@dte.vsnl.net.in

2 Star
President (220600-605) Fax: 230469 Website: www.fhrai.com

Budget
Kautilya Vihar, BSTDC (225411)
Satkar Int'l (220550) Fax: 22556 Website: www.fhrai.com
President (220600), **Anand Lok** (229273), **Rajasthan** (225103)
Marwari Awas Griha (220625-34), Fax: 220707
Website: www.fhrai.com E-mail: awas@vsnl.com
and many others within the city.

Best Season: Throughout the year.

Clothing: Summer- Light tropical, Winter- Light woollen.

137

A Speechless Wonder

JAMMU

Ex-Delhi

*L*egend has it that Raja Jambu Lochan discovered a tiger and a goat drinking water side by side from the same place in the Tawi river. This site of speechless wonder is today the city of Jammu, laid by the Raja. As if by divine ordination Jammu Tawi represents the entire Hindu pantheon with representative statues of gods, goddesses, and numerous *lingams*. Pilgrims throng the famous temples of 'Bawey Wali Mata', Raghunath Temple, and also the *Dargah* of Peer Budhan Ali Shah. The Bahu Fort on the bank of the Tawi river is scene to a fountain garden situated amidst its fearsome walls. The Amar Singh Palace is reminiscent of a French castle and is now a priceless museum featuring the region's culture. The city is partly located on a ridge and partly on the plains. The river Tawi meandering through the habitation can be a base for many memorable excursions.

Places to See: Peer Khoh; Rambireshwar Temple; Raghunath Temple; Bahu Fort; Bagh-e-Bahu; *Dargah* of Peer Budhan; Mahamaya Temple; Mubarak Mandi Palace; Amar Singh Palace Museum; Dogra Art Gallery.

Excursions: Katra (base camp to the Vaishno Devi shrine, 50 kms)
Kud (tourist resort 1738 mt above sea-level, 106 kms)
Patnitop (hill resort, 2024 mt on a plateau with meadows, forests and an opportunity to ski during the snowy winter, 112 kms)

Sanasar (a cup-shaped meadow with a golf course and paragliding opportunity, 119 kms)
Batote (resort at 1,560 mt overlooking the spectacular Chenab river gorge, 125 kms.)
Sudh Mahadev (1225 mt the shrine is situated, 120 kms)
Mantalai (believed to be the marriage place of Lord Shiva. Lush Deodar forests at 2000 mt)
Mansar Lake (excellent boating facilities, 60 kms)
Surinsar Lake (picturesque lake, 42 kms)

How to Reach: By Air:- Jammu Tawi is an airport.
By Rail / Road:- Jammu Tawi is well connected by both rail and road.

Plan your tour by rail

Route: Delhi – 585 kms – Jammu Tawi

Day	Train No./Name	Dep.	Arr.	From	To
One	2403 Jammu Exp.	2240	-	Delhi	-
Two	Enroute	-	0905	-	Jammu Tawi
Two/Three/ Four /Five	Stay at Jammu and Visit Environs				
Five	2404 Jammu Exp.	1800	-	Jammu Tawi	-
Six	Enroute	-	0420	-	Delhi

Where to Stay: Tel. Code- 0191

Hotels: Heritage
Hari Niwas Palace (543303, 547216) Fax: 543180
Website: www.fhrai.com E-mail: hariniwas@hotmail.com

4 Star
Asia Jammu Tawi (435757-60) Fax: 435756
Website: www.fhrai.com E-mail: asiahotels@vsnl.com
Jammu Ashok (543571) Fax: 543576, 547110 Website: www.fhrai.com

2 Star
Ambica (32062) Fax: 32064 Website: www.fhrai.com
Jammu Jewels (547630) Fax: 555076
Website: www.fhrai.com E-mail: info@jewels.myasa.com

Budget
K.C. Residency (520770-71) Fax: 575222
Website: www.fhrai.com, www.kcresidency.com
E-mail: kcr@kcresidency.com
Masar (543610) Website: www.fhrai.com
Premier (543436)
Samrat (548212) Fax: 575711 Website: www.fhrai.com
Moti Mahal
Vivek (577553)
Cosmo (547561)
Modern (543425, 546066) Fax: 433517 Website: www.fhrai.com
E-mail: kcindustries@hotmail.com
Air Lines
Tawi View
Vardaan Jammu (547414) Fax: 548286
Website: www.fhrai.com E-mail: vinns@vsnl.com
and many others.

Best Season: Throughout the year

Clothing: Summer - Light woollen, Winter – Woollen.

Home of Gandhi

AHMEDABAD

Ex-New Delhi

*A*hmedabad is a bulging metropolis of modern India with roots in medieval Indian history. It was founded in 1411 AD by Ahmed Shah. The Indo-Saracenic style of architecture makes Ahmedabad a delight for a tourist. The pencil thin minarets of the Rajpur Bibi and Sidi Bashir mosques appear to be shaking with the gusts of wind. The exquisitely carved screens of the Sidi Sayyid mosque in the centre of the city, carve most enchanting patterns in the sky, if you look through them. Bringing together the different styles of textiles, which evolved through ancient and medieval India is the Calico Museum of Textiles. The city served as one of the bases to Mahatma Gandhi's struggle for independence. His Sabarmati Ashram played an important role in the formulation of his thoughts and policy. It speaks brilliantly of the simple man who lived high.

Places to See: Rani Sipri's and Sidi Bashir Mosques; Jami Masjid and Ahmed Shah Masjid; the Calico Museum of Textiles; the Utensils Museum; the Kite Museum; Sabarmati Ashram.

Excursions: Vadodra (Baroda); Lothal (80 kms, civilization dating back to Harappan times); Modhera (104 kms); Palitana (there are 863 mindboggling temples); Dwarka (a flourishing port in ancient times, the temple of Dwarkadhish is an important pilgrimage); Porbandar (the birth place of Mahatma Gandhi).

How to Reach: By Air:- Ahmedabad is well connected by air. By Rail / Road :- Ahmedabad is well connected by both rail and road.

Plan your tour by rail

Route: New Delhi - 935 kms - Ahmedabad

Day	Train No./Name	Dep.	Arr.	From	To
One	2958 Rajdhani Exp. (Mon, Wed, Fri)	1935	-	New Delhi	-
Two	Enroute	-	1000	-	Ahmedabad
Two/Three/Four	Stay and visit Ahmedabad.				
Four	2915 Ashram Exp.	1745	-	Ahmedabad	-
Five	Enroute	-	1020	-	New Delhi

Where to Stay: Tel. Code- 079

Hotels: 5 Star
Inder Residency (6565222) Fax: 6560407
Website: www.fhrai.com
E-mail: inder@adl.vsnl.net.in
Sofitel Ummed (2864444) Fax: 2864454
Website: www.fhrai.com, sofitel.com
E-mail: sofummed@wilnetonline.net
The Trident (2864444) Fax: 2864454
Website: www.oberoihotels.com
E-mail: trident.ahmedabad@tta.ob.wiprobt.ems.vsnl.net.in

4 Star
Cama Park Plaza (5505281) Fax: 5505285
Website: www.fhrai.com,
http://www.camahotels.com E-mail: camahotel@vsnl.com
Radisson (6426967) Fax: 6560022 Website: www.fhrai.com

3 Star
Fortune Hotel Landmark (7552929) Fax: 7552919
Website: www.fhrai.com
E-mail: fortune@satyam.net.in

Holiday Inn (5505505) Fax: 5505501 Website: www.fhrai.com, http://www.holidayhospitaltyind.com E-mail: holiday.ahd@smlsprintrpg.ems.vsnl.net.in
Nest (6426255) Fax: 6426259, 6449926 Website: www.fhrai.com, http://hotelnest.webjump.com E-mail: nest@satyam.net.in
President (6421422) Fax: 6421421 Website: www.fhrai.com
Nalanda (6564123) Fax: 6426090 Website: www.fhrai.com
Royal Highness (5507450) Fax: 5507451
Website: www.fhrai.com, http://www.fhraindia.com/hotel/ahmedabad.royalhighness
Westend (6466464) Fax: 6469990 Website: www.fhrai.com

Budget
Quality Inn Shalin
Royal Balwas
Standard Karnavati
Kingsway (5501215) Fax: 5505271 Website: www.fhrai.com
Toran Gandhi Ashram (7559342) Fax: 6582183
Website: www.fhrai.com, http://www.gujrattourism.com
E-mail: tcgl.and@rmt.sprintrpg.vsnl.net.in
Prithvi
City Palace (2168145)
Ambassador (5502490) Fax: 5502327 Website: www.fhrai.com
Dimple Int'l (2141849) Fax: 2113276 Website: www.fhrai.com
Bombay (5506344) Fax: 5506296 Website: www.fhrai.com
E-mail: tahil23@bom5.vsnl.net.in
Rock Regency (6562101) Fax: 6423694
Website: www.fhrai.com, www.rock regency.com
and many others provide comfortable accommodation.

Best Season: Throughout the year.

Clothing: Summer- Light tropical, Winter –Woollen.

The Southern Eagle

TIRUCHIRAPALLI
Ex-Chennai

A giant fort on top of huge rocks dominates the landscape of Tiruchirapalli. Like an eagle, which sits pretty while on rest surveying the surroundings, Trichy's Fort rules the city. The place is an interesting blend of religion, traditions, and history. It was once the citadel of Chola kings. Then came the Pallavas, followed by the Pandyas. The present fort was erected by the Nayak rulers of Madurai. A thirteen century temple complex at Srirangam with its 21 *gopurams* is located on an island in the Kaveri river. The monumental *gopurams* of the place speak highly of the architectural skills and style, which evolved in South India. In the vicinity are caves with fine frescoes, pre-historic burial grounds and old churches.

Places of Interest: Rock Fort; Vinayaka Temple; Tiruvanaik; Jambukeshwara Temple; the Government Museum; Srirangam Temple.

Excursions: Grand Anicut (Kallanai, 24 kms); Mukkombu (Upper Anicut 18 kms); Vayaloor (08 kms); Samayapuram (20 kms); Viralimalai (30 kms); Sittannavasal (58 kms); Narthamalai (37 kms); Elakurichi; Puliancholai (72 kms) ; Kodumbalur (42 kms); Avudayar Kovil.

How to Reach: By Air :-Tiruchirapalli is well connected by air. By Rail / Road :- Tiruchirapalli is well connected by both rail and road.

Plan your tour by rail

Route: Chennai - 337 kms – Tiruchirapalli

Day	Train No./Name	Dep.	Arr.	From	To
One	6877 Rock Fort Exp.	2230	-	Chennai Egmore	-
Two	Enroute	-	0530	-	Tiruchirapalli
Two/Three/Four	Stay and Visit Tiruchirapalli				
Four	6878 Rock Fort Exp.	2200	-	Tiruchirapalli	-
Five	Enroute	-	0510	-	Chennai Egmore

Where to Stay: Tel. Code- 0431

Hotels: 4 Star

Sangam (414700, 414480) Website: www.hotelsangam.com
E-mail: hotelsangam@vsnl.com

3 Star

Jenneys Residency (414414) Fax: 461451
Website: www.fhrai.com
Royal Southern (4213030) Fax: 421307 Website: www.fhrai.com

Budget

Femina (414501) Fax: 410615 Website: www.fhrai.com
E-mail: femina@md3.vsnl.net.in
Ashby (460652) Website: www.fhrai.com
E-mail: chinoor@yahoo.com
Ramyas (415128) Fax: 412750 Website: www.fhrai.com
and many other budget hotels.

Best Season: Throughout the year.

Clothing: Summer-Light tropical, Winter –Tropical.

A Painting on Glass

THANJAVUR
Ex-Chennai

Exquisite like a painting on glass is the land of Thanjavur itself. The town is situated in the Kaveri delta amidst rich green rice fields. The Chola dynasty which ruled the area about a thousand years ago had made Thanjavur as its capital. That is the reason why Thanjavur has splendid specimens of Chola architecture. The palace structure rises pyramidically to the sky. Besides is a six-storeyed structure reminiscent of buildings in the Roman empire. A monolithic granite temple of Brihadeshwara, 66.5 m high, dominates the city skyline. The cupola on the top weighs 81.3 tonnes. The place was the repository of a rich culture. Therefore, manuscripts, palm leaf inscriptions, paintings on glass, bronze items, and silver/brass inlay work on copper plates are some of the art forms which flourished here. The world renowned exponent of Carnatic music also regarded as a saint, the legendary Thyagaraja has his birthplace nearby at Tiruvarur. The Thiruvaiyaru music festival is held here each January and the place reverberates with music.

Places to See: Saraswati Mahal Library; Brahmasirikandeswaran Temple; Harshavimochanna Perumal Temple; Sarangapani Temple; Nageswara Temple; Ramaswamy Temple.

Excursions:

Tharangambadi: (105 kms) There is a fort on the beach and a couple of old churches.

Swamimalai: (32 kms) There is a temple on the top of the hill dedicated to Lord Subramanya.

Thirubuvaiyaru: (13 kms) Thyagaraja lived and attained Samadhi.

Nagore (88 kms) Muslim pilgrimage, popular with people of all faiths.

Vailankanni: (90 kms) Noted church dedicated to 'Our Lady of Health.'

Point Calimere: (112 kms) Noted for its migratory water birds.

Tiruvarur: (55 kms) Thyagarajaswami Temple, notable as the biggest temple in Tamil Nadu.

How to Reach: By Air:- Trichy is the nearest airport (58 kms) By Rail / Road:- Thanjavur is well connected by both rail and road.

Plan your tour by rail

Route: Chennai - 387 kms - Thanjavur

Day	Train No./Name	Dep.	Arr.	From	To
One	6877A Rock Fort Express	2230	-	Chennai Egmore	-
Two	Enroute	-	0715	-	Thanjavur
Two/Three/Four	Stay and Visit Thanjavur				
Four	6878A Chennai Link Express	2000	-	Thanjavur	-
Five	Enroute	-	0510	-	Chennai Egmore

Where to Stay: Tel. Code- 04362

Hotels: 3 Star

Parisutham (31801, 31844) Fax: 30318 Website: www.fhrai.com, http://www.bayarea.net.judge/india/thanjavur.html E-mail: hotel.parisutham@vsnl.com

1 Star

Ganesh (31113, 32861) Website: www.fhrai.com E-mail: hotelganesh@yahoo.com

Budget

Sangam (34151) Fax: 36695
Website: www.fhrai.com, www.hotelsangam.com
E-mail: hotelsangam@vsnl.com
Oriental Towers (30724) Fax: 30770 Website: www.fhrai.com
E-mail: hotel.oriental.towers@theoffice.net
Ideal River View Resort (24533, 24633)
Tamil Nadu (30365, 31965), and other budget hotels.

Best Season: Throughout the year.

Clothing: Summer- Light tropical, Winter –Tropical.

Gateway to Heaven

VARANASI
Ex-New Delhi

Varanasi has for long enjoyed the status of the spiritual capital of India. It is the place where people come to die, in the hope of ascending heaven. The ghats of Varanasi, with imposing buildings at the backdrop and steps flowing down to the waters of the eternal river Ganga, have for long caught the fancy of visitors. Varanasi is an ancient city, which continues in its time warp in some parts. The Kashi Vishwanath Temple, one of the twelve *jyotirlingas*, is the most sacred shrine dedicated to Lord Shiva. The entire *Gita* is engraved on its marble walls. The other temples of Durga, Tulsi Manas, Vinayaka, Annapoorna, Kal Bhairav, etc., celebrate the spiritual traditions of Varanasi. All human life revolves round the temples. Along with the spiritual, the other dominant force is educational- there are three universities at Varanasi. The funeral pyres at Varanasi burn all twentyfour hours, in the hope of departed souls attaining *Moksha* (salvation in heaven).

Places to See: Kashi Vishwanath Temple; new Vishwanath Temple; Durga Temple; Tulsi Manas Mandir; Vinayaka Temple; Annapoorna Temple ; Kal Bhairav Temple; Jateshwar Mahadev Temple; Maha Mritunjay Temple; Bharat Mata Temple ; Sankatmochan Temple; Banaras Hindu University; Sarnath .

How to Reach: By Air :- Varanasi is an airport.
By Rail / Road :- Varanasi is a railhead and is also well connected by road.

Plan your tour by rail

Route: New Delhi - 698 kms - Varanasi

Day	Train No./Name	Dep.	Arr.	From	To
One	5206 Lichchavi Exp.	1625	-	New Delhi	-
Two	Enroute	-	0505	-	Varanasi
Two/Three/Four	Stay and Visit Varanasi.				
Four	5205 Lichchavi Exp.	1500	-	Varanasi	-
Five	Enroute	-	0420	-	New Delhi

Where to Stay: Tel. Code- 0542
Hotels: 5 Star
Clarks Varanasi (348501) Fax: 348186 Website: www.fhrai.com
E-mail: clarks.varanasi@dartmail/dartnet.com
Taj Ganges (345100-118) Fax: 348067, 344227
Website: www.fhrai.com, tajhotels.com
E-mail: tghgm.ben@tajhotels.com

Heritage
Pallavi International (356939) Fax: 392943
Website: www.fhrai.com
E-mail: pallaviinternational@epages.webindia.com

4 Star
Varanasi Ashok (346020) Fax: 348089 Website: www.fhrai.com
Hindustan International (351484) Fax: 350931
Website: www.fhrai.com, www.hindusthan.com
E-mail: hhivns@lw1.vsnl.net.in

3 Star
De Paris (346601-8) Fax: 348520 Website: www.fhrai.com
Ideal Tops (348091-92) Fax: 348685 Website: www.fhrai.com
Pradeep (344963) Fax: 344898 Website: www.fhrai.com,
http://www.angelfirecom/in E-mail: hotelpradeep@hotmail.com
India (342912) Fax: 348327 Website: www.fhrai.com,
http://epages.webindia.com/india/indiahotel
E-mail: india.hotel@epages.webindia.com

2 Star
Malti (351395) Fax: 392161 Website: www.fhrai.com
Barahdari (330581) Fax: 330581 Website: www.fhrai.com,
Hotel Baradari.web-page.net
E-mail: baradari@lw1.vsnl.net.in

Budget
Diamond (310696) Fax: 310703 Website: www.fhrai.com,
www.anglefire.com/in/diamondhotel
E-mail: diamotel@lw1.vsnl.net.in
Varuna (358524) Fax: 320690 Website: www.fhrai.com,
http://www.hotelvaruna E-mail: hotelvaruna@mailexite.com
Gautam (346239)
Siddharth (358161)
M.M. Continental (345272)
Tourist Bungalow, UPSTDC (343413), and others provide
comfortable accommodation.

Best Season: Throughout the year.

Clothing: Summer- Light tropical, Winter –Woollen.

Buddha's Retreat

RAJGIR

Ex-New Delhi

*R*ajgir is situated in a valley surrounded by rocky hills. Lord Buddha used to meditate and preach on Griddhkuta, the "Hill of Vultures." It was in Rajgir that he delivered some of his famous sermons and converted King Bimbisara of the Magadh dynasty and countless others to Buddhism. Lord Mahavir spent 14 years of his life at Rajgir and Nalanda. A peace pagoda dedicated to Lord Buddha has been built by the Japanese. It is said that on one of the hills in the cave of Saptparni, was held the first Buddhist Council. The sound of Buddhist *shlokas* recited in a sonorous voice, with a lot of feeling creates an atmosphere of peace and religiosity. Rajgir is also source to hot water springs, which are considered sacred.

Places to See: Amravana or Jivaka's Mango Garden; Venuvana; Ajatshatru's Fort; Bimbisara's Jail; Swarna Bhandar; the Cyclopean Wall; Griddhkuta or Vulture's Peak; Jain Temples; Pippala Cave; Hot Springs; Karnada Tank (where Lord Buddha used to bathe).

Excursions: Swarajpur—Baragaon (18 kms); Kundalpur (18 kms); Pawapuri (35 kms); Bihar Sharif (25 kms); Tomb of Makhdum Shah Sharif-ud-din (a Muslim saint of the 14th century).

How to Reach: By Air:-The nearest airport is Patna.
By Rail / Road:- Bhaktiyarpur is the nearest rail head. One can approach by road from Patna, which is 107 kms.

Plan your tour by rail

Route: New Delhi - 992 kms – Patna - 107 kms - Rajgir

Day	Train No./Name	Dep.	Arr.	From	To
One	2310/2306 Patna/Howrah Rajdhani Exp.	1715/1700 -		New Delhi	-
Two	Enroute	-	0545/0535 -		Patna
Two	By bus or taxi to Rajgir				
Two/Three	Stay and Visit Rajgir (back to Patna on fourth day)				
Four	2309/2305 Patna/Howrah Rajdhani Exp.	2115/ 2115 -		Patna	-
Five	Enroute	-	1010/0950 -		New Delhi

Where to Stay: Tel. Code- 06119

Hotels: Budget

Centaur Hokke (5245)
Gautam Vihar, BSTDC (25273)
Tathagat Vihar, BSTDC (25176)
Ajatshatru Vihar, BSTDC (25027)
Rajgir (25266, 25322)
Mamta (25044)
For more information contact Govt. of India Tourist Office at Patna, Ph: 0612-345776.

Best Season: Throughout the year.

Clothing: Summer-Light tropical, Winter- Woollen.

Romance of Art

Some dreams are pleasant, some ugly, and some remain just dreams. Full of earthly life, vivid colours, a strong mysticism, they seem to come from the other world. They speak of strange things; the divine spirit on earth, smoke and fire, sharp mountains, harsh elements, reflections and human will. The subconscious mysticism contained within comes to the fore in dreams. Man perhaps lives a fuller life in dreams than in reality. Much of this finds realisation in art forms.

So we have Indian art in many different aspects, spread over many centuries, celebrating the triumph of life. Early in ancient India the stone memorials, which consisted of great pillars, popular as lats, crowned by sculpted animals of metaphysical significance were set up at sites associated with the Buddha. On these pillars and other rocks were inscribed Ashoka's edicts on Dharma, in Pali. The stone, whether on railings or whether on gateway, was profusely decorated. Stupas, now built, have the same mathematical perfection of sheer architectural form and mass as in the pyramids. Above the square or circular base rose the solid and hemispherical dome. The dome symbolised the dome of heaven, enclosing the world mountain rising from earth to heaven. Symbolism found representation in the motifs of the carved railings. A frequent motif of that time is of the *yakshi* embracing a tree, usually a flowering *sal*. The embrace of the *yakshi* and the tree that yearns for her quickening touch is symbolic of some ancient fertility rite. *Yakshas* and *Yakshis* adorn many railings. The most beautiful representation of *yakshis* portrays swelling breasts and an ample pelvis. Jewelled ornaments are carved in sharpness and precision while the body curves in contrast, softly. The effect of drapery is created intelligently, emphatically defining borders and seams of the skirt. The exquisite precision of carving and the delight in

Frozen Time

surface decoration make sculpture appear to be a wood-carver's technique.

Then there are the most famous wall paintings in Cave I at Ajanta and date from the late Gupta to the early Chalukya period (late 5th to early 7th century). The colossal painted figures of Bodhisattvas "by their beauty and finality represent the imagined anatomy of a god. The face has the perfect oval of the egg, the brows curve as an Indian bow; the eyes are lotusform. The elephantine shoulders and arms, the leonine body, and perhaps loveliest of all, the hand, which in its articulation suggests the pliant growth of the lotus flower it holds." The representation of Shakti or female energy can be recognised in the beautifully drawn female figure of dusky complexion who wears a towering headdress.

The Sun Temple at Konark raises a storm in the eye, perhaps as powerful as the endeavour of the temple to emulate the stride of Sun god. The ambitions of King Narasimha of the Ganga dynasty in 1255 AD soared like the Sun's heat. Out boiled a temple, designed like a chariot drawn on twenty-four exquisitely carved giant stone wheels. A team of seven spirited horses, symbolising the ruthless, imposing, strident sun draws the temple chariot. Occasionally in such cities the sculptor is still at work and your gaze is arrested by a bright red conglomeration of sculpted figures. You cannot hold the impulse for a close encounter. The sculptures span the imagination of the sculptor as wide as it could be stretched. They dabble in themes of- reclining Ganesha, Sri Krishna, Lakshmi Narayan, Ram Sita, Durga, and the Buddha. Not bound by religious frontiers, the artist has made immortal a lady with a pitcher on shoulder, as a gazelle caresses her feet. These influences of religious learning and observations of beauteous representations combine to blaze a strong emotive trail.

Every Indian city celebrates some art form or the other and who should best discover it but you.

The Land of Erotic Art

KHAJURAHO

Ex- New Delhi

*K*hajuraho erotic art temples are India's unique gift to the world, representing as they do a celebration of life, of love, of joy. These temples were built in the years 950-1050 AD, in a short span of hundred years- a truly inspired burst of creativity. Of the 85 original temples, 22 have survived, constituting one of the world's greatest artistic wonders. The sculpture is so beautiful that it appears almost human. The lady holding the mirror, or beating the drum brings the temple walls alive. The human union is celebrated here in hundreds of styles. Even the unnatural seems so natural. Khajuraho is an education in art and life. Every year, a dance festival is organised in the backdrop of the charming Khajuraho temples to celebrate the beauty of life. The place has become a passion of every visitor to India. A visit to India is incomplete without admiring the passionate sculpture of Khajuraho.

Places to See: Temples of Khajuraho: Kandariya Mahadeo; Chaunsat Yogini; Chitragupta Temple; Vishwanath Temple; Lakshmana Temple; Matangeswara Temple; Parsvanath Temple; Ghantai Temple; Adinath Temple; Duladeo Temple; Chaturbhuj Temple.

Excursion: Panna National Park – 30 kms.

How to Reach: By Air:- Khajuraho is well connected by air.

By Rail / Road: - The nearest mainline railhead is Jhansi. All major mail and express trains stop at Jhansi. From Jhansi to Khajuraho by bus / taxi 175 kms on the Jhansi – Khajuraho Road (Regular bus services connect Khajuraho with Jhansi).

Plan your tour by rail

Route: New Delhi - 414 kms - Jhansi - 175 kms - Khajuraho

Day	Train No./Name	Dep.	Arr.	From	To
One	2002 Shatabdi Exp.	0600	1024	New Delhi	Jhansi
	By bus / taxi	1100	1500	Jhansi	Khajuraho
	(approx.)				
Two/Three	Stay and Visit Khajuraho				
Three	By bus/taxi	1330	1730	Khajuraho	Jhansi
	Travel back to Jhansi before 1700 hrs.				
Three	2001 Shatabdi Exp.	1755	2250	Jhansi	New Delhi

Where to Stay: **Tel. Code- 07686**

Hotels: 5 Star

Taj Chandela (42355, 42366) Fax: 42366
Website: www.fhrai.com
E-mail: chandgm.khj@tajgroup.sprint.rpg
Jass Oberoi (42344, 42376) Fax: 42345 Website: www.fhrai.com

4 Star

Clarks Bundela (42386-87) Fax: 42385 Website: www.fhrai.com
E-mail: clarksvaranasi@deartmaildarnet.com

3 Star

Khajuraho Ashok (44024, 44042) Fax: 42239
Website: www.fhrai.com

2 Star

Jhankar, MPT (2063, 2194) Website: www.fhrai.com
Payal, MPT (44064, 44076), and other budget hotels.

Best Season: Throughout the year.

Clothing: Summer - Light tropical; Winter-Light woollen.

The Black Pagoda

KONARK
Ex-New Delhi

Sun Temple

*T*his crowning piece of Orissan architecture and sculpture, built in the 13ᵗʰ century, the golden year of Orissan art, is poetry in stone, and on the World Heritage list. The Mukhashala, or entrance hall, continues to interest both devotees and visitors. The sun god *Surya* is celebrated in the three colossal statues installed over the three *dwars*. The walls of this magnificent temple portray exquisite sculptures covering all aspects of life. Scenes of love and war, trade and court transactions, hunting, catching of elephants, sages teaching, childbirth, amorous dalliances, dancers and mythical figures, all vie for attention on the panels and niches of this immortal work of art. *Surasundaris*, heavenly damsels, free standing, larger than life mono-block female statues playing the cymbals and drums, flutes and trumpets, adorn the top of the temple. The beautifully carved couples engaged in myriad modes of amorous union, with their incomparable charms, are an attraction for connoisseurs of art as well as for ordinary visitors.

Places to See: Sun Temple Konark is a many splendoured gem of Orissan art. Its beauty cannot be described in words. It is to be seen, enjoyed and savoured, not once but again and again, for it is truly a thing of beauty, a joy for ever.

Excursions: Ramachandi (8 kms). Temple of Goddess Ramachandi, meeting place of the river Kushabhadra with the sea— a nice picnic spot; Beleswar; Balighai; Kuruma; Kakatapur; Chaurasi; Pipili.

How to Reach: By Air:- Bhubaneswar is the nearest airport, 65 kms.
By Rail / Road:- Konark is well connected by both rail and road.

Plan your tour by rail

Route: New Delhi - 1258 kms - Bhubaneswar - 65 kms - Konark

Day	Train No./Name	Dep.	Arr.	From	To
One	2422 Bhubaneswar (Mon, Fri) Rajdhani Express	1715	-	New Delhi	-
Two	Enroute	-	1825	-	Bhubaneswar
Three	Stay and Visit Bhubaneswar				
Four/Five	Visit Konark and travel back to Bhubaneswar				
Six	2421 Bhubaneswar (Wed, Sun) Rajdhani Express	0910	-	Bhubaneswar	-
Seven	Enroute	-	1010	-	New Delhi

Where to Stay: Tel. Code- 06758

Hotels: Budget
Yatrinivas (35820)
Pantha Niwas, OTDC (35831)
Travellers Lodge (35823)
and others around the place.

Best Season: Throughout the year.

Clothing: Summer- Light tropical, Winter-Light woollen.

Romance of Sculpture and Paintings

AURANGABAD, AJANTA AND ELLORA CAVES

Ex-New Delhi

*A*urangabad is a 2200-year-old city known earlier as Rajtadok, Kirkee Fatehnagar, and finally renamed after Aurangzeb. Emperor Aurangzeb wanted to emulate his father Shahjahan who had built the wonderful Taj Mahal. He constructed a monument on the lines of the illustrious Taj Mahal which is popularly known as the duplicate Taj. Though built similarly, it could not equal the Taj. It, however, promises a delightful holiday.

Places to See: Bibi ka Maqbara; (tomb of Begum Rabia Durani, wife of Emperor Aurangzeb)

Pan Chakki: Aurangabad Caves (These caves dating back to around the 6th century AD are a fine example of contemporary life).

Excursions:

Daulatabad: 13 kms. It is famous for its fort that was once considered invincible. Constructed by Bhillama, Raja of the Yadav dynasty in the 12th century.

Khuldabad: A few kms. away from Daulatabad lies the tomb of Aurangzeb. Khuldabad is also famous for Bhadra Hanuman; Hanuman in sleeping posture.

Ghrishneshwar Temple: About half a km from Ellora lies one of the twelve *jyotirlingas* of India.

Pithalkora: 78 kms from Aurangabad, a cluster of 13 cave sanctuaries, Chaityas and Viharas that date back to the second century BC.

Ajanta: 106 kms from Aurangabad, Ajanta offers a rich tapestery of images that speak of palaces, royalty, culture and tales of everyday life in ancient India (a glorious past from 200 BC to 650 A.D.) These caves were built to offer seclusion to Buddhist monks, who lived, taught and performed rituals in the Chaityas and Viharas, which were the seats of learning and cultural movement. These enigmatic caves set deep in the Sahyadri hills, still illuminate with natural light during some parts of the day.

Ellora: 30 kms from Aurangabad, carved during 350 AD and 700 AD, the rock temples and monasteries represent three faiths-Hinduism, Buddhism and Jainism. The Vishvakarma Cave of the Buddhists, the Kailasha Hindu Temple and Jain Indrasabha present a captivating sight. These were carved out of a solid rock to provide sanctuaries to Buddhist monks.

How to Reach: By Air:-Aurangabad is well connected by air. By Rail / Road:- Aurangabad is well connected by both rail and road.

Plan your tour by rail and road

Route: New Delhi - 1394 kms - Aurangabad - 30 kms - Ellora
Aurangabad - 106 kms - Ajanta

Day	Train No./Name	Dep.	Arr.	From	To
One	2716 Sachkhand Exp. (except Tu, Fri)	1335	-	New Delhi	-
Two	Enroute	-	1215	-	Aurangabad
Two/Three	Stay and Visit Aurangabad				
Four	Stay and Visit Ajanta and Ellora caves				
Five	Travel back to Aurangabad before 1200 hrs.				
Five	2715 Sachkhand Exp. (except Wed, Sun)	1230	-	Aurangabad	-
Six	Enroute	-	1320	-	New Delhi

Hotels: 5 Star

Ambassador Ajanta (485211-14) Fax: 484367
Website: www.fhrai.com E-mail: amau@vsnl.com
Taj Residency (381106-10) Fax: 381053
Website: www.fhrai.com,
www.tajhotels.com E-mail: residency.aurangabad@tajhotels.com
Welcomgroup Rama International (485441-44)
Fax: 484768 Website: www.fhrai.com
E-mail: rama@welcomemail.wiprobt.vsnl.net.in

4 Star
President Park (486201-10) Fax: 484823
Website: www.fhrai.com,
www.presidenthotels.com E-mail: hpp@bom4.vsnl.net.in

3 Star
Raviraj (352124-25) Website: www.fhrai.com
The Meadows (677412-14) Fax: 677416
Website: www.fhrai.com, meadowsresort.com

1 Star
Khemi's Inn (484868) Fax: 482926 Website: www.fhrai.com
E-mail: khemis@vsnl.com

Budget
Aurangabad Ashok (332492-93) Fax: 331328, 331427
Website: www.fhrai.com
Amarpreet (351346-61) Fax: 351346-61
Website: www.fhrai.com
E-mail: hapmipag@bom4.vsnl.net.in
Quality Inn Vedant (350701-10)
Kailash
MTDC Holiday Resorts in Aurangabad and Fardapur (about 4
kms from Ajanta).

Best Season: October to March (Season extends all round the year).

Clothing: Summer- Light tropical, Winter- Light woollen.

Epics in Stone

BELUR, SHRAVANABELAGOLA, HALEBID

Ex-Bangalore

*H*assan: A place to experience unruffled calm in a pleasant climate. A convenient base to visit Shravanabelagola, Belur and Halebid. These places can be visited from Bangalore and Mysore, but if you'd rather explore them at leisure, Hassan offers a wide variety of accommodation.

Shravanabelagola: Wedged between two rocky hills, 51 kms south-east of Hassan, this is one of the most important Jain pilgrim centres and shrines. The monolithic statue 17 m high, the world's tallest of Lord Gomateshwara, a Jain saint, is standing atop one of the hills (Indragiri Hill). The symmetry in stone was created around 983 AD by Chamundaraya, a general and minister of King Rachamatta. The Mahamastakabisheka festival, an elaborate ritual, is held here every 12 years, the last one in 1993. Just opposite on the smaller Chandragiri Hill are some Jain temples and the tomb of King Chandragupta Maurya, the famous patron of Jainism.

Belur: 38 kms from Hassan, Belur is famous for its exquisite temple. Belur is known as the Dakshina Varanasi or Southern Banaras. The serenity of Belur is attributed to the celebrated temple of Channakeshava, built by Hoysala King Vishnuvardhana in 1117 AD.

Halebid: Halebid is 27 kms east of Belur, the ancient capital of Hoysalas- Halebid was then known as Dwaras Mudram (Gateway to Sea). The Hoysaleswara Temple here is a wealth of sculptural detail. The magnificent temple guarded by Nandi Bull was never completed despite 86 years of labour.

How to Reach: By Air:- The nearest airport is Bangalore. By Rail / Road:- Hassan is well connected by both road and rail from Bangalore.

Plan your tour by road

Route: Bangalore - 194 kms - Hassan - 51 kms - Shravanabelagola. Hassan - 38 kms - Belur. Hassan - 27 kms - Halebid

Day	Train No./Name	Dep.	Arr.	From	To
One		(morning) 0600	1130 (approx.)	Bangalore	Hassan
Two	Visit Shravanabelagola Post Lunch (Travel back to Hassan)				
Three	By bus/taxi	0900	1000	Hassan	Belur
Three	By bus/taxi	1400	1500	Belur	Halebid
		1700	2130	Halebid	Bangalore

Where to Stay: **Tel. Code- 08172**

Hotels: 3 Star
Hassan Ashok (68731-36) Fax: 67154, 68324
Website: www.fhrai.com, http://www.ashokgroup.com
E-mail: hsnashok@bgl.vsnl.net.in

Budget
Amblee Palika
Vishnu Prasad
Suvarna Regency (66774, 64279) Fax: 63822
and others.

Best Season: Throughout the year.

Clothing: Summer- Light tropical, Winter- Woollen.

Hidden with Sweet Beguile

TABO

Ex-New Delhi

*H*idden with sweet beguile are wonders that lie embedded like jewels in the mountains. Faith, the everlasting truth, flows like the current of a river, carrying away with itself all that is transient. Tabo monastery- the Buddhist *gompa* is the centre-piece of attraction in the Spiti Valley. This *gompa* was founded in 996 AD in the Tibetan year of the Fire Ape. Murals and stucco images distinguish the *gompa*. It is popularly called 'the Ajanta of the Himalayas.' The monastery complex has nine temples, twenty three *chortens*, a monks chamber and an extension housing the nuns' chambers. A series of caves earlier used by monks as dwelling units with an assembly hall make it the largest monastic complex in Spiti. The landscape is endowed with colour and fortitude.

Places of Interest: The Temple of Enlightened Gods (Gtsug Lha- Khang); Golden Temple (Gser- Khang); Mystic Mandal Temple (Dkyil-hkhor-khang); Bodhisattva Maitreya Temple (Byams-pa Chen-po Lha-khang); the Temple of Dromton (Brom-ston lha-khang); the Chamber of Picture Treasures (Z'al-ma); the Large Temple of Drom Ton (Brom-ston-lha-khang); Mahakala Vajra-bhairava Temple (Gon-khang); White Temple (Dkar-abyum Lha-khang).

Excursions:

Monasteries in Spiti- Mane Gogma, Dhankar, Gungri, Mud, Lha-lung, Lidang, Rangrik, Ki, Losar, Hikim.

Monasteries in Lahaul- Labrang, Shashin, Gondhla, Teling, Lapchang, Dalang, Tukchiling, Keylong, Galang, Kardang, Piukar, Tayul, Gemur, Darcha, Jispa, and Markula.

Monasteries in Kinnaur- Sangla, Ribba, Morang, Kanum, Nako, Leo, Chango, Shalkhar.

How to Reach: By Air :- Shimla is the nearest airport. By Rail / Road :- The nearest railhead is Shimla and Tabo is 365 kms by road from Shimla.

Plan your tour by rail

Route: New Delhi - 364 kms – Shimla - 365 kms - Tabo

Day	Train No./Name	Dep.	Arr.	From	To
One	2011 Shatabdi Exp. By bus/taxi to Shimla (night stay)	0740	1100	New Delhi	Chandigarh
Two	By taxi to Tabo (early morning) Three/Four/Five Stay and Visit Tabo				
Six	By taxi to Shimla (proceed to Kalka by road on day seven)				
Seven	2312 Kalka Mail	2345	-	Kalka	-
Eight	Enroute	-	0625	-	Delhi

Where to Stay:

Hotels: There are many budget hotels available at Tabo, a PWD and a Forest Rest House. Tented accommodation is also available for adventurous tourists.

For further information contact Himachal Tourism Office at Shimla: 0177- 78311, 78302, 6810.

Best Season: April to October.

Clothing: Summer- Woollen, Winter –Heavy woollen.

Jungle Safaris

$\mathcal{W}$hy do you and I sometimes have an irrepressible urge to run over plains, climb mountains and for a while disappear in a deep forest? Surely, becoming Tarzan the Ape-Man or finding a semi-naked beautiful maiden in a bower, is not the desire. Then why do we take to the jungle? I often wonder. If the line of man's descent is sliced off with a genealogical weapon, perhaps, we are inhabitants of the forest, hunting for a living, the cave our dwelling, the birds our music systems, the stars our compass, and goat paths our roads. For the Creator we do not have a name, but fear his wrath. The passing seasons our calendar and animal skin our clothing. Life is as pure as the elements themselves, so say the majestic sun and the romantic moon in their sure and steady stride. In a forest we are perhaps back to our roots.

Think like this and you find yourself heading for dense forests or sanctuaries. The road decides to reveal various faces of Nature on the way. Close by, a crooked road is in the grip of tall straight trees. The crooked road weans its way amidst dense forest and seems to be running away from straight angles. The forest, aflame with bright seasonal blossoms starts sucking you in its preserves. The road is narrow and shadows longer. Welcome is written boldly on the flaming hill and carpeted road. An excited bird call shifts the focus towards the sanctuary and this reverie is broken.

A day inside an Indian sanctuary is yet another day out of the jungle book for a visitor. The Indian forests have an abundant wildlife. Barking deer, bears, porcupines, wild boars, jackals, tigers, elephants, leopards, rhinos, spotted deer, sambhar, lions, panthers, blue-bulls, and scores of other species roam the wild. The sun spreads its forceful presence on men and animals below. Blue bull families are best swishing their tails or munching on a high bush. Spotted deer feel lazy and are not in a mood to jump and hop away. Wild boars, quite boorish, stroll in the company of sambhars. There is excitement in store. You can spot a tiger in its natural habitat. As you move scouring jungle pathways, ducking under low branches, craning necks from an open jeep to the right and left and finally stopping dead— pug marks of tiger, fresh on mud. A frightened call of a spotted deer confirms the majestic presence. If you are lucky you can see the ferocious beast chasing his breakfast. The thrills and pleasures of the wild are indeed more powerful in nature, than those of the civilised world.

However, it is in the birds that the forests again excel. Peacocks, wagtails, pond herons, kingfisher, magpie, parrots, pigeons, flamingos, cranes, cormorants, painted storks, white ibis, golden orioles, ducks, partridges, whistling thrush, wren and hundreds of other species inhabit Indian national parks. All these and more inhabit the forest. The prettiest are the young ones. The Siberian cranes come from as far as Siberia during the winter months.

Charming trek routes through trees and shadows are invigorating. The breeze blows as if in a stream motion and you can actually hear the sounds of the wind. A huge forest bungalow or rest house is perhaps a chapter on living in the woods. Immediately there runs a current in the body. You can carve and chalk out your own trek paths in the forest like a creature of Nature. Let the forests fill your being, as does the night to the forest.

Dusk falls to the surprised calls of a barking deer. The sunlight melts into a bluish-purple sky. Suddenly a crescent of white light is seen emerging over the sky. The sharp shape of a tree cuts into the rising sphere as if it is trying to hold the moon, for one last moment. The moon is but in a hurry to rule the sky for the night. Its hesitant yellow gives way to a brighter wl   It drifts into moods and windows with ease. Keep the w   )ws clear of curtains, for you shall have an unusual guest tc ght. Today, after the candle is sniffed out, it shall be time to slee̩ with the moon. The forest moon will hold you in its grip, and nothing can prevent you from falling into a moony swoon.

Are you watching me

Ready for a leap

Haven of Tigers

CORBETT NATIONAL PARK
Ex-Delhi

India's first National Park is situated in the hilly districts of Pauri Garhwal and Nainital. The Park was first established in 1936 by the then Governor, Sir Malcolm Hailey, and was named Hailey National Park. After Independence, the park was renamed Ramganga National Park and finally Corbett National Park in honour of the late Jim Corbett, the legendary author and photographer who helped in demarcating the Park's boundaries and setting it up. The Park is cradled in the foothills of the Himalayas and is spread over an area of 520 sq. kms.

Attractions within the Park:

i) The lake in the Park attracts a large number of species of water birds, both migrant and native.

ii) Among the reptiles, the snouted Gharial and Mugger (crocodiles) could be seen basking in the sun.

iii) Sporting fish such as Mahseer and Malee thrive in the lake and in the river- offer a great fishing temptation to anglers.

iv) The tiger is the biggest attraction of this Park (following an international appeal to save the world's most magnificent beasts Project Tiger was launched with the help of World Wildlife Fund on April I, 1973, making the Corbett Park a haven for tigers).

v) Elephant, leopard, beer, hog, sambhar, deer, and fox are the attractions of the Park.

vi) Different species of trees, shrubs, bamboo and grass make up the lush vegetation of the Park. The sanctuary is dominated by pure *sal* forest for which the Park is known.

How to Reach: By Rail / Road:- Corbett Park is well connected by both rail and road. The nearest railhead is Ramnagar.

Plan your tour by rail

Route: Delhi- 246 kms - Ramnagar - 56 kms - Corbett National Park

Day	Train No./Name	Dep.	Arr.	From	To
One	5013A Ranikhet Exp.	2245	-	Delhi	-
Two	Enroute	-	0450	-	Ramnagar
	By bus or taxi to Ramnagar Corbett Park.				
Two/Three	Stay and Visit Corbett National Park.				
Three (night)	Travel back to Ramnagar before 2100 hrs.				
	5014A Ranikhet Exp.	2110	-	Ramnagar	-
Four	Enroute	-	0445	-	Delhi

Where to Stay:

Forest Rest Houses at Dhikala, Sarapduli, Ghairal, Sultan, Bijrani, Malani, Kanda, Dhela, and other accommodation around the Corbett Park.

For booking contact: General Manager, Tourism, KMVN, Oak Park House, Nainital. Tel.: 05942- 36356.

Best Season: November 15 to June 15.

Clothing: Summer- Light tropical, Winter- Normal woollen.

Wildlife Bonanza

KANHA

Ex- New Delhi

*K*anha National Park forms the core of Kanha Tiger Reserve created in 1974 under Project Tiger. The Park is the only habitat of the rare hard ground barasingha (Cervus Duvaceli Branckri). Kanha's *sal* and bamboo forests, rolling grasslands and meandering streams stretch over 840 sq km in natural splendour. By a special statute in 1955, Kanha National Park came into being. Since then, a series of stringent conservation programmes for the projection of the Park's flora and fauna have given Kanha its deserved reputation for being one of the finest and best administered National Parks in Asia- an irresistible attraction for all wildlife lovers and a true haven for its animal and avian population.

What to See: Forest Department guides accompany visitors around the Park on mapped-out circuits. The best areas are the meadows around Kanha, where black buck, chital and barasingha can be seen throughout the day.

Bamni Dadar: Known as sunset point, this is one of the most beautiful areas of the Park.

Mammalian species: Kanha has some 22 species of mammals. Those easily spotted are- jackal, wild pig, chital, swamp deer, sambhar and black buck. Less commonly seen can be tiger, Indian hare and Indian wild dog.

Avian species: Kanha has some 200 species of birds.

Commonly seen species include: cattle egret, pond heron, black ibis, common peafowl, crested serpent, racket tailed drongo, Indian roller and grey hornbill.

How to Reach: By Air: - Nearest airport is Jabalpur.
By Rail / Road:- Most convenient railhead is Jabalpur and it is also well connected by road.

Plan your tour by rail

Route: New Delhi – 914 kms - Jabalpur - 165 kms - Kisli - 3 kms - Kanha

Day	Train No./Name	Dep.	Arr.	From	To
One	2412 Gondwana Exp.	1430	-	Nizamuddin	-
Two	Enroute	-	0540	-	Jabalpur
	Travel to Kanha by bus /taxi				
Three/Four/Five	Stay and Visit Kanha				
	Travel to Jabalpur by bus /taxi				
Five	2411 Gondwana Exp	1540	-	Jabalpur	-
Six	Enroute	-	0720	-	Nizamuddin

Where to Stay: Tel. Code- 07636

Hotels: 2 Star
Royal Tiger Resort (56418) Fax: 56345
Website: www.fhrai.com,
http://www.royaltiger.com E-mail: tiger@nde.vsnl.net.in

Budget
Tuli Tiger Resort (77221) Fax: 534473 Website: www.fhrai.com,
www.tuligroup.com E-mail: tuli@bom2.vsnl.net.in
Kanha Safari Lodge, Mukki (MPT)
Baghira Log Huts
Kanha Jungle Lodge
Wild Chalet Resort
Kisli (MPT)
Tourist Hostel Kisli (MPT)

For further details contact Tiger Resorts, New Delhi (011-6516770, 6853760).

Best Season: February to June (The park is closed from July to Oct. because of the monsoon). A stay of three nights is recommended in order to have a good chance of seeing the more elusive animals.

Clothing: Cottons, but woollens as well, as early morning and evening can be chilly. Try not to wear loud colours.

One-Horned Glory

KAZIRANGA

Ex-Calcutta

Kaziranga is situated in central Assam and is known for its National Park, the home of great Indian one-horned rhinoceros (unicorn). The activities of the rhino, its lazing in the forest ponds, its majestic walk, are a real treat to the wildlife enthusiast. Kaziranga is a sheer primeval forest of elephant grass, rugged reed, marsh, pools, and beds. It is situated 217 kms from Guwahati and covers an area of 430 sq. kms. It is also a breeding ground for pelicans and host to numerous resident and migratory birds. One can catch many photo opportunities of fledegling birds learning to fly, soaring flights of others and the pranks of many in the water. The harmony of wild creatures and indulgent environment is seen here at its best.

Attractions In the National Park: Rhinoceros; elephant; swamp deer; sambhar; hog deer; sloth bear; water buffalo; tiger; leopard; leopard cat; jungle cat; hog badger; capped langur; hoolock gibbon; jackal; goose hornbill; ibis; cormorant; heron; fishing eagle and other migratory and non- migratory birds.

How to Reach: By Air:- Guwahati is the nearest airport.
By Rail / Road:- Kaziranga is well connected by both rail and road via Guwahati.

Plan your tour by rail

Route: Calcutta - 991 kms - Guwahati - 334 kms - Jorhat - 60 - kms - Kaziranga.

Day	Train No./Name	Dep.	Arr.	From	To
One	2345 Saraighat Express (Wed, Thur, Sun)	1550	-	Howrah	-
Two	Enroute	-	0945	-	Guwahati
Two	5605 Inter City	1900	-	Guwahati	-
Three	Enroute	-	0720	-	Jorhat
Three/Four/Five	Stay and Visit Kaziranga National Park				
Five	5606 Inter City	2035	-	Jorhat	-
Six	Enroute	-	0730	-	Guwahati
Six	2346 Saraighat Express (M,Thu,F)	1915	-	Guwahati	-
Seven	Enroute	-	1305	-	Howrah

Where to Stay:
Hotels: Budget
Aranya, Bonani and Bonoshri Lodges
Wild Grass Resort
and Tourist Bungalow.
For further information contact: Director, Kaziranga National
Park, P.O. Bokakhat, Jorhat, Assam- 785612 OR Govt. of India
Tourist Office at Guwahati. Tel. : 0361- 547407.

Park Visit: By jeep or on elephant back.

Best Season: November to April.

Clothing: Summer- Cotton, Winter- Woollen.

61

Elephant Trail

PERIYAR

Ex-Chennai

The Periyar sanctuary in Idukki district of Kerala is a vast reservoir of water created by a dam on the Periyar river. In 1978 the sanctuary was declared a Tiger Reserve under Project Tiger. Forests in this sanctuary are grasslands, moist deciduous, tropical evergreen, and semi-evergreen. The Reserve covers hills and forest over an area of 777 sq.kms. Over 160 species of birds inhabit this Reserve. Birds sitting on the dried trees half submerged in water present wonderful viewing and picture opportunities. Elephant herds are numerous and can be seen lazily grazing on the banks of the water body. There are about 600 elephants and a wide range of animal life in the sanctuary. Except in December and January, the sanctuary receives rainfall throughout the year.

Attractions within the Sanctuary:

Birds: Great Indian Hornbill; Brahmini Kite; Black Winged Kite; Cormorant; King Fisher; Blue Winged Parakeet; Whistling Thrush; Golden Oriole.

Animals: Elephants; Sambhar; Barking Deer; Mouse Deer; Wild Boar; Porcupine; Nilgiri Langoor; Bonnet Macaque, Lion-Tailed Macaque; Tigers; Panthers; Malabar Squirrel; Sloth Bear and Wild Dogs.

How to Reach: By Air:- Madurai (140 - kms) is the nearest airport.

By Rail / Road:- Madurai is the most convenient railhead and Periyar is easily accessible by road.

Plan your tour by rail

Route: Chennai - 492 kms - Madurai – 140 kms - Periyar

Day	Train No./Name	Dep.	Arr.	From	To
One	2635 Vaigai Express	1225	2015	Chennai Egmore	Madurai
Two	By bus /taxi to Periyar (140 kms.).				
Two/Three	Stay and Visit Periyar (Travel back to Madurai)				
Four	2636 Vaigai Express	0645	1430	Madurai	Chennai Egmore

Where to Stay: Tel. Code- 04869

Hotels: Budget
Edapalayam Lake Palace, KTDC (22023, 22283)
Aranya Niwas, KTDC (22023, 22283)
Periyar House KTDC (22026)
For further information contact: Field Director, Project Tiger, Kanjikuzhi, Kottayam, Kerala or Govt. of India Tourist Office at Kochi. Tel. : 0484- 668352.

Best Season: December to May.

Clothing: Summer-Light tropical, Winter-Light tropical.

62

Tiger Country

RANTHAMBORE

Ex-New Delhi

anthambore needs very little introduction. Its national park has been one of India's conservation success stories. Nestling between the Aravalli and Vindhyachal Ranges, Ranthambore is an important town with its own historicity. Ranthambore was one of the first few areas to come under Project Tiger and has continued to be the most successful. It is home to an expansive variety of other animals in its 392 sq. km area. It is just the right place to accost the majestic tiger in its own habitat. Whether it emerges suddenly out of the bushes onto the track, or is seen sipping water at the water-hole on a moonlit night, the sight is truly thrilling. The majestic tiger at the royal sanctuary is a treat not to be missed.

Attractions within the Park:
One can spot — Tigers; sambhar; chital; wild boar; leopard; jackal; hyena.

Other Places: Ranthambore Fort (one of the oldest in Rajasthan); Ganesh Temple; Jogi Mahal and Tonk.

Tonk: 96 kms from Jaipur, a focal point of Tonk is the *Sunehri Kothi*, a fairly ordinary monument from outside, but with a richly ornamented interior, with stained glass, mirrors, stucco and gilt (Tonk was ruled by a tribe of Pathans from Afghanistan).

How to Reach: By Air:- The nearest airport is Jaipur.
By Rail / Road:- Ranthambore is well connected by both rail and road. The nearest railhead is Sawai Madhopur. It is also easily approachable by road from Jaipur.

Plan your tour by rail

Route: New Delhi - 308 kms - Jaipur - 65 kms - Ranthambore

Day	Train No./Name	Dep.	Arr.	From	To
One	2015 Shatabdi Exp. (except Su)	0610	1040	New Delhi	Jaipur
	By bus /taxi proceed to Sawai Madhopur and stay.				
Two/Three	Visit Ranthambore and Tonk.				
Three	By bus or taxi proceed from Ranthambore to Jaipur				
	2016 Shatabdi Exp. (except Su)	1755	2220	Jaipur	New Delhi

Where to Stay: Tel. Code- 07462

Hotels: Budget
RTDC Jhoomar Baori (20495)
RTDC Vinayak (21333)
Jogi Mahal
Sawai Madhopur Lodge (20541)
Maharaja Lodge
Ankur Resort (20792)
Tiger Safari Resort (21137)
The Ranthambore Bagh (22879),
PWD Rest House
For further information contact: Field Director, Ranthambore National Park, Sawai Madhopur, Rajasthan or Govt. of India Tourist Office at Jaipur, Tel. : 0141- 372200.

Best Season: October & March.

Clothing: Summer- Light tropical, Winter- Light woollen.

Where Birds Sing

BHARATPUR
Ex-New Delhi

*B*haratpur was founded by Maharaja Suraj Mal in 1733 AD. Legend has it that the place was named Bharatpur after the name of Bharat, the brother of Lord Rama. Today Bharatpur is better known for the Keoladeo National Park, a unique bird sanctuary. Inside the Park are many kilometres of shaded walks with unique bird views on both sides. One can also sit for long hours at a point and gaze the frolicking birds. Alternatively one can row a boat in the sanctuary and behave like a winged creature. The Siberian cranes come to Bharatpur every year flying across mountains, lakes and countries. They present an exclusive picture of global integration where it concerns avian life. It is more than peace within bird country. UNESCO has listed the Keoladeo National Park as a World Heritage Site.

Places to See:

Forts: The Palace; the Iron Fort; Purana Mahal; Deeg Fort.

Bird Sanctuary: Keoladeo National Park.

Buildings: Gopal Bhavan; Bengal Chamber; Suraj Bhavan; Nand Bhavan.

Others: Government Museum; Jawahar Burj; Fateh Burj; Deeg.

How to Reach: By Air:- The nearest airport is New Delhi. By Rail / Road:- Bharatpur is well connected by both rail and road.

Plan your tour by rail

Route: New Delhi - 179 kms - Bharatpur

Day	Train No./Name	Dep.	Arr.	From	To
One	2904 Golden Temple Express	0755	1050	New Delhi	Bharatpur
One/Two/Three	Stay and Visit Bharatpur				
Three	2903 Golden Temple Express	1540	1900	Bharatpur	New Delhi

Where to Stay: Tel. Code- 05644

Hotels: Budget
ITDC Forest Lodge (22760, 22722) Fax: 22864
Website: www.fhrai.com
Saras, RTDC (23700)
Laxmi Vilas Palace (23523) Fax: 25259 Website: www.fhrai.com
Eagle's Nest (25144)
Crane Crib (24224)
Paradise (23791)
Sunbird (25701)
Pelican (24221)
Jungle Lodge (25622)
and many other budget hotels.

Best Season: October to March.

Clothing: Summer- Light tropical, Winter- Woollen.

64

Lakes and Tiger Safari

ALWAR
Ex-New Delhi

Alwar is nestled between a cluster of small hills of the Aravalli Range. Perched on the most prominent of these hills is a massive ancient fort that whispers tales of rich history. The city, apart from its long history, has rich natural heritage with some beautiful lakes and thickly wooded picturesque valleys. Alwar has one of the finest wildlife sanctuaries in Rajasthan, *Sariska* which is an excellent tiger country. Even the city of Alwar is a most charming presentation of old havelies, narrow lanes and a largely medieval lifestyle and those who are bothered by a sweet tooth can partake of the best milk cake which is prepared here. The museum at Alwar has a series of miniature paintings, which are based on classical Indian music ragas. Perhaps this is the only attempt in the world to paint pure music styles.

Places to See: The Fort; City Palace or Vinay Vilas Mahal; Government Museum; Purjan Vihar; Sariska (wildlife sanctuary).

Excursions: Vijai Mandir Palace; Siliserh Lake and Palace Hotel; Jai Samand Lake; Sariska Palace.

How to Reach: By Air:- The nearest airport is Delhi.
By Rail / Road:- Alwar is a railhead on the Delhi-Jaipur route and is well connected by road.

Plan your tour by rail

Route: New Delhi - 156 kms – Alwar

Day	Train No./Name	Dep.	Arr.	From	To
One	2015 Shatabdi Exp. (except Su)	0610	0833	New Delhi	Alwar
One/Two	**Stay and Visit Alwar.**				
Two	2016 Shtabdi Exp. (except Su)	1943	2220	Alwar	New Delhi

Where to Stay: Tel. Code- 0144

Hotels: Heritage

Sariska Palace (41322, 41460) Fax: 6172346, 6188862
Website: www.fhrai.com, http://www.sariska./com
E-mail: sariska@del2.vsnl.net.in

Budget

Alwar (20012, 220341) Fax: 332250 Website: www.fhrai.com
E-mail: ukrustagi@hotmail.com
RTDC Lake Palace at Siliserh (86322, 86311)
Meenal (22852, 22991)
Tiger Den, RTDC at Sariska (41342)
Aravalli (332883), and many others.

Best Season: September to February.

Clothing: Summer- Light tropical, Winter-Light woollen.

Mystical Experiences

Have you ever heard of cities where spirituality is a way of life. Where life is more lived in the scriptures than in mundane pursuits. Where the mystic and supernatural overpower the physical urges of men and women. Where divine peace is embodied in frail human forms, which seem to effortlessly carry the gospel truth to a disturbed humanity. Yes, such cities exist in India beside the eternal rivers.

The river is regarded holy in India. And this holiness flows out onto the parched plains, leaving forever the secure embrace of the hills. The river waves have woven their presence into the lives of people here, as plaits braided in the hair-do of a sage. Brahma, Vishnu and Mahesh, the three lords of the Hindu pantheon, live in the vermilion marks pasted on the forehead of the devout; in the *shlokas* and *mantras* recited by the faithful; in the regimen of asceticism followed by *swamis;* in the ritual bath undertaken at the banks of the river early morning, worshipping the sun; in the *pravachan* (address) discharged by the *guru*; and even in the pure vegetarian food which is consumed by the township. It is an experience in spirituality to be at one such city.

A sea of humanity comes on holy days from all over to submerge itself, and its mental burdens in the river. Rarely does a sea flow towards a river. The life cycle of ordinary man is completed in such cities as they serve the common man's religiosity. Overenthusiastic *pandits* (priests) liberate the souls of the dead to a possible union with the spirit (*parmatman*). Others are content with dips in the icy waters, convinced that their sins have been carried away by the holy river. More involve themselves in ceremonies. This soul cleansing may satisfy the ordinary toiler, but it does not satisfy the seeker of

The Shades of Silence

The bridge to Salvation

truth. The truth beyond existence, past all comprehension, is a subject to be dabbled in at these cities. Exploring the frontiers of spirituality, much above the ordinary plane of life and the visible, is the aim of the solemn pursuer. Living close to gods, a divine life, is objective and resolution both. Self-love melts into introspective humility and living here becomes seminal. More than a sightseeing venture it is an experience in spirituality and an exposure to divinity. The ordinary fades into oblivion, the meaninglessness of all conspicuous consumption becomes acute, the hankering after this or that appears futile, and the enormity of the supreme force which rules puny lives is more pronounced than everything else. Thirst for knowledge and food for thought is what you desire here. The sentiment may not be articulate but the force of undercurrent cannot be undermined. Aspirations for godliness, blended into a pursuit of the divine creator, are visible here as the moving force of all humanity.

You may get answers here to so many questions, which you raise everyday and find no explanation. Like the faith of a group of pilgrims, who move onward their pilgrimage undeterred by everything, the mystic cities live on in unique godliness. The journey of a human being from man to seer begins, perhaps at one such mystic Indian city.

65

The City of Shrines

AMRITSAR

Ex-New Delhi

Situated on the north-western border of the country, the 400-year-old city, founded by the fourth Guru of the Sikhs, Guru Ramdas, has been the seat of Sikh religion and culture from its very inception. It is renowned for the famous Golden Temple. Amritsar literally means 'pool of nectar,' and derives its name from the holy panel around the temple. The land for the pool was gifted by the Mughal Emperor Akbar. Amritsar is also equally important to the Hindus with the Durgiana Temple being a pilgrimage place. Nationally it is famous for the Jallianwala Bagh, where many innocents were mowed down by a British General during the freedom struggle. The Punjabi spirit celebrates life in cuisine, in lifestyle, in camaraderie, in creating the best articles for use in day-to-day living.

Places to See:

Golden Temple-Built in the midst of a holy pool by Maharaja Ranjit Singh in 1803 it is also known as Darbar Sahib or Har Mandir Sahib. The dome of the temple is covered with an estimated 400 kg. of gold leaves hence popularly known as Golden Temple.

Jallianwala Bagh: The historical site, where hundreds of innocent Indians were massacred by British General Dyer on April 13, 1919.

Excursions: Taran Taran, 22 kms; Goindwal 22 kms; Hazoor Sahib; Sultanpur Lodhi 15 kms (Holy Gurdwara of Ber Sahib, where Guru Nanak spent the first 14 years of his life); Baba Bakala, 21 kms (a place associated with the ninth Guru, Shri Guru Tegh Bahadur; a magnificent gurdwara where people gather in thousands to worship).

How to Reach: By Air:- The airport is Sansi, Amritsar.
By Rail / Road:- Amritsar is well connected by both rail and road.

Plan your tour by rail

Route: New Delhi - 447 kms - Amritsar

Day	Train No./Name	Dep.	Arr.	From	To
One	2029 Shatabdi Exp.	0720	1300	New Delhi	Amritsar
Two/Three	Stay and Visit Amritsar.				
Three	2030 Shatabdi Exp.	1705	2250	Amritsar	New Delhi

Where to Stay: **Tel. Code- 0183**

Hotels: 4 Star
Mohan International (227801-8) Fax: 226520
E-mail: hotel@jla.vsnl.net.in

3 Star
Ritz Plaza (563836-39) Fax: 226657 Website: www.fhrai.com
E-mail: hotel@jla.vsnl.net.in

Budget
Grand (562424, 562977) Fax: 229677 Website: www.fhrai.com
E-mail: grand@jla.vsnl.net.in
Amritsar International
Neem Chameli
Magnolia
Sun City Towers (229636-38)

187

Astoria (566046, 566414) Fax: 564443 Website: www.fhrai.com
E-mail: astroia@epages.webindia.com
Guru Ram Das Niwas, and many others. The Golden Temple also provides night stay accommodation for pilgrims.

Best Season: Throughout the year.

Clothing: Summer - Tropical, Winter- Woollen

Symbol of Faith

CHITRAKOOT

Ex-New Delhi

The place is wrapped in peace and tranquillity, broken only by the flutter of birds or the murmur of gushing streams. Chitrakoot is a symbol of faith; dotted with myriad temples and filled with the reverberating sound of temple bells- truly an abode of God. Chitrakoot Dham is one of the most ancient holy pilgrim places of India situated on the banks of the river Paisuni (Mandakini). Legend has it that during his fourteen years' exile, Lord Rama along with his consort Sita and brother Lakshman came to Chitrakoot and in the solitude of its forests came into intimate contact with Sage Atri and Sati Ansuya. Goswami Tulsidas, the creator of the epic, *Shri Ramcharitmanas,* spent many years on the soil of Chitrakoot.

Places to See: Kamadgiri (the abode of Kamtanath); Ansuya-Atri Ashram; Gupt-Godavari; Sphatikshila; Hanuman Dhara; Bharatkoop; Jankikund; Ganesh Bagh; Rajpur- 42 kms (believed to be the birthplace of Goswami Tulsidas); Marbha - (4 kms from Gupt Godavari Marpha is famous for its natural beauty and waterfall). Fort of Kalinjar (88 kms from Chitrakoot lies the invincible Fort of Kalinjar, once desired by kings and dynasties. It houses within itself the Nilkanth Temple, Swarga Rahan Kund, and Balkhandeshwar Mahadev Temple).

How to Reach: By Air:- The nearest airport is Khajuraho (190 kms).

By Rail / Road: - The nearest railhead is Karvi 8 kms, but one can approach Chitrakoot from Allahabad or Jhansi by road. Chitrakoot itself is a railhead.

Plan your tour by rail

Route: New Delhi - 627 kms - Allahabad - 134 kms - Chitrakoot

Day	Train No./Name	Dep.	Arr.	From	To
One	1450 Mahakoshal Exp.	1620	-	Nizamuddin	-
Two	Enroute	-	0405	-	Chitrakoot
Two/Three	Stay at Chitrakoot				
Three	1449 Mahakoshal Exp.	2030	-	Chitrakoot	-
Four	Enroute	-	1040	-	Nizamuddin

Where to Stay:

Tourist Bungalow, Matushree Anadram, Jaipuria Guest House, and many dharamshalas provide simple and basic facilities.

For further information contact Regional Tourist Office, Allahabad: Ph. 0532- 601873.

Best Season: Throughout the year.

Clothing: Summer- Light tropical, Winter- Woollen.

Spiritual Quest

PUTTAPARTHY
Ex-New Delhi

*P*uttaparthy is situated 183 kms from Bangalore on the west bank of the river Chitravarti. It is one of southern India's most celebrated saintly villages, being the abode of Sri Satya Sai Baba. Sai Baba is credited with spiritual wisdom, and occult powers. A large number of his disciples from all over the country and abroad arrive at Puttaparthy in search of peace and truth in the Ashram. The Sai Baba following in the country has grown tremendously and the place now assumes a lot of significance in our country, where religious thought has prospered in a bid to uplift mankind. The teachings of Sri Satya Sai Baba convey a deep understanding of the Indian reality and work as a binding force amongst people following various faiths. The unity of God is stressed at Puttaparthy and the righteous way of life is shown to followers through discourse and sermons.

Places to See:
Le Pakshi: Famous for the temple built in the Vijayanagar style and dedicated to Lord Shiva, and shrine dedicated to Lord Vishnu.

Puttaparthy: Chosen as an abode by Sri Satya Sai Baba, the place has been transformed into a seat of knowledge transcending materialism in the world.

How to Reach: By Air:- Puttaparthy is well connected by air. By Rail / Road:- Puttaparthy is well connected by both rail and road via Bangalore.

Plan your tour by rail

Route: New Delhi - 2434 kms - Bangalore - 183 kms - Puttaparthy

Day	Train No./Name	Dep.	Arr.	From	To
One	2430 Bangalore Rajdhani Exp. (Mon,Tue,Fri,Sat)	2050	-	Nizamuddin (New Delhi)	-
Two/Three	Enroute By bus or taxi to Puttaparthy	-	0655	-	Bangalore
Three/Four/Five	Stay and Visit Puttaparthy (Travel back to Bangalore)				
Five	2627 Karnataka Exp.	1825	-	Bangalore	-
Six/ Seven	Enroute	-	1205	-	New Delhi

Where to Stay:

Puttaparthy- Stay at the Ashram, which has guest houses and dormitories, and is equipped with all facilities.

For more information contact Govt. of India Tourist Office at Bangalore: Tel. 080- 5585417.

Best Season: Throughout the year.

Clothing: Summer- Light tropical, Winter- Light woollen.

In the Lap of Tagore

SHANTINIKETAN
Ex- New Delhi

In 1863, Maharishi Debendranath, father of Rabindranath Tagore, founded an Ashram, and almost 40 years later, Rabindranath started an open air school at Shantiniketan that gradually developed into an international university. Vishwa Bharti was destined to be the place, where the cultures of the East and the West may meet in common fellowship and thereby strengthen the fundamental conditions of world peace. The thought of Tagore was meant for the entire humanity and he spoke a language of universal love. Shantiniketan in its existence is like a poem of the legendary Tagore. Rabindra Sangeet at Shantiniketan not only gives peace, but also brings out the best in an individual.

Places to See: Institutions under Vishwa Bharti; Vichitra and Art Gallery- Nanda; Deer Park; Joydev- Kenduli (30 kms); Nanoor (18 kms); Bakreshwar (58 kms); Tarapith (88 kms); famous Tara Devi Temple.

How to Reach: By Air:- Dum Dum, Calcutta, is the airport. By Rail / Road:- The main railhead is Howrah. Bolpur is also a railhead and well connected by road.

Plan your tour by rail

Route: New Delhi - 1441 kms - Calcutta- 159 kms - Bolpur - 2 kms - Shantiniketan

Day	Train No./Name	Dep.	Arr.	From	To
One	2302/2306 Rajdhani Exp.	1700/1700-		New Delhi	-
Two	Enroute	-	0955/1245 -		Howrah
Three	3017 Ganadevta Exp.	0605	0854	Howrah	Bolpur
	By taxi or rickshaw to Shantiniketan				
Three/Four	Stay and Vist Shantiniketan (Travel back to Calcutta)				
Five	2301/2305 Rajdhani Exp.	1700/1345 -		Howrah	-
Six	Enroute	-	0950/0950 -		New Delhi

Where to Stay:
Hotels: Budget

Tourist Lodge and Tourist Cottage run by Bengal Tourist Development Corpn.,
Vishwa Bharti Guest House
Chhuti Holiday Resort
Bolpur (03463- 52692), and other hotels and lodges in Bolpur. For more information contact Govt. of India Tourist Office at Calcutta: Tel. 033- 2821402, 2821475.

Best Season: Throughout the year.

Clothing: Summer-Light tropical, Winter- Tropical.

69

Lamp of Enlightenment

GAYA AND BODH GAYA

Ex-New Delhi

*G*aya is a very sacred pilgrim centre for Hindus. Who offer oblations for the salvation of their dead parents and forefathers. The temple of Vishnupad on the bank of the river Falgu attracts a large number of pilgrims.

Serene and quiet, this tiny little village of Bodh Gaya is holiest among holy places. Here the quest of Prince Siddharth was fulfilled after years of seeking the truth and the saga of Buddha thus began. He attained supreme enlightenment and became 'The Buddha,' the enlightened one. Thus Buddhism was born here under a peepal tree. The prince had been wandering in search of peace for six long years hither and thither. But it was at Bodh Gaya only where his holy mission was achieved. Lying in sylvan solitude this sacred place is situated on the bank of the river Niranjana (modern Falgu). It is 13 kms from Gaya town.

Places to See: The Bodhi Tree; Mahabodhi Temple; Vajrasana; Ancient Railings; Chankaramana; Animeshlochana; Ratnagar; Lotus Tank.

How to Reach: By Air:- The nearest airport is Patna, 112 kms. By Rail / Road:- The nearest railhead is Gaya and it is well connected by road.

Plan your tour by rail

Route: New Delhi - 984 kms - Gaya - 16 kms - Bodh Gaya

Day	Train No./Name	Dep.	Arr.	From	To
One	2302 Howrah Rajdhani Exp. (except Mon & Fri.)	1700	-	New Delhi	-
Two	Enroute	-	0416	-	Gaya
Two	Stay and Visit Gaya				
Three	Stay and Visit Bodhgaya by bus or taxi				
Four	2301 Howrah Rajdhani Exp. (except Wed & Sun.)	2211	-	Gaya	-
Five	Enroute	-	0950	-	New Delhi

Where to Stay: Tel. Code- 0631
Hotels: 3 Star
Bodhgaya Ashok (400700, 400790), Fax: 400788
Website: www.fhrai.com
Siddhartha International (436243, 436252) Fax: 436368
Website: www.fhrai.com E-mail: siddarthendf.vsnl.net.in

Budget
Tourist Bungalows
Siddharth Vihar (400445)
Buddha Vihar (400445) of Bihar State Tourism Development Corporation
Sujata (400761), and many other budget hotels in the city.
For more information contact Govt. of India Tourist Office at Patna: Tel. 0612- 345776.

Best Season: Throughout the year.

Clothing: Summer- Light tropical, Winter- Light woollen.

70

World's First Republic

VAISHALI
Ex-New Delhi

*L*ying on the northern bank of the Ganga river, it was the seat of the Republic of Vaijji. Vaishali is credited with being the world's first republic to have a duly elected assembly of representatives and an efficient administration. Lord Buddha visited Vaishali more than once during his lifetime and announced his approaching *mahaparinirvana* to his followers. Hundred years after he attained *mahaparinirvana*, it was the venue of the second Buddhist Council. According to one belief, the Jain Tirthankar, Lord Mahavir was born at Vaishali. Some places are blessed with holiness, and Vaishali is one of them.

Places to See: Ashoka Pillar; Bawan Pokhar Temple; Buddha Stupa-1; Buddha Stupa-II; Raja Vishal ka Garh; Shanti Stupa; Kundupur (birth place of Lord Mahavir); Coronation Tank.

How to Reach: By Air:- The nearest air port is Patna.
By Rail / Road:- Vaishali is well connected by rail. Hajipur is the nearest railhead (35 km) but one can go by road to Vaishali from Patna (56 kms).

Plan your tour by rail

Route: New Delhi - 992 Kms - Patna - 56 Kms - Vaishali

Day	Train No./Name	Dep.	Arr.	From	To
One	2310/2306 Patna/Howrah Rajdhani Exp.	1715/1700 -		New Delhi	-
Two	Enroute	-	0545/0535 -		Patna
Two/Three	Stay and Visit Vaishali				
Three	2309/2305 Patna/Howrah Rajdhani Exp.	2115/2115 -		Patna	-
Four		-	1010/0950 -		New Delhi

Where to Stay:
Hotels: Budget

Moderate accommodation is available in **Tourist Bungalow** and **Tourist Youth Hostel** of Bihar State Tourism Development Corporation.

For more information contact Govt. of India Tourist Office at Patna: Tel. 0612- 345776.

Best Season: Throughout the year.

Clothing: Summer- Cotton, Winter-Woollen.

71

Blessings

VAISHNO DEVI
Ex-Delhi

*V*aishno Devi is a world famous holy shrine where your prayers are answered. Legend has it that over seven centuries ago, Vaishno Devi was an ardent devotee of Lord Vishnu. Bhaironath, a *tantrik* gave Vaishno Devi a chase when she was going towards the Trikuta Mountains. When thirsty, the goddess shot an arrow into the earth and water gushed out at the place where the *Banganga* exists today. The imprints of her feet marked the spot *Charan Paduka*, where she rested. She meditated in the cave at Ardhkwari. Since Bhaironath took nine months to locate her, the cave is called *Garbh Joon*. When found by Bhaironath, the goddess made her way out by blasting an opening with the trident. When she arrived at the holy cave at Darbar, she took on the form of Maha Kali and chopped off the head of Bhaironath. A temple after his name too stands where the head fell on the ground.

How to Reach: By Air:- The nearest airport is Jammu Tawi. By Rail / Road:- The nearest railhead is Jammu Tawi. There is a regular rail / road service from Delhi / New Delhi. From Jammu Tawi to Katra one has to travel by bus / taxi, and from Katra to Mata Vaishno Devi on foot-13 kms.

Plan your tour by rail

Route: Delhi - 585 kms - Jammu Tawi - 47 kms - Katra - 13 kms Vaishno Devi Temple

Day	Train No./Name	Dep.	Arr.	From	To
One	2403 Jammu Exp.	2240	-	Delhi	-
Two		-	0905	-	Jammu Tawi
	by bus or taxi			Jammu Tawi	Katra
	On foot			Katra	Vaishno Devi
Two /Three	Visit Vaishno Devi shrine				
Three	Travel back to Jammu Tawi before 18.00 hrs.				
Three	2404 Jammu Exp.	1800	-	Jammu Tawi	-
Four		-	0420	-	Delhi

Where to Stay: Tel. Code- 0191

Hotels at Jammu:

Heritage
Hari Niwas Palace (543303, 547216) Fax: 543180
Website: www.fhrai.com, E-mail: harinivas@hotmail.com

4 Star
Asia Jammu Tawi (435757-60) Fax: 435756
Website: www.fhrai.com, E-mail: asiahotels@vsnl.com
Jammu Ashok (543571) Fax: 543576, 547110
Website: www.fhrai.com
Website: www.fhrai.com, E-mail: harinivas@hotmail.com

2 Star
Ambica (32062) Fax: 32064 Website: www.fhrai.com
Jammu Jewels (547630) Fax: 555076 Website: www.fhrai.com

Budget
K.C. Residency (520770-71) Fax: 575222
Website: www.fhrai.com, www.kcresidency.com
E-mail: ker@kcresidency.com
Masar (543610, 543030) Website: www.fhrai.com
Premier (543436)

Samrat (548212, 547402) Fax: 575711 Website: www.fhrai.com
Moti Mahal
Cosmo (547561, 577245)
Air Lines and
Tawi View many others.
Vardaan Jammu (547414, 573212) Fax: 548286
Website: www.fhrai.com, E-mail: vinns@vsnl.com

Hotels at Katra   Tel. Code- 01991

2 Star
Asia Vaishno Devi (32161, 32061) Fax: 33344
Website: www.fhrai.com

Budget
New Subhash (33044) Website: www.fhrai.com
Asia Shripati (33264, 32399) Fax: 33366
Website: www.fhrai.com
and others.

Best Season: Navratra (twice a year).

Clothing: Summer- Light tropical, Winter- Heavy woollen.

72

Temple Towns

OMKARESHWAR AND MAHESHWAR

Ex-New Delhi

*O*mkareshwar shaped like the holiest of all Hindu symbols *OM* has drawn generations of pilgrims. Here at the confluence of the rivers Narmada and Kaveri, the devout have gathered to kneel before the *jyotirlinga* (one of the twelve throughout India).

Places to See: Shri Omkar Mandhata Siddhnath Temple; 24 Avatars (a cluster of Hindu and Jain temples); Satmatrika temples (a group of 10th century Temples); Kajal Rani Caves.

Maheshwar: This temple town on the banks of the Narmada finds mention in the *Ramayana* and *Mahabharata*. Maheshwar was a glorious city at the dawn of Indian civilisation when it was Mahishmati, capital of King Kartivarjun. Revived to its ancient position of importance by the Holkar Queen, Rani Ahilyabai of Indore.

Places to See: Rajgaddi and Rajwada; Ghats; Temples; and Maheshwari sarees (introduced into Maheshwar 250 years ago by Rani Ahilyabai, these sarees are renowned throughout India for their unique weaves).

How to Reach: By Air:- The nearest airport is Indore (77 kms). By Rail / Road:- The nearest railhead is Omkareshwar Road (12 kms). Travel from Indore by bus or train.

Plan your tour by rail

Route: New Delhi – 835 kms Indore - 77 kms Omkareshwar
Indore - 91 kms Maheshwar

Day	Train No./Name	Dep.	Arr.	From	To
One	2416 Nizamuddin-Indore Exp.	2215	-	Nizamuddin	-
Two	Enorute By bus/taxi to Omkareshwar	-	1150	-	Indore
Three/Four/Five	Visit Omkareshwar and Maheshwar (Travel back to Indore before 16.00 hrs.)				
Five	2415 Nizamuddin - Indore Exp.	1630	-	Indore	-
Six		-	0610	-	Nizamuddin

Where to Stay: Tel. Code- 0731

Hotels at Indore :

5 Star

Taj Residency (557700) Fax: 555355 Website: www.fhrai.com,
http://www.tata.com/indian/hotels
E-mail: tajinder@bom4.vsnl.net.in

3 Star

Balwas International (524933) Fax: 517938
Website: www.fhrai.com
E-mail: balwas@bom2.vsnl.in
Kanchan Tilak (538606-08) Fax: 431884
Website: www.fhrai.com
E-mail: kanchan@bom4.vsn.net.in
Shreemaya (514081) Fax: 527680 Website: www.fhrai.com
E-mail: krishna@bom4.vsn.nt.in
Surya (517701-06) Fax: 518774 Website: www.fhrai.com
E-mail: ecelsurya@cudindere
Tulsi (524920-22) Fax: 519552 Website: www.fhrai.com

Budget

Amaltas International (432631-32) Fax: 495145
Website: www.fhrai.com

Crown Palace (528855) Fax: 523014 Website: www.fhrai.com
E-mail: crown@bom4.vsnl.net.in
Mashal (856230) Fax: 856138 Website: www.fhrai.com
President (528866) Fax: 512230 Website: www.fhrai.com
Princes Palace (517940) Fax: 517314 Website: www.fhrai.com
E-mail: princespalace@usa.net.in
Sunder (523314) Fax: 409423 Website: www.fhrai.com
Sayaji (552121) Fax: 553131 Website: www.fhrai.com
E-mail: sajikmfb@hotmail.com
and others.

At Omkareshwar and Maheshwar: Ahilyabai Charity Trust,
Omkareshwar Mandir, Forest and PWD Rest House and a
number of Dharamshalas offer accommodation with basic
amenities.

Best Season: July to March.

Clothing: Summer-Light tropical, Winter- Woollen.

73

Pilgrimage Cities

AJMER AND PUSHKAR

Ex- New Delhi

*A*jmer was invaded in early 7th century by Ajaipal Chauhan and named Ajaimer. Today, Ajmer is a popular pilgrimage centre for Muslims as well as Hindus, especially famous for Dargah Sharif, tomb of the Sufi saint, Khwaja Moinuddin Chisti. The Mughal Kings were so much in obeisance to the Sufi saint that they have built mosques inside the tomb complex, in reverence. Every year, the *Urs* of the saint is celebrated with gusto and pilgrims from all over the world come for this celebration. As per popular belief, a wish made at the Dargah is answered without fail. All you have to do is to pray to the saint, say a wish in your mind, and tie a thread on one of the marble screens. The fulfilment of the wish will bring you back to untie the thread.

Places to See: The Dargah; Shahjahan's Mosque; Adhai-din-ka-Jhonpra; Taragarh Fort; the Museum; the Circuit House.

*P*ushkar is sacred to the Hindus and located 11 kms west of Ajmer. The lake at Pushkar is believed to have been created by Lord Brahma himself. According to Hindu mythology, "no pilgrimage is complete without a visit to Pushkar." Today, there are as many as 400 temples in Pushkar and the lake is circled by 52 ghats. Pushkar is also the site for one of the largest cattle fairs in the world (for 12 days) which falls some time in November. The cattle fair is believed to be the most colourful one in the world.

Places to See: Pushkar Lake; Temple of Lord Brahma and Shiva; Manmahal; Pushkar Fair.

How to Reach: By Air:- The nearest airport is Jaipur.
By Rail / Road:-Ajmer is well connected by both rail and road.

Plan your tour by rail

Route: New Delhi - 442 kms - Ajmer - 11 kms - Pushkar

Day	Train No./Name	Dep.	Arr.	From	To
One	2015 Shatabdi Exp. (except Su)	0610	1245	New Delhi	Ajmer
Two/Three	Stay and Visit Ajmer and Pushkar.				
Three	2016 Shatabdi Exp. (except Su)	1530	2220	Ajmer	New Delhi

Where To Stay: Tel. Code- 0145

Hotels at Ajmer:

3 Star
Mansingh Palace (425855) Fax: 425858
Website: www.fhrai.com, www.mansinghhotels.com

2 Star
Regency (620296) Fax: 420747, 621750 Website: www.fhrai.com

Budget
Khadim RTDC (52490)
Ambassador (425095)
Ajaymeru.

Hotels at Pushkar
Budget
Sarovar RTDC (72040)
Peacock Holiday Resort 72093)
Pushkar Palace (72001) and
RTDC Tourist Village (72074).

Best Season: Throughout the year.

Clothing: Summer- Light tropical, Winter- Woollen.

74

Spirituality by the River

RISHIKESH
Ex-New Delhi

$\mathcal{I}$t is said that when Kaibhya Rishi did a hard penance, God appeared by the name of "Hrishi Kesh" and this area henceforth came to be known as Rishikesh. Surrounded by the Shivalik range of the Himalayas on three sides, it is the starting point for the Char (four-place) pilgrimage (Yamunotri, Gangotri, Kedarnath and Badrinath) to seek spiritual salvation. It is here that the Ganga cut its passage through the last foothills on her journey down the mountains and enters the plains. Rishikesh is a city of renunciation. Ascetics, and those who have opted for living a life in prayer and meditation , explore the frontiers of spiritualism by the banks of the eternal river Ganga , which flows here.

Places to See: Triveni Ghat; Bharat Mandir; Lakshman and Ram Jhoola; Shivanand Ashram.

Yoga Centres: Divine Life Society; Kailash Ashram, Omkara Nanda Ashram, Parmarth Niketari, Swami Ram Ashram, Yog Niketan.

Haridwar: Haridwar, a mirror of the Hindu religion, is situated at the base of the Shivalik hills. It is perhaps one of the oldest Hindu cities and believed to date back to 1700 BC. The most sacred place in Haridwar remains Har-ki-Pauri, where people take a dip in the holy river Ganga to cleanse themselves of their sins. It is the place where the comman man fulfils his religious aspirations. The rituals of devout Hindus right from birth to death are performed at Har-ki Pauri, and are an education in the Hindu way of life.

Places to See: Mansa Devi Temple; Daksh Mahadev Temple; Chandi Devi Temple; Sapt Rishi Ashram.

How to Reach: By Air:- There is no airport at Haridwar or Rishikesh.

By Rail / Road:-Rishikesh and Haridwar are well connected by both rail and road.

Plan your tour by rail/road

Route: New Delhi - 347 kms - Haridwar - 24 kms - Rishikesh

Day	Train No./Name	Dep.	Arr.	From	To
One	2017 Shatabdi Exp.	0700	1122	New Delhi	Haridwar
One	Visit Haridwar (Travel by bus or taxi to Rishikesh in the evening).				
Two/ Three	Stay and Visit Rishikesh. (Travel back to Haridwar in the evening)				
Three	2018 Shatabdi Exp.	1810	2240	Haridwar	New Delhi

Where to Stay: Tel. Code- 0135
Hotels:
2 Star
Ganga Kinare (431658, 435243) Fax: 435243
Website: www.fhrai.com, yogaindia.com
E-mail: hotelgangakinare@hotmail.com
Inderlok (430555) Fax: 432855 Website: www.fhrai.com
E-mail: interlok@nde.vsnl.net.in

Budget
Natraj (431099, 431262) Fax: 433355 Website: www.fhrai.com
E-mail: natraj@nde.vsnl.net.in
Mandakini Int'l (430781, 431081) Website: www.fhrai.com
E-mail: gupta1@del3.vsnl.net.in
Aakash Ganga

Baseraa (432138, 430720) Fax: 433106
Website: www.fhrai.com, http://websearch.india.com./
hotel.basera.htm
E-mail: combis@nde.vsnl.net.in
Ganga View (436146), Fax: 431081, 430781
Website: www.fhrai.com, www.yogaindia.com
E-mail:hotelgangaview@hotmail.com
Shivalik
Suruchi
Tourist Complex at Muni-ki-Reti (430373), and dharamshalas
in and around the city providing basic amenities to pilgrims.

Best Season: Throughout the year.

Clothing: Summer- Light tropical, Winter- Woollen.

75

Confluence of Mythical and Real Rivers

ALLAHABAD

Ex-New Delhi

From the mists of mythology and legend, the history of Allahabad moves through time to 1575 AD when Emperor Akbar founded a city on lavish proportions and called it by this name. The monarch realised its strategic importance as a waterway landmark in North India and also built a magnificent fort on the banks of the holy *sangam*. Hindu mythology has it that for the Prakrishta Yagna, Lord Brahma, the creator God of the Trinity, chose a land on earth on which the three rivers- the Ganga, the Yamuna and the mythical Saraswati- would flow into a quiet confluence. That land, blessed by the gods, came to be called Prayag or Allahabad, as it is known today. It is one of the most sacred pilgrimage centres of India. Perhaps, foreseeing the sanctity, the place would command over the ages to come, Lord Brahma also referred to it as *Tirth Raj* or the King of all pilgrimage centres. Today Allahabad is an important city where history, culture and religion create a confluence- much like the sacred rivers that caress this God graced land.

Places to See: *Sangam*; Allahabad Fort; Patalpuri Temple; Ashoka Pillar; Akshayavat; Hanuman Temple; Shankar Viman Mandapam; Mankameshwar Temple; Minto Park (Madan Mohan Malviya Park); Anand Bhawan; Swaraj Bhawan; Beni Madhav Temple.

Festivals:

Kumbh Mela: One of the largest congregations of devout Hindus from all across the world, the Kumbh Mela is held every 12 years on the banks of the *sangam*.

Ardh Kumbh Mela: This festival is held every six years on the banks of the *sangam*.

Magh Mela: (Mini Kumbh Mela)- Held in the years other than the years of Kumbh and Ardh Kumbh the Magh Mela is no less than an annual mini- Kumbh Mela.

How to Reach: By Air:- There is no airlink to Allahabad. The nearest airport is Varanasi.
By Rail / Road:- Allahabad is well connected by both rail and road.

Plan your tour by rail

Route : New Delhi - 627 - kms - Allahabad

Day	Train No./Name	Dep.	Arr.	From	To
One	2418 Prayagraj Exp.	2130	-	New Delhi	-
Two	Enroute	-	0650	-	Allahabad
Two/Three	Stay and Visit Allahabad.				
Three	2417 Prayagraj Exp.	2130	-	Allahabad	-
Four	Enroute	-	0705	-	New Delhi

Where to Stay: Tel. Code- 0532

Hotels:
4 Star
Kanha Shyam (420281-290) Fax: 622164, 621568
Website: www.fhrai.com, www.kanhashyam.com
E-mail: info@kanhashyam.com

3 Star
Yatrik (601713) Fax: 601434 Website: www.fhrai.com

2 Star
Presidency (623308) Fax: 623897
Website: www.fhrai.com, www.rodeostar.com
E-mail: star@del3.vsnl.net.in

Budget
Allahabad Regency (601519, 601735) Fax: 611107
Website: www.fhrai.com
Samrat (420780-83) Fax: 420785 Website: www.fhrai.com
E-mail: atulgoswamy@hotmail.com
Vilas (622878, 420796) Fax: 621009 Website: www.fhrai.com
E-mail: parmarth@nde.vsnl.net.in
Prayag (656329, 656325) Website: www.fhrai.com
YMCA
Dharamshalas and charitable trusts are also available.

Best Season: Throughout the year.

Clothing: Summer- Light tropical, Winter- Light woollen.

76

The Home of Kalidasa

UJJAIN
Ex-New Delhi

The names of Kalidasa and Ujjayni (Ujjain) are inextricably linked together in the Indian tradition. It is in *Meghdoot*, a poem of a little over hundred verses, describing the anguish of a *yaksha*, separated from his beloved by a curse, sending a message to her in the city of Alaka through a rain cloud from his exile in Ramagiri (now identified as Kamtek near Nagpur), that Kalidasa's love of Ujjayni finds full expression. Modern Ujjain is situated on the banks of the Shipra, regarded since time immemorial as sacred Ujjayni. Ujjain has a legend that in the hoary past, the godlike King Shiva of Avanti commemorated his victory over the demon-ruler of Tripura or Tripuri on the banks of the Narmada by changing the name of his capital, Avantipura, to Ujjayni (one who conquers with pride).

Places to See:

Prime Sites: Mahakaleshwar (one of the 12 *jyotirlingas* in India); Bade Ganeshji ka Mandir; Chintaman Ganesh Temple; Harsiddhi Temple; Kal Bhairava Temple; Gadkalika Temple; Mangalnath Temple; Vikram Kirti Mandir; Gopal Mandir; Navagraha Mandir, (this temple is dedicated to the nine planets, and attracts large crowds on new moon days falling on Saturdays).

Other Places: Siddhaval (an enormous banyan tree on the bank of the Shipra); Sandipani Ashram; the Vedha Shala (observatory); Vikram University; Kalidasa Academy.

How to Reach: By Air:- The nearest airport is Bhopal. By Rail / Road:-The most convenient railhead is Bhopal. It is also well connected by road.

Plan your tour by rail

Route: New Delhi - 705 kms - Bhopal - 184 kms - Ujjain

Day	Train No./Name	Dep.	Arr.	From	To
One	2002 Shatabdi Exp.	0600	1410	New Delhi	Bhopal
	By bus/taxi to Ujjain				
Two/Three	Stay and Visit Ujjain				
Four	Travel from Ujjain to Bhopal and reach before 14.00 hrs.				
Four	2001 Shatabdi Exp.	1450	2250	Bhopal	New Delhi

Where To Stay: **Tel. Code- 0734**

Hotels:
3 Star
Ashray (519301-04) Fax: 519300 Website: www.fhrai.com
E-mail: ashray@bom4.vsnl.net.in

2 Star
Shipra (551495-96) Website: www.fhrai.com
E-mail: nicner@mpujainmpnicin

Budget
Palash (MPT)
Panchanan (MPT)
Ashok Lake View (MPT/ITDC)
Yatri Niwas (551398)
Raj Tilak
Atlas, and many others in the city.

Best Season: Throughout the year.

Clothing: Summer- Light tropical; Winter- Woollen.

Ghats and Temples

MATHURA
Ex-New Delhi

$\mathcal{M}$athura, a little town on the river Yamuna, is the birthplace of Lord Krishna. Krishna is fondly remembered for his divine charm and pranks. Krishna revealed to the world the supreme truths of life. Shri Krishna, 'an incarnation of Lord Vishnu,' was born in the *Dwapar Yuga* as the eighth son of Yadava prince Vasudev and his wife Devaki. Mathura is an ancient city whose origins fade into mists of history. Mathura's strategic location at the cross roads of various ancient trade routes-that went westwards to West Asia and the Roman Empire; northwards via Taxila and Pushkalavati Purushapur to Central Asia and the silk route, and eastwards to China, ensured its position as a centre of trade and a meeting point for varied cultures. Today Mathura is an important place of pilgrimage.

Places to See:
Temples: Dwarikadhish Temple, Pipaleshwar Temple, Rangeshwar Temple, Gokarneshwar Temple, Bhuteshwar Temple.

Ghats/Kunds: Vishram Ghat; Surya Ghat; Dhruva Ghat; Somatirtha Ghat; Asikunda Ghat; Shiv Tal; Balbhadra Kund; Potara Kund; Saraswati Kund.

Others: Kankhal Tirtha; Rangabhumi; Krishna Janmasthan; Saraswati Sangam; Govt. Museum; Mathura.

Excursions: Gokul (15 kms S.E. Mathura); Mahavan (18 kms); Baldeo (20 kms); Govardhan (26 kms W. Mathura); Barsana (50 kms N.W. Mathura); Nandgaon (56 kms); Radhakund (26 kms W. Mathura.).

Vrindavan: Vrindavan, 15 kms from Mathura, is also a major place of pilgrimage. Vrindavan is noted for the numerous temples, both old and modern. The name Vrindavan evokes the playfulness of Shri Krishna. This is the wood where he frolicked with the *gopis*.

Important temples: Madan Mohan Temple; Radha Vallabh Temple; Govind Deo Temple; Banke-Behari Temple; Jaipur Temple; Shahiji Temple; Rangaji Temple; Shri Krishna-Balram Temple; Sewa Kunj.

How to Reach: By Air:- Delhi is the nearest airport.
By Rail / Road:- Mathura is well connected by both rail and road.

Plan your tour by rail

Route: New Delhi - 145 kms - Mathura - 4 kms - Vrindavan

Day	Train No./Name	Dep.	Arr.	From	To
One	2180 Taj Express	0715	0857	Nizamuddin	Mathura
One/Two	Stay and Visit Mathura and Vrindavan.				
Two	2179 Taj Express	1930	2145	Mathura	Nizamuddin.

Where to Stay at Mathura: Tel. Code- 0565
Hotels:
3 Star
Best Western Radha Ashok (405557) Fax: 409557
Website: www.fhrai.com E-mail: Radhaanila@hotmail.com
Madhuban (420064, 420058) Fax: 420684 Website: www.fhrai.com
E-mail: Bhul@nde.vsnl.net.in

Budget

Mansarovar Palace (408686, 409966) Fax: 401611
Website: www.fhrai.com
Dwapar Resorts
Mukund Palace (410316)
Satyam
Modern UPSTDC Tourist Bungalow Krishna Lodge and
Dharamshalas.

Hotels at Vrindavan   Tel. Code- 0565.

International Rest House (443478)
Yatrika
Geet Govind Tourist Complex (442517)
Bitko Cottage, and many Dharamshalas.

Best Season: Throughout the year.

Clothing: Summer- Light tropical, Winter- Woollen.

Forts and Palaces

The call of the hills is commanding, the call of the sea is enchanting, but the call of forts and palaces is magically inviting. And if something as beautiful as a lone flower in stone in a barren desert, rich in colours, proud in heritage is the cause *célèbre*, can one resist an impulse to travel?

Past the narrow lanes as you drive by, heavily turbaned and thickly mustachioed men, whom you encounter, remind you of the times past. The road starts winding itself round the solid rock formation on which stands a fort. The plains below were field to many battles. The earth is soaked in the blood of thousands of proud, defiant soldiers. To them, freedom and independence was more meaningful than a mere life. What is built on the hill or a hillock is awesome splendour. In its sheer look it appears unconquerable. It wraps the hill on which it stands like an eagle picking up its prey.

Once upon a time these forts and palaces were a celebration of life. The difficult Indian terrain could not deter the undaunted spirit of warriors who were flushed with the thought of only conquer and nothing else. They celebrated life to such an extent through their deeds of valour, songs of pride, forts of glory and palaces of speaking stones, that the fierceness of death pales into insignificance before their romancing life spirit.

As you look at a fort, your gaze travels along the gigantic bastions, goes round past the visibly menacing cannons, rises up the fortress- palace structure and gets lost in the voices rising from the *chattris* and carved teeny-weeny *jharokhas*. As you alight below one such fort, its size and reach appears alarming. On seeing the fort you proclaim like Kipling- "a work of angels, fairies and giants." Below, down below, the immensely peopled city appears an orderly confusion of houses and streets.

The palaces conjure up images of a lavish lifestyle. *Mahals* have courtyards, geometrical and arabesque patterns,

Timeless grandeur

A peep into the royal past

ornamental arches, beautiful brackets, and an assemblage of rooms linked by galleries and corridors. The effect cast upon the eye is profuse yet delicate. It is the decorative aspect that first strikes then fascinates a visitor. Sometimes on white marble has been exquisitely done an inlay work. Precious and semi-precious stones have been filled in carefully carved grooves and sockets. The patterns— sometimes geometric, floral, and sometimes representative of fruit or delicate trees, accentuate in a certain finish the entire effect of the building. The inlay work became the precursor of later embellishments to Mughal buildings. *Khas Mahal*, with a *bagh* in front completing a concept, is a most charming presentation. The white marble buildings have been lavishly painted in different patterns. The cool effect, created by siting the palace beside a river on one side and the water fountains of a bagh on the other, is unbeatable. As a concept it owes an origin only to kingly overtures. Many palaces have *Sheesh Mahals* (palaces of glass) decorated by glass mosaic work. Precision, patience and artistry are at their best here. If you light a candle inside such a chamber, the reflections from a thousand and more mirrors, quivering like emotions, approach you nudgingly. Dreams were not dreamt in slumber, but felt and seen here with waking eyes.

Administrative needs of palace buildings were satisfied in the *Diwan-i-Am* and *Diwan-i-Khas*. The arches of these buildings are works of mathematical accuracy and a paint brush delivery. The *Diwan-i-Khas* is always ornate and is truly the preserve of kings. Religious needs gave birth to many exquisite mosques in the Mughal era. Some notable ones are the Mina Masjid, Nagina Masjid and Moti Masjid. The arches, pillars, *chhatris* and the perfect domes create a spectacular effect. They befit kingly worship.

Forts and palaces are undoubtedly the best specimen of· architecture in medieval India. Grace, purity and sanctity combine in a harmonious relationship with the Creator. Come, let's go back in the time zone and live the lives surrounded by beauty, grandeur and pomp.

78

City of Eternal Love

AGRA
Ex- New Delhi

*O*f you think of some place on earth where successively fortunes have been made; where gems as precious as the irresistible Kohinoor have passed hands; which has remained the cynosure of kings for many centuries; where lofty buildings as high as ambitions themselves, have been erected; a city which has ruled the hearts and minds of people; a capital which defined the borders of a nation; a place where love blossomed in the hearts of kings; a sky under which dreams have been realised — the only name that comes instantly to lips is that of Agra. Agra has long been renowned as the city of the Taj Mahal. This has often overshadowed the fact that this royal Mughal city has, in addition to the legendary Taj, many magnificent monuments that epitomise the high point of Mughal architectural achievement. Not even Delhi, the seat of kings and emperors for over a thousand years, can boast such a heritage of architectural and cultural splendour from the golden age of the great Mughals. The Taj was built by Emperor Shahjahan in memory of his royal consort Begum Mumtaz Mahal, as a dream in white marble. No singular building is worth comparison to the beauty of the Taj. At Agra was born the delicate art of pietra-dura, that is, engraving precious and semi-precious stones in designs and floral patterns on white marble. Not many know that the legendary Mirza Ghalib, Urdu poet, philosopher, litterateur par excellence, was born at Agra on December 27, 1797.

Places to See: Taj Mahal; Ram Bagh; The great Red Fort of Agra; Akbar's Tomb at Sikandra; Tomb of Itmad-ud-Daula; Chini ka Rauza; Fatehpur Sikri; Dayal Bagh.

How to Reach: By Air:- Agra is well connected by air. By Rail / Road:- Agra is well connected by both rail and road.

Plan your tour by rail

Route: New Delhi - 204 kms - Agra

Day	Train No./Name	Dep.	Arr.	From	To
One	2002 Shatabdi Exp.	0600	0755	New Delhi	Agra
One/Two	Stay and Visit Agra				
Two	2001 Shatabdi Exp.	2018	2250	Agra	New Delhi

Where to Stay: Tel. Code- 0562

Hotels:
5 Star

Agra Ashok (361223-32) Fax: 361620 Website: www.fhrai.com
Jaypee Palace (330800) Fax: 330850 Website: www.fhrai.com, http://www.jaypeehotels.com E-mail: jaypeeag@nde.vsnl.net.in
Clarks Shiraz (361421-27) Fax: 361428
Website: www.fhrai.com E-mail: clarkraz@nde.vsnl.net.in
Taj View (331841-59) Fax: 331860, 332705
Website: www.fhrai.com E-mail: tjagra@nde.vsnl.net.in
Mughal Sheraton (331701-728) Fax: 331730, 330701
Website: www.fhrai.com
E-mail: gm.mughal@welcomemail.wiprobt.ems.vsnl.net.in
Howard Park Plaza (331870, 331878) Fax: 330408
Website: www.fhrai.com E-mail: howard@nda.vsnl.net.in

3 Star
Atithi (330879) Fax: 330878 Website: www.fhrai.com
Trident Agra (331818) Fax: 331827 Website: www.fhrai.com, http://www.oberoihotels.com E-mail: ttag@tridentag.com

Mansingh Palace (331771) Fax: 330202 Website: www.fhrai.com
www.mansinghhotels.com E-mail: mansingh.agra@mailcity.com
Grand (364320) Fax: 364271 Website: www.fhrai.com
E-mail: grand@nde.vsnl.net.in
Amar (331885-89) Fax: 330299 Website: www.fhrai.com

Budget

Kant (331332, 333806-07) Fax: 331046 Website: www.fhrai.com
Ranjit (364446) Fax: 364271 Website: www.fhrai.com
Amar Yatri Niwas (333800-804) Fax: 333805
Website: www.fhrai.com
Sunrise (330602-04) Fax: 330606 Website: www.fhrai.com
E-mail: komal@nde.vsnl.net.in
Lauries (364536), Fax: 268045 Website: www.fhrai.com
E-mail: laurieshotel@hotmail.com
Joshi (05613 - 44238, 44294) Fax: 310433
Website: www.fhrai.com
E-mail: joshiresorts@advantage2you.com
and Taj Khema, UPSTDC (330140).

What to Buy: The craftsman at Agra is still labouring on
making exquisite marble inlay work pieces that made its
monuments famous. Boxes, table-tops, trays, etc., in white or black
with fine inlay decorations are still the best buy. Agra is also a
centre for fine leather- wear.

Best Season: Throughout the year.

Clothing: Summer- Light tropical, Winter- Woollen.

79

The Pink City

JAIPUR

Ex-New Delhi

Jaipur was founded in 1727 AD by one of the greatest rulers of the Kachhawaha clan, the Sawai Raja Jaisingh, and designed by architect Vidayadhar. Jaipur today epitomizes the spirit of Rajputana. For long called the Pink City, because of extensive usage of the locally abundant pink stone, Jaipur has massive forts, magnificent palaces, exquisite temples and marvellous gardens. The city has straight roads and planned intersections. Hawa Mahal is an experience of a windy palace in the desert. Closeby is the City Palace Museum (where arms and artefacts are displayed) and the Jantar Mantar (observatory). Riding an elephant up the Amer Fort approach is a royal experience. Inside one comes across a fusion of Indo-Mughal art. Beyond the neighbouring hill is a beautiful garden-cum-palace complex called Sisodia Rani ka Bagh. Neatly tucked away between the folds of hills this palace is exquisite.

Places to See: Forts and Palaces: Amer Fort; Jaigarh Fort; Nahargarh Fort; Hawa Mahal; Jal Mahal; City Palace.

Other Interesting Places: Galtaji; Sisodia Rani ka Bagh; Gaitor; Sanganer; Bagru; Albert Museum; Jantar Mantar; Birla Mandir.

How to Reach: By Air:- Jaipur is well connected by air.
By Rail / Road: - Jaipur is well connected by both rail and road.

Plan your tour by rail

Route: New Delhi - 308 kms - Jaipur

Day	Train No./Name	Dep.	Arr.	From	To
One	2015 Shatabdi Exp. (except Su)	0610	1040	New Delhi	Jaipur
One/Two/Three	Stay and Visit Jaipur				
Three	2016 Shatabdi Exp. (except Su)	1755	2220	Jaipur	New Delhi

Where to Stay: Tel. Code- 0141

Hotels: 5 Star

Jal Mahal Palace (371616) Fax: 365237 Website: www.fhrai.com
Rambagh Palace (381919) Fax: 381098 Website: www.fhrai.com
E-mail: rambagh@jp1.dot.net.in
Rajvilas Oberoi (640101) Fax: 640202 Website: www.fhrai.com,
www.oberoihotels.com E-mail: reservations@rajvilas.com
Clarks Amer (549437, 550616) Fax: 550013
Website: www.fhrai.com
E-mail: clkamer@jp1.dot.net.in
Rajputana Palace Sheraton (360011) Fax: 367848
Website: www.fhrai.com, www.welcomgroup.com
E-mail: rajputana@wecomgroup.com
Mansingh (378771-79) Fax: 377582 Website: www.fhrai.com,
www.mansinghhotels.com
E-mail: mansinghjaipur@mailcity.com
Jaipur Palace (512961-63) Fax: 512966 Website: www.fhrai.com,
http://www.hotel.jaipur.palace.com E-mail: hjpj@jp1.dot.net.in

4 Star

Jaipur Ashok (204491-96) Fax: 202099 Website: www.fhrai.com
Meru Palace (371111-16) Fax: 378882, 563767
Website: www.fhrai.com,
www.fhraindia.com/hotel/jaipur/merupalace
E-mail: kotawaha@jpi.dot.net.in

Heritage
Bissau Palace (304371, 304391) Fax: 304628
Website: www.fhrai.com,
www.bissaupalace.com E-mail: sanjai@jpl.dot.net.in
Khasa Kothi (375151-54) Fax: 374040 Website: www.fhrai.com
Narain Niwas Palace (561291, 563448) Fax: 561045
Website: www.fhrai.com
Raj Mahal Palace (381757, 381625) Fax: 381887
Website: www.fhrai.com
Samode Haveli (632370, 632407) 631397 Website:
www.fhrai.com,
http://www.samode.com E-mail: reservations@samode.com
Ramgarh Lodge (55217, 52078) Fax: 52078 Website:
www.fhrai.com

3 Star
Mansingh Towers (378771) Fax: 377582
Website: www.fhrai.com, www.mansinghhotels.com
E-mail: mansinghtower.jaipur@mailcity.com
Holiday Inn Jaipur (609000) Fax: 609090
Website: www.fhrai.com,
http://www.holiday.inn/com/hotel.jaiin
E-mail: hijaiin@jpl.vsnl.net.in
Kanchandeep (364500) Fax: 364518, 369218
Website: www.fhrai.com,
http://www.kanchandeep.com
E-mail: kanchandeep@kanchandeep.com
Hawa Mahal (381201-02) Website: www.fhrai.com
Great Value Kohinoor (368238) Fax: 360822
Website: www.fhrai.com
Maharani Palace (204702, 204378) Website: www.fhrai.com,
maharanihotels.com E-mail: maharani@jp1.dot.net.in
LMB Hotel (565844) Fax: 562176 Website: www.fhrai.com,
www.lmbswets.com E-mail: info@imp.sweets.com
Trident Jaipur (630101) Fax: 630303 Website: www.fhrai.com,
E-mail: reservations@tridentjp.com

2 Star

Broadway (641275) Fax: 640576 Website: www.fhrai.com,
http://datainfosys.com/broadway
E-mail: broadway@datainfosys.net

Khetri House Fax: Website: www.fhrai.com

Budget

Neelam (377274) Fax: 370609 Website: www.fhrai.com
Vatika (513359) Fax: 0141-513359 Website: www.fhrai.com
Chokhi Dhani (583534) Fax: 580118 Website: www.fhrai.com,
www.chokhidhani.com E-mail: cokidani@datainfosys.net
Jaipur Emerald (370476) Website: www.fhrai.com
Welcomheritage Khimsar Fort (382314, 378682) Fax: 381150
Website: www.fhrai.com, http://www.rajasthanonline.com/
khimsarfot
E-mail: khimsar@jpl.vsnl.net.in

Gangaur (RTDC)

Aditya
and many others in the city.

Best Season: Throughout the year.

Clothing: Summer- Light tropical, Winter- Woollen.

80

Palaces and Lakes

UDAIPUR
Ex-New Delhi

Udaipur, the jewel of Mewar, is a fascinating blend of sights, sounds and experiences- an inspiration for the imagination of poets, painters and writers. Its kaleidoscope of fairy- tale palaces, lakes, temples, gardens, and narrow lanes strewn with stalls never fail to enchant. The exquisite Lake Palace of Udaipur, shimmering like a jewel on Lake Pichola, is overwhelming in splendour. An imaginative garden in seclusion for the royal Princesses, the Saheliyon ki Bari fulfilled the dual demands of the purdah system and a garden for frolic. Inside the museum of Shiv Niwas Palace, one comes across the indomitable Rajput spirit and valour which find expression in various arms, paintings and artefacts displayed here. It is the same city where the famous James Bond movie, *Octopussy*, was filmed. It is undoubtedly the most beautiful city of Rajasthan.

Places to See: Lake Palace; City Palace; Jagdish Temple; Bharatiya Lok Kala Museum; Saheliyon-ki-Bari; Pratap Memorial; Eklingji; Fateh Sagar; Pichhola Lake; Sajjan Garh; Ahar; Gulab Bagh.

How to Reach: By Air:- Udaipur is well connected by air.
By Rail / Road:- Udaipur is well connected by both rail and road.

Plan your tour by rail

Route: New Delhi – 739 - kms - Udaipur

Day	Train No./Name	Dep.	Arr.	From	To
One	9615 Chetak Exp.	1410	-	Delhi Sarai Rohilla	-
Two	Enroute	-	1025	-	Udaipur
Three/Four	Stay and Visit Udaipur.				
Five	9616 Chetak Exp.	1815	-	Udaipur	-
Six	Enroute	-	1310	-	Delhi Sarai Rohilla

Where to Stay: Tel. Code- 0294

Hotels:
5 Star
Lake Palace (527961-973) Fax: 527974 Website: www.fhrai.com
E-mail: lpugm.udp@tajgroup.sprintrpg.ems.vsnl.net.in

Heritage
Fateh Prakash Palace (528016, 528019) Fax: 528006
Website: www.fhrai.com, hrhindia.com
E-mail: shelley@udaipur.hrindia.com
Shivniwas Palace (528016-19)) Fax: 528006
Website: www.fhrai.com,
hrhindia.com E-mail: 1phm.hrh@axcess.net.in
Laxmi Vilas Palace (529711-15) Fax: 525536
Website: www.fhrai.com
E-mail: lvp.hotel@gems.vsnl.net.in
Shikarbadi (583200-04) Fax: 584841 Website: www.fhrai.com,
http://www.hrhindia.com E-mail: hrhindia.com

3 Star
Heritage Resorts (440382, 430628) Fax: 430549
Website: www.fhrai.com E-mail: hresort@usa.net
Hilltop Palace (521997-99) Fax: 525106
Website: www.fhrai.com
Rajdarshan (526601-5) Fax: 524588 Website: www.fhrai.com

Jaisamand Island Resort (02906-2222, 2200) Fax: 431406
Website: www.fhrai.com E-mail: resort@ad1.vsnl.net.in
Lake Pichola (421197) Fax: 430575 Website: www.fhrai.com
Trident Udaipur (432200) Fax: 432211 Website: www.fhrai.com,
www.oberoihotels.com E-mail: bhushan@tridentudo.com

2 Star

Chandralok (560011) Website: www.fhrai.com
Oriental Palace Resorts (412360, 412373) Fax: 411238
Website: www.fhrai.com E-mail: opr@bom5.vsnl.net.in
Lakend (415100-03) Fax: 523898 Website: www.fhrai.com
E-mail: resort@adl.vsnl.net.in
Pratap Country Inn (583138) Fax: 583058
Website: www.fhrai.com

Budget

Hermitage Inn (527128, 524586) Website: ww.fhrai.com
E-mail: a-bapna@hotmail.com
Ashish Palace (525558) Fax: 525558 E-mail: www.fhrai.com
Raj Inn (524275) Website: www.fhrai.com
Damanis (525675) Fax: 526380 Website: www.fhrai.com
Fountain (560272) Fax: 560251 Website: www.fhrai.com
Paras Mahal (483394)
Anand Bhawan (523256, 523018) Fax: 523247
Website: www.fhrai.com
Heritage Resort Nagda
Green View International (422222, 419556) Fax: 412555
Website: www.fhrai.com
and many other budget hotels.

Best Season: September to March.

Clothing: Summer- Light tropical, Winter- Woollen.

Tales of Grandeur

JODHPUR
Ex-Delhi

*J*odhpur, the former capital of Marwar State, set at the edge of the Thar desert, was founded in 1459 AD by Rao Jodha. A flourishing trading centre in the 16th century, Jodhpur is still one of the leading centres for wood, cattle, camels, salt and agricultural crops. However, the past is never very far behind and Jodhpur boasts of some very fine reminders of a glorious history. Once upon a time this region of Marwar was known as the land of death. But the difficult terrain could not deter the undaunted spirit of the Rathores who peopled this inhospitable rocky extravaganza. They celebrated life to such an extent through their deeds of valour, songs of pride, fort of glory and a palace of speaking stones, that the fierceness of death pales into insignificance before the romancing life spirit. A view of the Jodhpur fort rising proudly, its skyline framed upon the sky is both enchanting and uplifting. Like the fort, strong and independent, were the warriors of this clan. Inside one can see beautiful palanquins and howdahs used by kings and queens, relating a tale of yesteryear. Closeby, beside a water-body is Jaswant Thada, a marble memorial to a king. The city is unique and interesting.

Places to See: Prime Sites: Mehrangarh Fort; Jaswant Thada; Umaid Bhawan Palace; Museum.

Excursions: Balsamand Lake and Garden; Mandore; Mahamandir Temple; Kailana Lake; Rohit Fort and Luni Fort.

How to Reach: By Air:- Jodhpur is well connected by air.
By Rail / Road:- Jodhpur is well connected by both rail and road.

Plan your tour by rail

Route: Delhi - 623 kms - Jodhpur

Day	Train No./Name	Dep.	Arr.	From	To
One	2461 Mandore Exp.	2100	-	Delhi	-
Two	Enroute	-	0800	-	Jodhpur
Two /Three	Stay and Visit Jodhpur.				
Three	2462 Mandore Exp.	1930	-	Jodhpur	-
Four	Enroute	-	0615	-	Delhi

Where to Stay: Tel. Code- 0291

Hotels:
5 Star
Welcomheritage Umaid Bhawan Palace (510101) Fax: 510100
Website: www.fhrai.com, www.welcomeheritage.com
E-mail: ubp@ndf.vsnl.net.in

Heritage
Ajit Bhavan Palace (510410, 510610) Fax: 510674
Website: www.fhrai.com, www.ajitbhawan.com
E-mail: abhawan@del3.vsnl.net.in
Balsamand Lake Palace (545991) Fax: 542240
Website: www.fhrai.com, www.welcomeheritage.com
E-mail: marwar@del3.vsnl.net.in
Karni Bhavan (639380, 432220) Fax: 433495
Website: www.fhrai.com, www.karnihotels.com
E-mail: marwar@del3.vsnl.net.in

4 Star
Ratanada Polo Palace (431910-14) Fax: 433118
Website: www.fhrai.com E-mail: serena@ndf.vsnl.net.in

2 Star
City Palace (431933, 649911) Fax: 639033
Website: www.fhrai.com
Adarsh Niwas (624066, 615871) Fax: 627314
Website: www.fhrai.com, www.fhraindia.com/hotel/jodhpur/
adarshniwas
Sandhu Palace (640154, 432611) Fax: 432611
Website: www.fhrai.com

Budget
Residency Palace (431747, 640747) Fax: 640747
Website: www.fhrai.com & www.fhraindia.com/hotel/jodhpur/
residencypalace E-mail: residencypalace@hotmail.com
Shanti Bhawan Lodge (637001, 621689) Fax: 639211
Website: www.fhrai.com
Ghoomar, RTDC (544010)
Rajputana Palace (431672, 438059)
and many other budget hotels.

Best Season: October to March.

Clothing: Summer- Light tropical, Winter- Woollen.

82

Golden City of the Desert

JAISALMER

Ex-Delhi

Rising from the heart of the Thar desert like a golden flower is the city of Jaisalmer. The golden city was founded by Rawal Jaisal, a descendant of Yadav, a Bhati-Rajput, in 1156 AD. Legend has it that Lord Krishna visited this place and said that a descendant of the Yadav clan would raise his capital over here. Today the Desert City blooms with intricately carved *havelis* and old Jain temples. The imposing walls of the Fort of Jaisalmer defeated many a royal ambition in the past. But today they fulfil many photographic ambitions of the common man. The landscape is conclusive, and the sea of sand dunes has made it one of the most important tourist destinations in the country.

Places to See: Prime Sites: The Fort; Manak Chowk and Haveli's; Jain temples; Gadi Sagar Lake; Patwon-ki-Haveli; Salim Singh ki Haveli.

Excursions: Lodurva 16 kms; Wood Fossil Park, 17 kms; Sam Sand-Dunes (42 km.) and Desert National Park (45 km.).

How to Reach: By Air:-Jodhpur is the nearest airport
By Rail / Road:- Jaisalmer is well connected by both rail and road.

Plan your tour by rail

Route: Delhi - 623 kms - Jodhpur - 295 kms - Jaisalmer

Day	Train No./Name	Dep.	Arr.	From	To
One	2461 Mandore Exp.	2100	-	Delhi	-
Two	Enroute	-	0800	-	Jodhpur
Two	By Rail/Road			Jodhpur	Jaisalmer
Three/Four	Stay and Visit Jaisalmer				
Five	By Rail/Road			Jaisalmer	Jodhpur
Five	2462 Mandore Exp.	1930	-	Jodhpur	-
Six	Enroute	-	0615	-	Delhi

Where to Stay: Tel. Code- 02992

Hotels:
3 Star
Himmatgarh Palace (52002, 52004) Fax: 52005
Website: www.fhrai.com
Dholamaru (52863, 53122-25) Fax: 52761, 531254
Website: www.fhrai.com
Heritage Inn (52769, 50200) Fax: 51638 Website: www.fhrai.com
2 Star
Narain Niwas (52408, 51901-04) Fax: 52101
Website: www.fhrai.com
Budget
Gorbandh Palace (51511-13) Fax: 52749
Website: www.fhrai.com, http://www.hrhindia.com
E-mail: hrhindia.com
Deoki Niwas Palace (52599, 51202) Fax: 51202
Website: www.fhrai.com, www.indian-hotels/devkijaisalmer.com
Moomal, RTDC (52392)
Sam & Hani, Rawalkot (51874, 52638)
Nachna Haveli (52110)
Rang Mahal (50907-08)
Khushboo International, and many other budget hotels.

Best Season: October to February.

Clothing: Summer- Light tropical, Winter-Woollen.

234

83

A Silvered Past

GWALIOR
Ex-New Delhi

A multitude of reigning dynasties, of the great Rajput clans of the Pratiharas, Kachhwahas and Tomars have left indelible etchings of their rule in this city of palaces, temples and monuments. Gwalior's history is traced back to a legend; in 8 AD a chieftain called Suraj Sen was stricken by a deadly disease. He was cured by a hermit saint, Gwalipa, and in gratitude founded a city which he named after the saint who had given him the gift of a new life. Gwalior gained fame as a kingdom of the Scindia rulers. A fort stands testimony to their fighting spirit. The greatest music maestro, Tansen, who in the Mughal period achieved unparalleled fame, has his memorial here. Today Gwalior is a modern Indian city, vibrant and bustling.

Places to See: The Fort, Gujari Mahal; Man Mandir Palace; Suraj Kund; Teli ka Mandir and Sas Bahu ka Mandir; Gurdwara Data Bandhi Chhod; Jai Vilas Palace and Museum; Tansen's Tomb; Ghaus Mohammed's Tomb; Memorials; Kal Vithika and Municipal Museum; Sarod Ghar; Sun Temple.

How to Reach: By Air:- Regular flights connect Gwalior to New Delhi.
By Rail / Road:- Gwalior is well connected by both rail and road.

Plan your tour by rail

Route: New Delhi - 317 kms - Gwalior

Day	Train No./Name	Dep.	Arr.	From	To
One	2002 Shatabdi Exp.	0600	0915	New Delhi	Gwalior
One/Two	Stay and Visit Gwalior.				
Two	2001 Shatabdi Exp.	1900	2250	Gwalior	New Delhi

Where to Stay: Tel. Code- 0751

Hotels:
Heritage
Welcomgroup Usha Kiran Palace (323993-94) Fax: 321103
Website: www.fhrai.com

2 Star
Tansen Gwalior (MPSTDC, 340370, 342606) Fax: 340371
Website: www.fhrai.com E-mail: intoworld@poboxes.com
Regency Resorts (3320, 3321) Fax: 3321
Website: www.fhrai.com

Budget
Fort View
Grace (340110)
Gwalior Regency (340670-74) Fax: 343520
Website: www.fhrai.com
Shelter (326209, 326210) Fax: 326212
Website: www.fhrai.com E-mail: hotelshelter@hotmail.com
Midway
Vivek Continental (432721, 422938) Fax: 320432
Website: www.fhrai.com
Meghdoot
Safari.

Best Season: Throughout the year.

Clothing: Summer- Light tropical, Winter- Light woollen.

84

City of the Nawabs

BHOPAL
Ex- New Delhi

*B*hopal today presents a multi–faceted profile; the old city with its teeming market places and fine old mosques and places, still bears the aristocratic imprint of its former rulers, amongst them a succession of powerful *Begums* who ruled Bhopal from 1879 to 1926. The Nawabs of Bhopal gave to the city a royal tradition and many architecturally splendid buildings. Glimpses of the royal tradition are still visible in the city life. Equally impressive in the new city are exquisitely laid out parks and gardens, broad avenues and modern edifices. Bhopal is an interesting city with many monuments displaying medieval architecture. In the middle of the city is a lake which has been a mute witness to the ups and downs of history. Bhopal is giving to modern India a spirit of unity through a novel way of concerts.

Places to See: Taj-ul Masjid; Shaukat Mahal; Sadar Manzil; Bharat Bhawan; Jama Masjid; Gohar Mahal; Tribal Habitat; Moti Masjid; Laxminarayan Temple; Van Vihar; Regional Science Centre; Upper and Lower Lakes.

How to Reach: By Air:- Bhopal is well connected by air. By Rail / Road:- Bhopal is on the Delhi-Chennai grand trunk route and is well connected by road.

Plan your tour by rail

Route: New Delhi - 705 kms - Bhopal

Day	Train No./Name	Dep.	Arr.	From	To
One	2002 Shatabdi Exp.	0600	1410	New Delhi	Bhopal
One/Two	Stay and Visit Bhopal				
Three	2001 Shatabdi Exp.	1450	2250	Bhopal	New Delhi

Where To Stay: Tel. Code- 0755

Hotels:
Heritage
Noor-Us-Sabah Palace (749101-7) Fax: 749110
Website: www.welcomeheritage.com
E-mail: welcome@ndf.vsnl.net.in
Jehan Numa Palace (540100) Fax: 540720
Website: www.fhrai.com
E-mail: jehanuma@bom6.vsnl.net.in

4 Star
The Residency (556001-6) Fax: 557637 Website: www.fhrai.com

3 Star
Amer Palace (272110) Fax: 575308 Website: www.fhrai.com,
www.bhopalnet.com/amer E-mail: amer@bhopalnet.com
Lake View Ashok (541601) Fax: 541606
Website: www.fhrai.com,
www.indiatourism.com E-mail: hlvashok@bom6.vsnl.net.in
Nisagra (555701-03) Fax: 555701-03, 272701-03
Website: www.fhrai.com E-mail: nisarga@bom4.vsnl.net.in

2 Star
Palash, MPT (553076, 553066) Fax: 553076
Website: www.fhrai.com
Panchanan, MPT (551647) Website: www.fhrai.com

Budget
Raj Tilak, Best Western Residency
Ranjit (533511, 534411) Fax: 532242 Website: www.fhrai.com
E-mail: ranjit@bom6.vsnl.net.in
Surendra Vilas (760061-5) Fax: 760065 Website: www.fhrai.com
E-mail: surendravilas@hotmail.com
and many others in the city.

Best Season: Throughout the year.

Clothing: Summer- Light tropical; Winter -Light woollen.

85

City of Palaces and Birds

DEEG

Ex-New Delhi

*D*eeg is a popular tourist rendezvous today, located at a distance of 153 kms from Delhi and 11 kms from Mathura. An 18th century stronghold of the Jat *rajas* it has picturesquely contrived garden-cum-water palaces. The Deeg Fort, built by Raja Suraj Mal, stands majestically over a slightly elevated location. The fort is surrounded by impressive moats, ramparts and gateways. The Jat rulers were warriors to the core, and a swing captured from a Mughal fort is testimony to their daring. Closeby is the Keoladeo Bird Sanctuary, home to thousands of birds. Even the rare Siberian crane migrates to this water paradise during the severe Siberian winter.

Places to visit in Palace: Gopal Bhawan; Sawan-Bhadon Pavilions; Watch Tower (over it is placed a gun captured from the Agra Fort).

How to Reach: By Air:- The nearest airport is Delhi.
By Rail / Road:- Deeg is well connected by both rail and road.

Plan your tour by rail

Route: New Delhi - 179 kms – Deeg (Via Mathura)

Day	Train No./Name	Dep.	Arr.	From	To
One	2180 Taj Exp.	0715	0857	Nizamuddin	Mathura
	By bus or taxi	0930	1030	Mathura	Deeg
One/Two/Three	Stay at Deeg / Bharatpur and visit Keoladeo Bird Sanctuary.				
Three	By bus or taxi	1800	1900	Deeg	Mathura
	2179 Taj Express	1930	2145	Mathura	Nizamuddin

Where to Stay: **Tel. Code- 05644**
RTDC Midway (near Bus Stand, Deeg).

Hotels at Bharatpur:
Budget
Laxmi Vilas Palace (23523) Fax: 25259 Website: www.fhrai.com
Bharatpur Forest Lodge (22760, 22722) Fax: 22864
Website: www.fhrai.com
Saras, RTDC (23700)
Eagle's Nest (25144).

Best Season: Throughout the year.

Clothing: Summer- Light tropical, Winter- Light woollen.

86

City of Joy

MANDU
Ex- New Delhi

*M*andu was once the capital of Parmar rulers of Malwa. Mandu is a celebration of life and joy in stone. The pervading spirit of the place was gaiety. A tribute to love shared between poet Prince Baz Bahadur and his beautiful consort Rani Roopmati. The balladeers of Malwa still sing this euphoric romance. Under the sway of Mughal rulers, Mandu became a pleasure resort. Percy Brown, the great historian, has fondly described Mandu as a place "......with undulating tracts shaded by trees, are dark pools nestling in the hollows and larger lakes glistening in the sunshine, while rocky ravines alternate with sloping swards, the entire effect being almost unreal in its beauty." The ruins of Mandu relate a tale of grandeur and a hoary past. It is rare in history that a king is credited with excellence in poetry. The ruler of Mandu, Baz Bahadur, is remembered more for his songs than his kingship.

Places to See: Marble Tomb of Hoshang Shah; Jama Masjid; Jahaj Mahal; Hindola Mahal; Hindola Fort.

How to Reach: By Air:- The nearest airport is Indore.
By Rail / Road:- Indore is the nearest railhead, where all Mail / Express trains halt. Mandu is 99 kms by road from Indore.

Plan your tour by rail

Route: New Delhi - 829 kms - Indore - 99 kms - Mandu

Day	Train No./Name	Dep.	Arr.	From	To
One	2416 Nizamuddin Indore Exp.	2215	-	Nizamuddin	-
Two	Enroute	-	1150	-	Indore
Two/Three	Stay and Visit Mandu				
Four	Travel by bus or taxi to Indore and reach before 16.00 hrs.				
Four	2415 Nizamuddin Indore Exp.	1630	-	Indore	-
Five	Enroute	-	0610	-	Nizamuddin

Where to Stay: Tel. Code- 07292

Hotels: Budget
Traveller's Lodge, MPT (63221)
SADA Rest House, Tourist Cottage, MPT (63235).

Best Season: Throughout the year.

Clothing: Summer- Light tropical, Winter- Woollen.

87

A Medieval City Frozen in Time

ORCHHA
Ex-New Delhi

Orchha is a medieval city existing in the time warp of the then rulers of Orchha. Here a palace was erected by the ruler in honour of the visiting Emperor Jehangir for the brief duration of his stay. A grandiose temple was constructed to house the royal deity, after a dream command by the deity to the then King. The river Betwa flows on a rocky bed and by the bank are several *chhatris* (memorials) to the erstwhile rulers. It was the hideout to freedom fighter Chandrashekhar Azad during the freedom struggle. A rich forest surrounds the entire palace-cum-fort complex. The palaces display rich carving and sculpture. The legend of the installation of Ram Raja statue rules the place. A visit to Orchha is like going back in time.

Places to See: Jehangir Mahal; Raj Mahal; Rai Praveen Mahal; Ram Raja Temple; Sunder Mahal; Siddh Baba ka Sthan; Jugal Kishor; Janki Mandir; Hanuman Mandir; *chhatris* (There are fourteen *chhatris* or memorials to the rulers of Orchha, grouped along the Kanchana Ghat of the river Betwa).

How to Reach: By Air: - Gwalior is the nearest airport. By Rail / Road: - The nearest railhead is Jhansi. All major Mail / Express trains stop at Jhansi. From Jhansi to Orchha travel 16 kms by bus / taxi (regular bus services are available on the Jhansi-Khajuraho Road).

Plan your tour by rail

Route: New Delhi - 414 kms - Jhansi - 16 kms - Orchha.

Day	Train No./Name	Dep.	Arr.	From	To
One	2002 Shatabdi Exp.	0600	1024	New Delhi	Jhansi
	By bus/taxi			Jhansi	Orchha
Two/Three	Stay and Visit Orchha (travel back to Jhansi)				
Three	2001 Shatabdi	1755	2250	Jhansi	New Delhi

Where to Stay: Tel. Code- 07680

Hotels: Budget
Betwa Cottages, MPSTDC (52618)
Mansarovar
Palki Mahal
Sattar Yatri Niwas of Sada
Sheesh Mahal, MPSTDC (52624).

Best Season: Throughout the year.

Clothing: Summer- Light tropical; Winter- Woollen.

88

The Land of Fragrance

MYSORE
Ex-Bangalore

Once the capital of Wodeyars, this enchanting city still retains its old world charm, that never fails to bewitch. This serene city abounds in tourist attractions. The most imposing sight in the city is the palace of Mysore that never fails to enchant. Inside the palace is heady grandeur, displayed from the richly painted palace interiors. The palace has been maintained most responsibly and it appears that a charming princess may step out any time from an adjoining door. The smell of palace intrigue still wafts from the columns of the palace halls. The strong scent of sandal and agarbathis, the aroma of fresh roasted coffee beans, the heady fragrance of Mysore Mallige and a thousand roses blossoming...., yes Mysore is a land of fragrance. Mysore's most famous festival is the 10-day Dusshera in Oct.-Nov. each year

Places to See: Mysore Palace; St. Philomena's Church; Chamundi Hills; Jaya Chamarajender Art Gallery; Folk Art Museum; the Oriental Research Institute; the Railway Museum; Mysore Zoo; Brindaban Garden.

How to Reach: By Air:- The nearest airport is Bangalore. By Rail / Road:- Mysore is a railhead and is also easily approachable by road from Bangalore.

Plan your tour by rail

Route: Bangalore - 140 kms - Mysore

Day	Train No./Name	Dep.	Arr.	From	To
One	2007 Shatabdi Exp. (except Tue.)	1100	1300	Bangalore	Mysore
Two/three	Stay and Visit Mysore				
Three	6221 Mysore-Chennai Exp.	1800	2055	Mysore	Bangalore

Where to Stay: Tel. Code- 0821

Hotels:
5 Star
Lalitha Mahal Palace (571265) Fax: 571770
Website: www.fhrai.com, http://www.ashokgroup.com
E-mail: htlashok@giasmd01.vsnl.net.in

3 Star
Ramanshree Comforts (563056, 522202)
Website: www.fhrai.com
The Viceroy (424001, 428001) Fax: 433391
Website: www.fhrai.com
Kaynes (420931-933) Fax: 402934 Website: www.fhrai.com,
http://www.kaynes.com E-mail: kaynes@blr.vsnl.net.in

2 Star
Kadur Inn (402210, 402840) Fax: 402209
Website: www.fhrai.com

1 Star
Dasaprakash (442444, 444455) Fax: 443456
Website: www.fhrai.com
The Paradise 410366, 515655) Fax: 514400
Website: www.fhrai.com,
http://fhraindia.com/hotel.mysore/paradise
E-mail: Paradise@blr.vsnl.net.in

Budget

Mayura Hoysalo
Air Lines (23280, 520345) Website: www.fhrai.com
Rajendra Vilas Palace (420664) Website: www.fhrai.com
Siddharta (522999, 522888) Fax: 520692
Website: www.fhrai.com E-mail: giri@giadbgol.vsnl.net.in
Roopa (443770, 440044) Website: www.fhrai.com
E-mail: nrshreya@bir.vsnl.net.in
Indra Bhavan (423933) Fax: 422290 Website: www.fhrai.com
E-mail: grame Indian
Kabani River Lodge (32181, 44401) Fax: 32181
Website: www.fhrai.com, http://www.india.internet.com/
junglelodges E-mail: jungle@giasbg01.vsnl.net.in
Kings Kourt (421142) Fax: 438384 Website: www.fhrai.com
E-mail: king@giasbg01.vsnl.net.in
Bombay Indra Bhavan (4205221, 40295)
Website: www.fhrai.com
Quality Inn Southern Star (438141, 429686) Fax: 421689
Website: www.fhrai.com, http://www.southernstarmysore.com
E-mail: Southernstar@.vsnl.com
and other budget hotels.

Best Season: Throughout the year.

Clothing: Summer-Light tropical, Winter- Light woollen.

The Unconquerable Fort

CHITTORGARH

Ex-New Delhi

To trace the antiquity of Chittorgarh is difficult, but it is believed that Bhim the legendary figure of the *Mahabharata*, visited this place to learn the secrets of immortality and became a disciple of Soga. But his impatience to perform all the rites deprived him of his goal, and out of sheer anger he stamped on the ground creating a water reservoir, now known as Bhim Lat. Later on, it came under the Muri Rajputs, and remained the capital of Mewar till 1568 AD. The town of brave men, known for its massive forts atop a hill, has a chequered history. It witnessed some of the bloodiest battles in history, and most heroic deeds of valour. People of Chittorgarh still sing ballads to heroic grandeur. The hymns of Meerabai, dedicated to Lord Krishna, were originally sung by Meerabai at her temple in the fort of Chittor.

Places to See: The Fort; Vijay Stambh or Victory Tower; Kirti Stambh or Tower of Fame; Rana Kumbha's Palace; Kumbha Shyam Temple; Mahasati Cenotaphs; Kalika Mata Temple; Jaimal and Patta's Palace; Government Museum; Gaumukh (cow's mouth) Reservoir; Mohar Magri (Hill of Gold Coils).

Excursions: Nagri (20 kms); Baroli (130 kms); Bassi Village (25 kms); Bassi Wildlife Sanctuary; Sanwariaji Temple (40 kms); Bhainsrorgarh Wildlife Sanctuary (90 kms); Bijapur (40 kms); Sitamata Sanctuary; Deogarh (125 kms); Menal (90 kms).

How to Reach: By Air:-The nearest airport is Udaipur. By Rail / Road:-Chittorgarh is a railhead and is also easily approachable by road.

Plan your tour by rail

Route: New Delhi - 622 kms - Chittorgarh

Day	Train No./Name	Dep.	Arr.	From	To
One	9615 Chetak Exp.	1410	-	Delhi Sarai Rohilla	-
Two	Enroute	-	0630	-	Chittorgarh
Two/Three/Four	Stay and Visit Chittorgarh				
Four	9616 Chetak Exp.	2200	-	Chittorgarh	-
Five	Enroute	-	1310	-	Delhi Sarai Rohilla

Where to Stay: **Tel. Code- 01472**

Hotels:
Heritage
Castle Bejaipur
Basri Fort Palace (79248)

Budget
Panna, RTDC (41238)
Pratap Palace (40099, 43563)
Padmini Palace (41718, 46297)
Gaurav Palace (46207, 43107)
Chetak, Meera (40266)
Shalimar and many others.
Government accommodation can also be availed at Circuit House, Dak Bungalow and Railway Retiring Rooms.

Best Season: September to March.

Clothing: Summer-Light tropical, Winter- Light woollen.

Basket of Unusuals

o you have such simple ambitions – like becoming a leaf to the wind, scurried away once here on the path, once there under the tree; or of becoming part of an apricot tree in bloom, just one of those thousand pink flowers blossoming sensuously on each twig, leaving no space for leafy neighbours; or still higher of becoming a rolling stone, carried by a flowing river and lulled to sleep by the Moon's romancing rays. If you do, then come to a place away from the glare, away from the prying eyes, away from the eventful day, to something that is unusual.

Such a place can be the confluence of a river with the sea. Experience the forces of a delta celebrating Nature. See how the river, land, animals and birds combine to cart you away from the usual routine of your life. Let for once the beauty of nature submerge you completely. Allow Nature to release your mind from the hassles of unpaid bills, salary dues, promotional avenues, jealousies, unsettled scores, and the like. Try and dream your dreams with God's own creatures. Such an unusual taste can also lead you to row a boat in a river flowing at ease, with high rugged walls of marble to its side instead of banks. Look up the marble gorge- how purely it holds the river in between its white palms. Such caress of stone to river may lead you to become perhaps more expressive.

Or if you wish to playact a Bollywood hero, singing a song in the rains, there is a city for you too! Then there can be an island situated within a turbulent river- can you believe it ordinarily! We have heard of islands in the sea or even human beings as islands of excellence, but never of an island surfaced in a swollen river. Discover the secrets of evolution, of the time when thought was God, and God was stone, tree, or any other

251

ferocious or incomprehensible form. The banks have cradled one such island as a gem and the river waters have washed it each day, making it shine like a jewel.

Another option to be unusual is to go to the caves and wonder what the primeval man conceptualised, and painted on their uneven walls. Explore the motions of life in such rudimentary art forms and wonder upon the creative urge of man. Whether he lived in Stone Age or the present, this urge to give, to create, has been basic in man. This urge has led him to unusually establish such cities where all differences of creed, caste, colour, all prejudices of position, status melt into an unusual cauldron of humanity. What remains is a human being in communion with his Creator.

Yes, it is difficult to do the unusual, to think differently, to carve out a distinct place for oneself in society and history, but it is not impossible. And to conquer the small impossibilities of life, to do the unusual, visit this Basket of Unusuals at least once in a lifetime.

Possibilities

Enjoy Life

A River Island

MAJULI
Ex-Guwahati

*N*estled in the lap of the Brahmaputra, her face uplifted to the limitless frontiers of the blue sky, feet perpetually caressed by the lapping waters of the holy river and vision stretched to the distant hills, is Majuli. Perhaps the largest river island in the world, Majuli is a creation of the master craftsman– God. Multifaceted in its attractions, Majuli unfolds a variety of interests to the tourist- rare migratory birds, traditional handicrafts and pottery, ethnic culture and dance forms, and water sport. The main tribes of Majuli are the Misings, Deoris and Sonowal Kacharis. The father of Assamese culture, Sankardeva, took shelter in the 15th century AD at Majuli and spent a couple of months at Beloguri. He contributed the first "satra," -the Manikanchan Sanjog (Propagation of socio-cultural ideals). Twenty-two "satras" still flourish in Majuli and are the treasure house of various dance forms.

Places to See: Dakhinpat Satra; Garamurh Satra; Auniati Satra; Kamalabari Satra; Bengenaati Satra; Shamaguri Satra.

Other Attractions:
1. Various species of rare migratory birds like Pelican are found in Majuli.
2. The pottery-making centre is situated at upper Majuli.
3. The Paal Naam at Auniati Satra is a huge mela, held at the end of autumn.

4. Another festival performed by the Sonowal Kacharis tribe is "Bathow Puja," where Lord Shiva is worshipped with high veneration.
5. There are many places for viewing the sunset during winter.

How to Reach: By Air:-The nearest airport is Rowriah (Jorhat).
By Rail / Road: - Mariani (Jorhat) is the nearest railhead and is also approachable by road.

Plan your tour by rail

Route: Guwahati - 400 kms - Majuli

Day	Train No./Name	Dep.	Arr.	From	To
One	˄ 2424 A Rajdhani Exp. (Tue, Sun)	2200	-	Guwahati	-
Two	Enroute	-	0505	-	Mariani
Two/Three/Four	Stay and Visit Majuli				
Five	2423 A Rajdhani Exp. (Tue, Thur)	2100	-	Mariani	-
Six	Enroute	-	0430	-	Guwahati

Where to Stay:

Hotels:

Budget

Circuit House at Garamurh, P.W.D (Kamalabari)
Guest House Kamalabari Satra and Tourist Lodge.
For further information contact Govt. of India Tourist Office at Guwahati: Ph. 0361- 547407.

Best Season: Throughout the year.

Clothing: Summer-Light tropical, Winter- Woollen.

In the Neolithic Age

BHIMBETKA

Ex-New Delhi

*B*himbetka is the rocky terrain spread amongst dense forest and craggy cliffs. Over 600 rock shelters belonging to the Neolithic age were discovered recently. These are surrounded by the northern fringe of the Vindhyan ranges. An archaeological treasure, Bhimbetka has in panoramic detail paintings in over 500 caves depicting the pre-historic cave dwellers. Executed mainly in red and white with an occasional splash of green and yellow, portraying themes of hunting, dancing, music, horse and elephant riding, animal fights, household scenes, etc. Many animal designs such as lizards, crocodiles, dogs and wild boar and popular religious and ritual symbols also occur frequently. It is a study in the evolution of man.

Attractions within the Caves:

Upper Paleolithic: Linear representations of animal figures in green and red.

Mesolithic: Stylised figures showing linear decorations. Apart from animals, human pictures and primitive hunting tools.

Chaleolithic: Paintings reveal trade and agriculture.

Early Historic: Schematic and decorative depiction in red, white and yellow. Religious beliefs and symbols are prominent.

Medieval: Paintings become geometric and more schematic but artistic style degenerates.

Excursion:

Bhojpur: Bhojpur (28 kms from Bhopal) was founded by the legendary Parmar King, Raja Bhoj (1010-1053 AD). It is known for its magnificent Shiva Temple and Cyclopean Dam. Remains of a vast lake, west of Bhojpur, display the skill of the people and their kingdom.

Places to See: Bhojeshwar Temple; Cyclopean Dam; Jain Shrine; Ruins of Lake and Dam.

How to Reach: By Air:- The nearest airport is Bhopal. By Rail / Road:- Bhimbetka is well connected to railhead Bhopal (46 kms) and is easily approachable by road.

Plan your tour by rail

Route: New Delhi - 705 kms – Bhopal - 46 kms - Bhimbetka

Day	Train No./Name	Dep.	Arr.	From	To
One	2002 Shatabdi Exp.	0600	1410	New Delhi	Bhopal
One/Two	Stay at Bhopal and Visit Bhimbetka and Bhojpur.				
Three	2001 Shatabdi Exp.	1450	2250	Bhopal	New Delhi

Where to Stay: **Tel. Code- 0755**

Hotels at Bhopal:
Heritage
Noor-Us-Sabah Palace (749101-7) Fax: 749110
Website: www.welcomheritage.com
E-mail: welcome@ndf.vsnl.net.in
Jehan Numa Palace (540100) Fax: 540720
Website: www.fhrai.com
E-mail: jehanuma@bom6.vsnl.net.in

4 Star
The Residency (556001-6) Fax: 557637 Website: www.fhrai.com

3 Star
Amer Palace (272110) Fax: 575308 Website: www.fhrai.com/
amer
E-mail: amer@bhopalnet.com
Lake View Ashok (541601) Fax: 541606
Website: www.indiatourism.com
E-mail: hlvashok@bom6.vsnl.net.in
Nisagra (555701-03) Fax: 555701-03 Website: www.fhrai.com
E-mail: nisagra@bom4.vsnl.net.in

2 Star
Palash, MPT (553076, 553066) Fax: 553076 Website:
www.fhrai.com
Panchanan, MPT (551647) Website: www.fhrai.com

Budget
Raj Tilak
Best Western Residency
Ranjit (533511, 534411)
Surendra Vilas (760061-5), and many others in the city.

Best Season: July to March.

Clothing: Summer-Light tropical, Winter- Woollen.

Romance with a Song

KHANDALA- LONAVALA -KARLA

Ex-Mumbai

*H*ill stations of the Western Ghats, set in serene surroundings, almost entice a tourist to romance over a song. The heat and humidity of Mumbai is left far behind and one comes to live amidst breath-taking views of sprawling valleys, cascading waterfalls and out of the world sunsets. The clean crisp air invigorates and pleases to the core. At Karla one is face to face with the best preserved caves dating back to 160 BC. The caves are in the green hills of the Western Ghats and speak volumes for the primitive man. The Lohagad and Visapur forts in the distant horizon provide a magnificent backdrop to a viewer. The places are a favourite with Bollywood for filming songs and film sequences. Whether it be abduction or rendezvous, or fights, or the filming of quaint countryside, no Mumbai film is complete without the shooting unit coming to any of the three places.

Attractions in the Western Ghats:
* Khandala: Breath-taking views of cascading waterfalls.
* Lonavala: Scenic views and a place of solitude.
* Karla caves: One of the best preserved caves dating back to 160 BC.
* Bhaja caves: Caves excavated in the 2nd century BC.
* Lohagad Fort ruins.
* Visapur Fort ruins.

How to Reach: By Air:- Mumbai is the nearest airport. By Rail / Road:- Khandala, Lonavala, and Karla are well connected by both rail and road.

Plan your tour by rail

Route: Mumbai - 124 kms - Khandala - 4 kms - Lonavala - 12 kms - Karla

Day	Train No./Name	Dep.	Arr.	From	To
One	2027 Shatabdi Exp.	0640	0905	Mumbai	Lonavala
One/Two /Three Stay and Visit					
Three	2028 Shatabdi Exp.	1825	2100	Lonavala	Mumbai

Where to Stay: Tel. Code- 02114
Hotels at Khandala

3 Star
The Dukes Retreat (73817, 73819) Fax: 73836
Website: www.fhrai.com
E-mail: duke@ccmob.sprintsmx.ems.vsnl.net.in

Budget
Girija (72062, 73426) Website: www.fhrai.com
Fun-N-Food (73117, 73118) Website: www.fhrai.com
Vallerina (74108, 73410) Fax: 74109 Website: www.fhrai.com
E-mail: bvlf@vsnl.com
Mount View Resort (472335, 6496401) Fax: 71178, 6462513
Website: www.fhrai.com
E-mail: topbeat@bom2.vsnl.net.in
Velvet Hills Retreat (70149) Fax: 70154
Website: www.fhrai.com, www.vikasgroup.com/velvethills
E-mail: velvethills@vikasgroup.com

Hotels at Lonavala

5 Star
Fariyas Holiday Resort (73852-55) Fax: 72080
Website: www.fhrai.com

4 Star

Rainbow Retreat (72128, 73445) Fax: 73998
Website: www.fhrai.com
Valvan Village Resort (74111, 74112) Fax: 74114
Website: www.fhrai.com

3 Star

Biji's Hill Retreat (73023) Fax: 72965 Website: www.fhrai.com,
www.bijis hotels.com E-mail: bijis@boms.vsnl.net.in
Highland Resort (73608, 71191) Fax: 71192
Website: www.fhrai.com

2 Star

Lions Den (72954, 72246) Fax: 70642 Website: www.fhrai.com
Lunav (73457) Fax: 5517120 Website: www.fhrai.com

Budget

Savshanti (73524, 71138) Website: www.fhrai.com
Star Regency (73331, 72825) Fax: 74217
Website: www.fhrai.com
Chandralok (72294, 72921) Website: www.fhrai.com

Best Season: October to May.

Clothing: Summer-Light tropical, Winter- Tropical.

93

Kingdom of Sculpture

HAMPI
Ex-Bangalore

The erstwhile capital of the Vijayanagar kingdom that flourished in 1443 is now only a kingdom of sculpture. Hampi is full of surprises in its ruins. A 700-m long street is reminiscent of the bazaar that prospered in the kingdom. A monolith of Ugra Narasimha seated under a canopy of a seven-hooded snake still instills fear in the mind of an onlooker. A stone chariot with wheels that actually revolve is a proud contribution of the artisans. The palace structure, and the queens' bathing enclosure with lotus fountains, conveys delicacy and style. It has been said about Hampi by Abdul Razaq (a Muslim envoy) that "The pupil of the eye has never seen such a place like it." One can still feel the splendour of Hampi in its ruins. Needless to say, it has been declared as a World Heritage Site.

Places to See: King's Balance; Queen's Bath; Lotus Mahal; Elephant Stables; Vithala Temple Complex; Virupaksha Temple; Ugra Narasimha; Mahanavami Dibba; Hazara Rama Temple.

Excursions: Tungabhadra Dam; Chitradurga Fort.

How to Reach: By Air:- Bellary is the nearest airport (74 kms). Belgaum is another airport 190 kms away.
By Rail / Road:- Hospet is the nearest railhead (13 kms) and is easily approachable by road.
Hampi is just 350 km from Bangalore by road.

Plan your tour by rail

Route: Bangalore - 607 kms – Hampi

Day	Train No./Name	Dep.	Arr.	From	To
One	6592 Hampi Exp.	2200	-	Bangalore City	-
Two	Enroute (Travel to Hampi by bus/taxi)	-	0750	-	Hospet
Two/Three	Stay and Visit Hampi. (Travel to Hospet by bus/taxi)				
Three	6591 Hampi Exp.	2010	-	Hospet	-
Four	Enroute	-	0625	-	Bangalore City

Where to Stay: Tel. Code- 08394
Hotels:
Budget
Mayura Vijayanagar
KSTDC (48270)
Mayura Adil Shahi (20934)
Priyadarshani
Mayura Bhuvaneshwari
Mallige, and many others provide comfortable accommodation.

Best Season: Throughout the year.

Clothing: Summer- Light tropical, Winter –Light woollen.

94

City of the Deccan Dome

BIJAPUR
Ex-Mumbai

*B*ijapur for long remained the capital of Deccan India. Any emperor who desired to conquer the South had to necessarily control Bijapur. It was here that the Mughals stationed their governors for the Deccan. A magnificent dome 44 m in diameter, reputed to be the world's second largest, caps the tomb of Mohammed Adil Shah and boasts of the most sensitive echo-chamber. The ticking of a clock can be heard 125 ft. away, and a slight whisper echoes seven times over! Bijapur has one of the finest mosques in India which displays a most exciting *mehrab*. Exploring the history of the Deccan in its various monuments at Bijapur is quiet involvement. A wish granting medieval cannon 14 ft. long now does not boom with a roar, but fulfils silently.

Places to See: Gol Gumbaz; Ibrahim Roza; Jumma Masjid; Malik-e-Maidan; Afzal Khan's Cenotaph; Arakilla; Anand Mahal; Mehtar Mahal; Bara Kaman; Gagan Mahal; Amin Durgah; Asar Mahal; Chota Asar; Faroukh Mahal; Jahaz Mahal; Jod Gumbaz.

Excursions: Aihole (129 kms); Pattadakal (148 kms) and Badami (132 kms). These are the rock-cut temples close to each other within a radius of 13 kms and project Chalukyan architecture.

How to Reach: By Air:- Belgaum is the nearest airport (205 kms).

By Rail / Road:- Solapur (via Mumbai) is the most convenient railhead. However, Bijapur itself is a railhead. The distance between Solapur and Bijapur is approx. 108 kms by rail.

Plan your tour by rail

Route: Mumbai - 562 kms - Bijapur

Day	Train No./Name	Dep.	Arr.	From	To
One	7001 Hussain Sagar Exp.	2150	-	Mumbai CST	-
Two	Enroute	-	0540	-	Solapur
	By bus or taxi to Bijapur				
Two/Three/Four	Stay and Visit Bijapur				
Five	By bus or taxi to Solapur				
Five	7002 Hussain Sagar Exp.	2100	-	Solapur	-
Six	Enroute	-	0525	-	Mumbai.CST

Where to Stay: Tel. Code- 0217

Hotels at Solapur:
Budget
Ajanta (626519, 726518)
Surya International (729501-04)
Poonam Lodge (723212, 723213)
Pratham (312581/ 82/ 84).

Hotels at Bijapur:
Mayura Adil Shahi
Mayura Adil Shahi Annexe
Sanman
Samrat
Meghraj
Midland Lodge and many other budget hotels provide comfortable accommodation.

Best Season: September to February.

Clothing: Summer- Light tropical, Winter –Light woollen.

264

95

A Little Bit of France

PONDICHERRY
Ex-Chennai

The unknown village of Puddu Cherry was sold by the Raja of Jinji in 1683 AD to M. F. Martin. This was the beginning of French influence upon a hitherto unknown village, which today has become quintessentially French. The city saw its origin in 1739 AD and in 1815, passed into the hands of French colonisers. Like any colonial city, Pondicherry had two distinct city portions, the *Ville Blanche* and the *Ville Noire*, the latter being for the natives. Pondicherry grew in the French tradition with city architecture imitating that of French buildings. The Doric pillars topped by Greek arches, and French domes, gave it a unique look. Ancient churches with beautifully decorated façade dot the landscape. The names of streets and places are reminiscent of the French. Later Shri Aurobindo Ghosh established the Aurobindo Ashram, the city of dawn, north of Pondicherry. This ashram brought about a synthesis of yoga and modern science in an effort to unite the spirit and matter. It endowed Pondicherry with a spiritual character and is now renowned the world over.

Places to See: Matri Mandir; Auroville; Raj Niwas; Romain Rolland Library; Pondicherry Museum; Statue of Mahatma Gandhi; Goubert Salai; Church of the Sacred Heart of Jesus; Botanical Gardens; Church of Notre Dame; Institute of Indology; Aurobindo Ashram.

Excursion: Chidambaram: (65 kms) famous for Nataraja Temple with the roof of the sanctum sanctorum covered with golden plates.

How to Reach: By Air:- Chennai is the nearest airport (166 kms)

By Rail / Road:- Pondicherry is a railhead and is also well connected by road.

Plan your tour by rail

Route: Chennai - 197 kms - Pondicherry

Day	Train No./Name	Dep.	Arr.	From	To
One	855 Pondicherry Fast Passenger	1545	2135	Chennai Beach	Pondicherry
Two/Three/Four	**Stay and Visit Pondicherry**				
Four	854 Villupuram Pass.	1925	2025	Pondicherry	Villupuram
Four	814 Chennai Fast Passenger	2330	0415	Villupuram	Tambaram (Chennai)

Where to Stay: Tel. Code- 0413

Hotels:
3 Star
Pondicherry Ashok (655160-68) Fax: 655140
Website: www.fhrai.com
Anandha Inn (330711) Fax: 331241 Website: www.fhrai.com, www.anandhainn.com E-mail: checkin@anandhainn.com

Budget
International Guest House (336699, 221812) Fax: 334447
Website: www.fhrai.com, http://www.sriaurobindosociety.org
E-mail: sasocty@md2.vsnl.net.in
Seaside Guest House (36494, 21825) Fax: 34447
Website: www.fhrai.com, http://www.sriaurobindosociety.org.in
E-mail: sasocty@md2.vsnl.net.in
and others.

Best Season: Throughout the year.

Clothing: Summer - Light tropical, Winter–Tropical.

96

Nature's Own Habitat

SUNDERBANS
Ex-New Delhi

Sunderbans is the world's largest estuarine forest. Innumerable rivers spanning the entire delta belt flow in criss-cross patterns into the Bay of Bengal. In the land, left by the march of the flowing rivers, is spread the Sunderbans forest. The delta is home to thousands of animals, birds and insects species. Every day the tides of the bay wash in and ebb out of these forests leaving behind the wet earth and several forms of animal life. One of the largest mangrove forest; which is formed by the mixing of river and sea waters, is spread at Sunderbans. Needless to say the winged creatures populate the territory with countless pictures of frolic. Those of the animal kingdom, that can only crawl or slither, live incredible lifestyles. The forest region owes its name to Sundari trees, which once were the pride of the delta.

Places to See: Gosaba (Sir David Hamilton's settlement); Sajnekhali (bird sanctuary on the banks of the Matla and Gumdi rivers); Kalas Dwip (wooded island near the confluence of the river Matla); Bhagabatpur (crocodile project with hatchery and sanctuary); Kanak (nestling place of Olive Ridley turtles); Piyali (gateway to the Sunderbans);Tiger Reserve (a luxurious view of the Bengal tiger).

Animals and Birds in the Park: Tiger, jungle cat, fishing cat, cheetal, wild boar, rhesus monkey, mongoose, crocodiles, Olive Ridley turtle, Salvator lizard, pythons, cobras, herons, egrets, cormorants, fishing eagles, seagulls, kingfishers, black-tailed godwit, little stint, eastern knot, curlew, saintpiper, golden plovers, pintails, white eyed pochards, whistling teals, etc.

How to Reach: By Air:- Calcutta is the nearest airport. By Rail / Road:- Suburban trains take you to Canning, which is near the embarkation points. The entry points at Raidighi, Basanti, Namkhana, and Najat are connected by regular buses to Calcutta.

Plan your tour by rail

Route: New Delhi – 1441 kms – Calcutta - 80 kms - Sunderbans

Day	Train No./Name	Dep.	Arr.	From	To
One	2302/2306 Rajdhani Exp.	1700/1700 -		New Delhi	-
Two	Enroute	-	0955/1245 -		Howrah
	By road and waterway reach Sunderbans.				
Three/Four	Stay and Visit Sunderbans.				
	Back to Calcutta by road on 5th day.				
Five	2301/2305 Rajdhani Exp.	1700/1345 -		Howrah	-
Six	Enroute	-	0950/0950 -		New Delhi

Where to Stay:
Tourist Lodges:
Sajnekhali, Bakkhali and at Piyali.

Conducted trips on vessels with living arrangements on board, are also available.

For further information contact West Bengal Tourist Bureau, 3/2, B.B.D. Bagh, Calcutta. (Ph. 033- 2488271).

Best Season: September to March.

Clothing: Summer - Light tropical, Winter – Tropical.

97

Unfolding a Time Warp

BHUJ (KUTCH)

Ex-Ahmedabad

*U*nexposed and unvisited lies the land of Kutch in Northern Gujarat. Kutch, tempered by the sea and land both, is an experience in unusuals. The virgin sea beaches, a breathtaking landscape, pulsating wildlife, much-celebrated forts, palaces, temples, isolated wastelands, all combine to give Kutch a vibrance of unmatched quality. Nature is blended with the lifestyle of people. The traditions followed are many, as almost eighteen different tribes thrive with their cultural diversity within Kutch. While on a visit to Kutch, there is nothing urbane. Cultural heritage dating back to the original man attracts and captivates a visitor. The region is unusually rich in art ranging from sculpture, plaques, pottery, crowns, coins, cloth embroidery, musical instruments to arms. The designs are unique and close to the earth. It is an experience in history, one of the most rare, to be at Kutch.

Places to See: Ainamahal; Royal Cenotaphs; Sharad Bagh Palace; Pragmahal Palace; Kutch Museum; Ethnology Museum.

Excursions:

Mata No Madh: 1,200-year-old temple.

Lakhpat: Ancient port city, deserted, uninhabited with gigantic tombs and ruins.

Narayan Sarovar: A secret pilgrim centre with temples and five holy lakes

Anjar: Jesal Toral Samadhi and bungalow of James Mac Murdo-specimens of Kutch art.

Bhadreshwar: Stepwells, mosques, temples, a pilgrim centre of the Jain religion.

Mandvi: A beach with tranquil shores, Vijay Vilas Palace, Hawa Mahal.

Banni/Khavda: Desert lands of huge dimensions. Quaint villages warped in time.

Dhola Veera: Archaeological site where excavations led to discoveries.

How to Reach: By Air:- Gandhidham is the nearest airport. By Rail / Road:- Bhuj is a railhead. It is also approachable by road from Gandhidham and Ahmedabad.

Plan your tour by rail

Route: Ahmedabad – 360 kms – Bhuj (Kutch)

Day	Train No./Name	Dep.	Arr.	From	To
One	9601 Sayaji Nagri Exp.	2355	-	Ahmedabad	
Two		-	0645	-	Gandhidham
Two	By road	0800	1000	Gandhidham	Bhuj
Two/Three/ Four/Five	Stay Bhuj and visit environs.				
Five	By Road	1800	2000	Bhuj	Gandhidham
Five	9602 Sayaji Nagri Exp.	2200	-	Gandhidham	-
Six	Enroute	-	0420	-	Ahmedabad

Where to Stay:
Hotels at Bhuj:
Budget
Prince
Garha Safari Lodge
Abha
Anam
Sahara Palace

270

Lakeview
Parkview, and other deluxe / budget hotels provide comfortable accommodation.
For further information contact TCGL, H.K. House, Ashram Road, Ahmedabad. (Ph. 079- 6589172, 6587217).

Best Season: Throughout the year.

Clothing: Summer - Light Tropical, Winter – Tropical.

98

Between the Marble Gorge

JABALPUR
Ex-New Delhi

Jabalpur was the capital of Gond kings in 12th century AD and later it was under the sway of the Kalchuri dynasty, then the Marathas. The skyline is dominated by the 12 century fort, but the singularly striking aspects are the marble rocks at Bheda Ghat. Amidst the highlands of Central India lies the infinitely varied beauty of the marble rocks that rise like pinnacles casting long shadows on the flowing river below. As high as a hundred feet on either side of the Narmada, they produce an effect of encasing the flowing beauty in arms, and convey a serenity beyond words. Captain J. Forsyth has described this spectacle eloquently – "The eye never wearies of the .... effect produced by the broken and reflected sunlight, now glancing from a pinnacle of snow-white marble reared against the deep blue of the sky as from a point of silver; touching here and there with bright lights, the prominence of the middle heights; and again losing itself in the soft bluish grey's of their recesses." The purity of white marble and water vies for your undisturbed attention.

Places to See: Bheda Ghat; Madan Mahal Fort; Sangram Sagar; Baijnamath; Rani Durgavati Museum; Tilwara Ghat; Marble Rocks; Dhuandhar Falls; Chausat Yogini Temple; Soapstone Artefacts.

Excursions: Kanha National Park (165 kms)
Bandhavgarh National Park (164 kms)

How to Reach: By Air:- Jabalpur is an airport.
By Rail / Road:- Jabalpur is a railhead and is also easily approachable by road.

Plan your tour by rail

Route: New Delhi – 916 kms – Jabalpur

Day	Train No./Name	Dep.	Arr.	From	To
One	1450 Mahakoshal Exp.	1620	-	H. Nizamuddin	-
Two	Enroute	-	1030	-	Jabalpur
Two/Three/Four	Stay and Visit Jabalpur.				
Four	2411 Gondwana Express	1540	-	Jabalpur	-
Five	Enroute	-	0720	-	H.Nizamuddin

Where to Stay:.   Tel. Code- 0761

Hotels:
3 Star
The Samdariya (316800-803) Fax: 316354
Website: www.fhrai.com

2 Star
Kalchuri, MPT (321491-93) Fax: 321490
Website: www.fhrai.com E-mail: tigris@gwrl.dot.net.in
Ashoka (318777, 318779) Fax: 341746 Website: www.fhrai.com
Jackson's (323412, 33413/14) Fax: 322066 Website: www.fhrai.com

Budget
Krishna (310318, 21263) Fax: 315153 Website: www.fhrai.com
E-mail: hotelkrishna@hotmail.com
Utsav (26038)
Kartik (24945)
Marble Rocks (MPT)
Lower and Upper Rest House (PWD) and others provide comfortable accommodation.

Best Season: October to May.

Clothing: Summer - Light tropical, Winter – Woollen.

273

Seven Days in a Silver Spoon

ROYAL ORIENT EXPRESS

Ex-Delhi Cantt.

Route: Delhi Cantt. - Chittorgarh - Udaipur - Mehsana - Patan - Ahmedabad - Sasangir - Ahmedpur Mandvi - Diu - Palitana - Sarkhej - Ranakpur - Jaipur - Delhi Cantt.

ON-BOARD ROE: The Royal Orient Express beckons you on a tour of Rajasthan and Gujarat. The train is fully air-conditioned. New coaches have replaced the original saloons of Maharajas and comfort has edged out nostalgia. The two steam engines, with polished brass, shining black body, steam pouring out from nooks, a golden crest, lead you on this pleasurable trip. The magnificent fort of Chittorgarh, ramparts spread out in warlike fashion, the legend of Rani Padmini ,and an evening at Udaipur fill up the day. The site of the Lake palace floating like an iridescent bubble of light on the Pichola Lake is stuff that dreams are made of. The next day in Gujarat brings you the Sun Temple at Modhera, Ran ki Vav stepwell, and the weaving centre at Patan followed by descending down the stepwells of Ahmedabad, being one with the Mahatma's thought at Gandhi Ashram, Sabarmati, and other interesting exposures. The next day, the Sasangir irresistible wild and a peek at the Siddis, the descendants of Abyssinian slaves who mimic the dance of wild animals and birds, almost charm you. The Portuguese flavour at the island of Diu and a visit to Palitana temples and a village and the trip weaves its way to Jaipur, the Pink City, and ends in a grandeur unparalleled.

ITINERARY:

Day 1 – Leave Delhi Cantt. on Wednesday at 1500 hours. Tea and Dinner on-board.

Day 2 –Visit Chittorgarh and Udaipur.

Day 3 –Visit Mehsana, Patan, and Ahmedabad.

Day 4 –Visit Sasangir Lion Sanctuary, Ahmedpur Mandvi beach and Diu.

Day 5 – Visit 863 Jain temples at Palitana and Vishalla Village, Sarkhej.

Day 6 –Visit Ranakpur Jain temples.

Day 7 –Visit Jaipur.

Day 8 –Arrive at Delhi Cantt. in the morning (0700 hrs.)

Stay: On-board The Royal Orient Express.

Season: September to April

Tariff: September and April (single occupancy US $ 263 per day, sharing US $ 150/ per day, 3- berth Cabin sharing US$ 132 per day).

October to March (single occupancy US $ 350/ per day, sharing US $ 200/ per day, 3- berth Cabin sharing US$ 175 per day). (Half fare for children between 5 and 12 years of age if accompanied by parents).

Clothing: Summer - Light Tropical, Winter– Tropical

Booking: Central Reservation Office,A/6, State Emporia Building, Baba Kharak Singh Marg, New Delhi-110001. Tel: 3744015,3364724. Fax: 3367050
E-mail: tcgl.del@rmt.sril.in
Website: www.royalorienttrain.com
www.gujarattourism.com

Romance of the Orient

PALACE ON WHEELS

Ex-Delhi Cantt.

Route: Delhi Cantt. - Jaipur - Jaisalmer - Jodhpur - Ranthambore - Chittorgarh - Udaipur - Bharatpur - Agra - Delhi Cantt.

ON-BOARD POW: The mystique and exotica of the East can be experienced in the royal extravaganza that rolls on the wheels – the *Palace On Wheels.* The romance of Rajasthan and its Maharajas is known the world over. They celebrated the land and lived in a lavish lifestyle. Numerous royal ceremonies and an elaborate hunt, filled up the terrain. The Maharajas have gone but not the romance associated with them. The royal palaces, courts, gardens, forts, and the cities that they fondly laid and embellished are all there under the Rajasthan sun. Each city on the itinerary has a distinctive culture to unfold. The artefacts, armaments, and the ornamentation of buildings too differ from place to place. Spread on a canvas is a beautiful picture of once famous royalty, decorated to the hilt, with tales of valour and an indomitable spirit. The sandstone fort at Jaisalmer with 99 bastions over the yellow sand presents a unique sight. The gigantic buildings, palaces, and the Mehrangarh fort of Jodhpur, stilled like a cry in the desert, are quite an attractive proposition. In the middle of the tour, the tigers of Ranthambore bring the excitable wild close to the tourists. The birds of the sanctuary at Bharatpur bring the pleasures of the avian kingdom to camera-happy tourists. The crowning glory comes when one is face to face with the Taj Mahal. No experience on earth can be equal to being at the Taj. Travelling on POW is as if one is living a pipe dream with different patterns becoming visible with each puff. The flavour is strong, heady, and lasting. The metropolis of Delhi welcomes you back on the last day of the tour before royal exclusivity is lost in the crowd.

ITINERARY:

Day 1 – Leave Delhi Cantt. on Wednesday at 1745 hours. Tea and Dinner on-board.

Day 2 –Visit Jaipur.

Day 3 – Witness the spirit of the desert at Jaisalmer.

Day 4 – Visit and imbibe the magnificence of Jodhpur.

Day 5 – See the royal tiger at Ranthambore, and the impregnable fort of Chittorgarh.

Day 6 – Visit the royal city of Udaipur.

Day 7 – Visit Bharatpur and the dream in marble at Agra-Taj Mahal.

Day 8 – Arrive at Delhi Cantt. in the morning at 0600 hours.

Stay: On-board the *Palace On Wheels.*

Season: September to April.

Tariff: September and April (single occupancy US $ 395 per day, double occupancy US $ 295/ per day and triple occupancy US $ 240/ per day).
October to March (single occupancy US $ 485/ per day, double occupancy US $ 350/ per day and triple occupancy US $ 285/ per day).
(Half fare for children between 5 to 12 years of age).

Clothing: Summer - Light tropical, Winter– Woollen

Booking: Tourist Reception Centre, Bikaner House, New Delhi-110001. Tel: 3381884, 3386069. E-mail address at Jaipur office: rtdc@jp1.dot.net.in

The Reservations/cancellation of bookings on Palace on Wheels is as per the following terms & conditions.

Booking:
  i) 20% of ticket value at the time of booking.
  ii) 80% of the ticket value 30 day prior to the departure.

Cancellation:
  i) 5% of ticket value 60 days prior to the departure.
  ii) 20% of ticket value 30-59 days prior to the departure.
  iii) 50% of the ticket value 15-59 days prior to the departure.
  iv) 100% of the ticket value 14 days prior to the departure.

Exclusive Charter:
The total capacity of the trains is 104 pax. The entire train can be chartered by paying for 98 pax.

Index

Achalgarh, 32
Adhai-din-ka-Jhonpra, 205
Adinath Temple, 156
Agatti, 71, 72
Agha Khan Palace, 103
Agra, 220, 221, 276, 277
Aguada Fort, 67
Aguada, 66
Ahmed Shah Masjid, 141
Ahmed Shah, 141
Ahmedabad, 141, 269, 270, 274, 275
Ahmedpur Mandvi, 275
Aihole, 263
Ainamahal, 269
Aizawl, 52
Ajaipal Chauhan, 205
Ajanta, 155, 161
Ajatshatru's Fort, 152
Ajmer, 205
Akbar, 186
Akbar's Tomb, 221
Akshayavat, 210
Alappuzha, 81
Allahabad Fort, 210
Allahabad, 190, 210, 211, 28
Allen Forest Zoo, 132
Almora, 59, 60
Alwar, 182
Amar Singh Palace, 138
Amarnath Caves, 3
Amer Fort, 223
Amravana, 152
Amritsar, 186
Anand Bhawan, 210
Anjar, 270
Anjuna, 66
Annadale, 12
Arabian Sea, 66

Aravalli hills, 32
Aravalli Range, 182
Aravalli, 178
Ardhkwari, 199
Ashoka Pillar, 197, 210
Ashoka(s), 154
Ashoka, 136
Assam, 174
Auniati, 253
Aurangabad Caves, 160
Aurangabad, 160
Aurangzeb, 125, 160
Aurobindo Ashram, 265
Auroville, 265
Avantipur, 3
Avantipura, 213
Awadh, 122
Ayodhya, 15
Azeemabad, 136

Badami, 263
Bade Ganeshji ka Mandir, 213
Badrinath Temple, 28
Badrinath, 27, 28, 29, 207
Bagdogra, 7, 21
Bageshwar, 59
Bagh-e-Bahu, 138
Bagru, 223
Bahadurshah, 74
Bahu Fort, 138
Baijnath, 23, 59
Bakkhali, 107
Bakreshwar, 193
Balighai, 158
Balsamand Lake, 230
Bamni Dadar, 171
Banaras Hindu University, 149
Bandhavgarh National Park, 272

Bangalore, 118, 163, 164, 191, 246, 261
Banganga, 199
Bangaram, 71
Bangla Sahib, 98
Banke-Behari Temple, 216
Bara Bazaar, 37
Bara Imambara, 122
Baroli, 249
Barsana, 216
Basilica of Bom Jesus, 66
Bassi Wildlife Sanctuary, 249
Batasia Loop, 6
Batote, 47
Bay of Bengal, 267, 76, 79
Baz Bahadur, 242
Beleswar, 158
Belgaum, 261, 263
Bellary, 261
Belur Math, 107
Belur, 163
Betwa, 244
Bhadra Hanuman, 160
Bhadreshwar, 270
Bhagamathi, 111
Bhagat Singh, 132
Bhagirathi, 28
Bhainsrorgarh Wildlife Sanctuary, 249
Bhaironath, 199
Bhaja caves, 258
Bharat Bhawan, 237
Bharat Mandir, 207
Bharat Mata Temple, 149
Bharatpur, 180, 276, 277
Bheda Ghat, 272
Bhillama, 160
Bhimbetka, 255
Bhimtal, 56
Bhitargaon, 132
Bhojeshwar Temple, 256
Bhojpur, 256
Bhopal, 237, 256
Bhubaneswar, 159, 77, 79
Bhuj, 270

Bhuntar, 16
Bhutia Basti, 6
Bhutia language, 20
Bibi ka Maqbara, 160
Bihar Sharif, 152
Bihar, 136
Bijapur, 249, 263, 264
Bijli Mahadev Temple, 15
Bimbisara's Jail, 152
Bir and Billing, 23
Birla Mandir, 223
Birla Planetarium, 107
Bithoor, 132
Bodh Gaya, 195
Bodhgaya, 136
Bodhi Tree, 195
Bodhisattva Maitreya Temple, 165
Bolpur, 193
Bom Baim, 102
Bombay, 102
Brahma Temple, 67
Brahmaputra, 253
Brihadeshwara Temple, 146
Brindaban Garden, 246
Buddha Stupa, 197
Buddha, 154, 195
Buddhism, 152
Buddhist Council, 152, 197
Buddhist Philosophy, 19
Buddhists, 19
Bhutan, 18
Byrant Park, 25

C.P. Muzzey, 25
Calangute, 66
Calcutta, 6, 7, 21, 79, 107, 174, 18, 193, 268,
Calico Museum of Textile, 141
Calicut, 128
Camel's Back, 9
Canning, 268
Capt. Young, 9
Captain J. Forsyth, 272
Chail, 12
Chakratirath Beach, 74

Chamba, 62, 63
Chamoli, 28
Champavati, 62
Champhai, 52
Chamunda Devi Temple, 62
Chamundi Hills, 246
Chandi Devi Temple, 208
Chandigarh, 12, 13, 16, 125
Chandni Chowk, 97
Chandragupta Maurya, 136, 163
Chandrashekhar Azad, 132, 244
Channakeshava Temple, 163
Char Chinar, 3
Charan Paduka, 199
Charlotte Lake, 54
Charminar, 111
Chashme Shahi, 3
Chath Puja, 135
Chaturbhuj Temple, 156
Chaugan, 62
Chaunsat Yogini, 156
Chaurasi, 158
Chausat Yogini Temple, 272
Chenab, 47
Chennai, 25, 26, 34, 81, 93, 265, 114,
    144, 146, 176,
Cherapunji, 37
Cheriapalli, 81
Chidambaram, 265
Chilika Lake, 79
China, 18
Chintaman Ganesh Temple, 213
Chitradurga Fort, 261
Chitragupta Temple, 156
Chitrakoot, 189, 190
Chitravarti, 191
Chittor Fort, 249
Chittor, 249
Chittorgarh, 249, 274, 275, 276, 277
Chota Imambara, 122
Chowpatty, 102
Christ Church, 12
Chungthang, 20
Church of St. Francis of Assissi, 66
City Palace Museum, 223

Cochin, 72, 84
Coimbatore, 34, 35
Colva, 66
Coonoor, 34
Corbett National Park, 56, 169
Cubbon Park, 118
Cycloopean Wall, 152

Dakhinpat, 253
Daksh Mahadev Temple, 208
Dal Lake, 3, 5
Dalai Lama, 23
Dalhousie, 43
Daman Ganga, 91
Daman, 91
Darbar Sahib, 186
Darbar, 199
Dargah of Peer Budhan, 138
Dargah Sharif, 205
Darjeeling Himalayan Railway, 6
Darjeeling, 6, 7
Daulatabad, 160
Dayal Bagh, 221
Deccan, 263
Deeg, 180, 240
Dehradun, 10
Delhi Cantt. 274, 276
Delhi, 3, 23, 27, 28, 32, 40, 43, 45, 47,
    50, 56, 59, 62, 74, 97, 138, 169,
    199, 220, 230, 233, 240, 277
Deogarh, 249
Devaka, 91
Devaki, 215
Dhanolti, 10
Dharamsala, 23, 24
Dhauladhar mountain, 43
Dhuandhar Falls, 272
Digha, 107
Dilwara Jain temples, 32
Dimapur, 31
Diu Fort, 74
Diu, 74, 274
Doddabetta Peak, 34
Dodi Tal, 28
Do-Drul Chorten, 20

Dona Paula, 66
Dorothy's Seat, 56
Drass, 45
Dubdi Monastery, 19
Dudhsagar, 67
Duladeo Temple, 156
Durgiana Temple, 186
Durtlang, 52
Dussehra, 15
Dwarikadhish Temple, 215
Dwarka, 141

Eklingji, 227
Elephanta Caves, 102
Ellora, 161
Emperor Jehangir, 3
Enchey Monastery, 19
Ernakulam, 72, 84
Essel World, 102
Ethipothala Waterfalls, 111
Ettumanoor, 81

F.J. Shore, 9
Falaknuma Palace, 111
Fambong La Wildlife Sanctuary, 20
Fateh Burj, 180
Fateh Sagar, 227
Fatehpur Sikri, 221
Fidai Khan, 125
Fishing Nets, 84
Forest Research Institute, 10
Fort St. George, 114
Fortem Du Mar, 74

Gadi Sagar Lake, 233
Gandhi Ashram, 274
Gandhi Chowk, 43
Gandhi Memorial, 93
Gandhi Stupa, 130
Gandhidham, 270
Ganga, 132, 149, 197, 207, 210, 27,
  28
Gangotri, 207, 27, 28, 29
Gangtok, 20, 21
Garamurh, 253

Gateway of India, 102
Gaumukh, 32
Gaya, 195
General Dyer, 186
Ghantai Temple, 156
Ghoom, 7
Ghrishneshwar Temple, 161
Gita, 149
GMVN, 29
Goa, 66
goddess Meenakshi, 128
Goindwal, 187
Gokarneshwar Temple, 215
Gokul, 216
Gol Gumbaz, 263
Golconda Fort, 111
Golden Temple, 186
Golghar, 136
gompa, 165
Gomti, 122
Gopal Bhawan, 240
Gopalpur-on-sea, 79
Gosaba, 267
Govardhan, 216
Grand Anicut (Kallanai), 144
Griddhkuta, 152
Gser-Khang, 165
Gtsug Lha-Khang, 165
Gujarat, 269, 274
Gujari Mahal, 235
Gulmarg, 3
Gun Hill, 9
Gupt-Godavari, 189
Guru Gobind Singh, 27, 136
Guru Ramdas, 186
Guru Rimpoche, 20
Guru Tegh Bahadur, 187
Gurushikhar, 32
Guwahati, 38, 174, 253
Gwalior, 235, 244

H.S. Taylor, 25
Hailey National Park, 169
Hajipur, 136, 197
Halebid, 163

Hampi, 261
Hanuman Dhara, 189
Hanuman Temple, 210
Har Mandir Sahib, 186
Haridwar, 28, 29, 207, 208
Hariyala, 50
Har-ki-Pauri, 207, 208
Harmandir, 136
Harshavardhana, 134
Harshavimochanna Perumal Temple, 146
Harsiddhi Temple, 213
Hassan, 163, 164
Hathipaon, 9
Hawa Mahal, 223
Hawaldar Sohan Singh, 27
Hazoor Sahib, 187
Hazrat Ubaidullah, 71
Hazratbal Shrine, 3
Hazratganj, 122
Hemkund Sahib, 27
Himachal Pradesh, 12, 15
Himalayan   Mountaineering Institute, 6
Hindola Mahal, 242
Hindus, 19
Holy Guru Lhedo, 20
Hospet, 261
Howrah, 21, 193
Hoysaleswara Temple, 163
HPTDC, 12
Humayun's Tomb, 98
Hurka, 59
Hussain Sagar, 111
Hyder Mahal, 111
Hyderabad, 111, 130

Ibrahim Roza, 263
Idukki, 176
Imphal, 30
India Gate, 97
Indian Military Academy, 10
Indore, 242
Iron Fort, 180

J & K Govt. Tourist Reception Centre, 5
Jabalpur, 172, 272, 273
Jagannath Temple, 76
Jagannathi Devi Temple, 15
Jagdish Temple, 227
Jageshwar, 59
Jahaj Mahal, 242
Jai Samand Lake, 182
Jai Vilas Palace, 235
Jaigarh Fort, 223
Jain Glass Temple, 132
Jain Indrasabha, 161
Jaipur, 178, 179, 223, 274, 275, 276, 277
Jaisalmer, 233, 276, 277
Jajmau, 132
Jakhu Hill, 12
Jal Mahal, 223
Jalandhar, 74
Jalan Museum, 136
Jallianwala Bagh, 186
Jama Masjid, 97
Jambukeshwara Temple, 144
Jami Masjid, 141
Jammu Tawi, 4, 46, 199
Jammu, 41, 138
Jampore, 91
Janamashtmi, 28
Janki Mandir, 244
Jankikund, 189
Jantar Mantar, 98, 223
Jaswant Thada, 230
Jateshwar Mahadev Temple, 149
Jawahar Burj, 180
Jehangir Mahal, 244
Jew Town, 84
Jhamwar, 62
Jhansi, 157, 190, 244
Jim Corbett, 169
Jivaka's Mango Garden, 152
Job Charnock, 107
Jodhpur, 230, 276, 277
Jogi Mahal, 178
John Sullivan, 34

Juhu, 102
Jumma Masjid, 263
Jwalamukhi Temple, 23
jyotirlingas, 149,161, 202

Kabi Lungchok, 20
Kadmath, 72
Kaibhya Rishi, 207
Kailana Lake, 230
Kailasha Hindu Temple, 161
Kajal Rani Caves, 202
Kakatapur, 158
Kal Bhairav Temple, 149, 213
Kalai, 91
Kalas Dwip, 267
Kalashetra, 114
Kalhatti Waterfalls, 34
Kalidasa, 213
Kalijai, 79
Kalika Mata Temple, 249
Kalimath, 59
Kalinjar, 189
Kalpeni, 71, 72
Kamadgiri, 189
Kamtek, 213
Kanak, 267
Kanchenjunga, 6
Kandariya Mahadeo, 156
Kangra Museum of Art, 23
Kangra Valley, 24
Kangra, 23, 24, 43, 63
Kanha National Park, 171, 272
Kannauj, 134
Kanniyakumari, 93
Kanpur, 132
Kapaleeswarar Temple, 114
Kargil, 45
Karla, 258, 259
Karnada Tank, 152
Kasar Devi Temple, 59
Kashi Vishwanath Temple, 149
Kathgodam, 57, 60
Katra, 138, 199
Kausani, 59
Kavaratti, 71, 72

Kaveri, 144, 202
Kaziranga, 174
Kedarnath, 27, 28, 29, 207
Kempty Falls, 9
Keoladeo Bird Sanctuary, 240
Keoladeo National Park, 180
Kerala, 71, 176
Khajjiar, 43, 62
Khajuraho, 156, 157, 189
Khandala, 258, 259
Khecheopalri Lake, 19
Khonghampat Orchidarium, 30
Khuda Baksh Oriental Library, 136
Khuldabad, 160
Khurpa Tal, 56
Khwairamband Bazaar, 30
Khwaja Moinuddin Chisti, 205
King Bimbisara, 152
Kinnaur, 166
Kirkee Fatehnagar, 160
Kirti Stambh, 249
Kite Museum, 141
Kochi, 81
Kodaikanal Lake, 25
Kodaikanal, 25, 26
Kodumbalur, 144
Kohinoor, 220
Kohinoor, 95
Kolak, 91
Kolhapur, 102
Kollam, 81
Konaka Dugra Temple, 130
Konark, 155
Konark, 76
Kovalam beach, 88
Krishna, 215
Kud, 138
Kud, 47
Kufri, 12
Kullu valley, 15, 16
Kullu-Manali, 16
Kumaon, 50, 59
Kumarakom, 81
Kumbh Mela, 211
Kumbha Shyam Temple, 249

Kundupur, 197
Kuruma, 158
Kushabhadra, 158
Kutch, 269
Ladakh, 40
Lahaul, 166
Lake Palace, 227
Lakhpat, 269
Lakshadweep, 71
Lakshman Jhoola, 207
Lakshmana Temple, 156
Lakshmi Narayan (group of) temples, 62
Lakshmi Narayan Temple, 98
Lal Chowk, 3
Lal Tibba, 9
Lambs' Rock, 34
Landour, 9
LBS National Academy of Administration, 9
Le Corbusier, 125
Le Pakshi, 191
Lebong Race Course, 6
Leh, 40, 41
Lepcha, 19
Lhasa, 40
Loktak Lake, 30
(Lord) Shiva, 27, 32
(Lord) Vishnu, 66
Lodhi Gardens, 98
Lodurva, 233
Lohagad Fort, 258
Lonavala, 258, 259
Lord Brahma, 205, 210
Lord Buddha, 134, 152, 197
Lord Dalhousie, 43
Lord Gomateshwara, 163
Lord Mahavir, 152, 197
Lord Maleswara Temple, 130
Lord Raghunathji, 15
Lord Shiva, 130, 191
Lord Sundareswarar, 128
Losar, 165
Lothal, 141
Lotus Temple, 98

Lucknow Residency, 122
Lucknow, 122
Lunglei, 52
Luni Fort, 230

M. F. Martin, 265
Madan Mahal Fort, 272
Madan Mohan Temple, 216
Madhurapuri, 128
Madurai, 128, 144, 176, 25
Mahabharata, 27, 130, 202, 249
Mahabodhi Temple, 195
Mahakaleshwar, 213
Mahamandir Temple, 230
Mahamastakabisheka festival, 163
Mahamaya Temple, 138
mahaparinirvana, 197
Mahatma Gandhi, 141
Mahavan, 216
Maheshwar, 202
Mahishmati, 202
Maitreya, 45
Majuli, 253
Malayalam, 84
Malcolm Hailey, 169
Malik-e-Maidan, 263
Man Mandir Palace, 235
Manak Chowk, 233
Manali, 15, 16, 41
Mandore, 230
Mandu, 242
Mandvi, 270
Manipur, 30
Manmahal, 205
Mansa Devi Temple, 208
Mansar Lake, 139
Mapusa, 66
Marble Palace, 107
Marble Rocks, 272
Margao, 66
Mariani, 254
Marina Beach, 114
Marine Drive, 102
Mark Twain's, 6
Martyrs' Memorial, 136

Mata No Madh, 269
Matangeswara Temple, 156
Matheran, 54
Mathura, 215, 216, 240
Matri Mandir, 265
Mawsynram, 38
McLeodganj, 23
Mecca, 71
Meenaskhi Sundareswarar Temple, 128
Meerabai, 249
Meghdoot, 213
Mehrangarh Fort, 230
Mehrangarh, 276
Mehsana, 275
Menal, 249
Mewar, 227
Minicoy, 72
Miramar, 66
Mirza Ghalib, 220
Modhera, 141, 274
Mogalarajapuram Cave, 130
Mohammed Adil Shah, 263
Mormugao, 66
Moti Daman, 91
Moti Jheel, 132
Moti Tibba, 43
Mount Abu, 32
Mt. Khangchendzonga, 19, 20
Mudumalai Sanctuary, 34
Mulbek, 45, 46
Mumba Devi, 102
Mumbai, 54, 66, 71, 97, 102, 258, 259, 263, 264
Mumtaz Mahal, 220
Murshidabad, 107
Mussoorie, 9, 10
Mysore Palace, 246
Mysore, 246

Nagaraj Temple, 93
Nagarjunasagar, 111
Nagore, 147
Nagpur, 102

Nagpur, 213
Nagri, 249
Nahargarh Fort, 223
Naina Peak, 56
Naini Lake, 56
Nainital, 56, 169
Nakki Lake, 32
Nalabana, 79
Nalanda University, 134
Nalanda, 134, 136, 152
Namchi, 19
Namgyal Tsemo, 40
Nanarao Peshwa, 132
Nandan, 107
Nandgaon, 216
Nandi, 32, 164
Nani Daman, 91
Narayan Sarovar, 269
Narmada, 202, 213, 272
Nawabganj Bird Sactuary, 122, 132
Nek Chand, 125
Nepal, 18, 50
New Delhi, 9, 12, 13, 15, 16, 21, 30, 37, 41, 66, 84, 88, 91, 102, 107, 111, 114, 118, 122, 125, 132, 134, 136, 141, 149, 152, 156, 158, 160, 165, 171, 178, 180, 182, 186, 189, 191, 193, 195, 197, 202, 205, 207, 210, 213, 215, 220, 227, 235, 237, 240, 242, 244, 249, 255, 267, 272,
New Jalpaiguri, 7, 21
Nilgiri, 34
Nilkanth Temple, 189
Nirnajana, 195
Nishat Bagh, 3
Nubra Valley, 40

Observatory Hill, 6
Omkareshwar, 202
Ooty, 35
Orchha, 244
Osman Sagar, 111
Osmania University, 111

286

Padmanabhaswami Temple, 88
Padmini, 274
Pahalgam, 3
Paisuni, 189
Paithan, 102
Palace on Wheels, 277
Palampur, 24
Palaruvi Waterfalls, 88
Palitana, 275
Panaji, 66
Panna National Park, 156
Pantnagar, 50, 57, 60
Parliament House, 97
Parshurama, 66
Parsvanath Temple, 156
Parthasarathy Temple, 114
Parvati, 93
Patal Bhuwaneshwar, 50
Patalpuri Temple, 210
Pathankot, 24, 43, 63
Patliputra, 136
Patna, 136, 195, 197
Patnitop, 47, 48, 138
Pattadakal, 263
Pauri Garhwal, 169
Pawapuri, 134, 136, 152
Peer Khoh, 138
Pemayangtse Monastery, 18
Percy Brown, 242
Periyar sanctuary, 176
Phensong Monastery, 20
Phodong Monastery, 20
Pichola Lake, 227, 274
Pinjore Garden, 125
Pipaleshwar Temple, 215
Pipili, 158
Pippala Cave, 152
Pirpanjal mountains, 47
Pirpanjal range, 43
Pirpanjals, 62
Pithalkora, 161
Pithoragarh, 50
Piyali, 267
Point Calimere, 147
Pondicherry, 265

Ponmudi, 88
Porbandar, 141
Portuguese, 74, 91, 274
Prayag, 210
Prince of Wales Museum, 102
Prince Siddharth, 195
Project Tiger, 169, 171, 178
Prophet Muhammad, 71
Pulinkunnu, 81
Purana Quila, 97
Puri, 76, 77, 79
Pushkar Fair, 205
Pushkar, 205
Pushpapur, 136
Puttaparthy, 191

Queen's Bath, 261
Queen's Necklace, 102
Quli Qutub shah, 111
Qutub Minar, 98

Rabdentse Ruins, 18
Rabindra Sangeet, 107, 193
Rabindranath Tagore, 43, 193
Rachamatta, 163
Rachol Seminary, 67
Raghunath Temple, 138
Raghunathji Temple, 15, 32
Rai Gufa, 50
Rai Praveen Mahal, 244
Raja Jagat Singh, 15
Raja Jambu Lochan, 138
Raja Kelkar Museum, 103
Raja Sahil Varman, 62
Raja Sansar Chand, 23
Rajaji Sanctuary, 10
Rajasthan, 182, 274, 276
Rajgaddi, 202
Rajghat, 98
Rajgir, 134, 136, 152
Rajpur Bibi, 141
Rajtadok, 160
Rajwada, 202
Ram Bagh, 221
Ram Jhoola, 207

287

Ramachandi, 158
Ramagiri, 213
Ramaswamy Temple, 146
Ramayana, 202
Ramcharitmanas, 189
Ramganga National Park, 169
Ramnagar, 170
Rangaji Temple, 216
Rangeshwar Temple, 215
Rani Ahilyabai, 202
Rani Durgavati Museum, 272
Rani Roopmati, 242
Ranikhet, 59
Ranjit Singh, 186
Ranthambore Fort, 178
Ranthambore, 178, 179, 276, 277
Rao Jodha, 230
Rashtrapati Bhawan, 97
Rathyatra, 76
Ratnagar, 195
Rawal Jaisal, 233
Red Fort, 97, 221
Reis Magos Church, 67
Rishikesh, 28, 29, 207, 208
Rock Fort, 144
Rock Garden, 125
Roerich's, 15, 118
Rohit Fort, 230
Rowriah (Jorhat), 254
Royal Orient, 274, 275
Rudreshwar Temple, 67
Rudyard Kipling, 66

Sabaramti, 274
Sabarmati Ashram, 141
Sadar Manzil, 237
Saheliyon-ki-Bari, 227
Sai Baba, 191
Sajnekhali, 267
Salarjung Museum, 111
Sanasar, 47, 48, 139
Sandipani Ashram, 213
Sangacholing Monastery, 18
sangam, 210, 211
Sangam, 28

Sanganer, 223
Sankar Gompa, 40
Sansi, 187
Sanskrit manuscripts, 19
Sapt Rishi Ashram, 208
Saptparni, 152
Sarangapani Temple, 146
Saraswati Kund, 215
Saraswati Mahal Library, 146
Saraswati, 210
Sariska Palace, 182
Sariska, 182
Sarnath, 149
Sas Bahu ka Mandir, 235
Sasangir, 274, 275
Sat Tal, 56
Satapada, 79
Sati Ansuya, 189
Satmatrika Temples, 202
Sawai (Raja) Jaisingh, 223
Sawai Madhopur, 179
Second World War, 30
Sengge Namgyal(s), 40
Shaheed Minar, 31, 107
Shahjahan, 220
Shahjahanabad, 97
Shakti Sthal, 98
Shalimar Bagh, 3
Shankaracharya temple, 3
Shankaracharya, 27
Shanti Stupa, 197
Shantiniketan, 193
Shaukat Mahal, 237
Shenbaganur Museum, 25
Shergol, 45
Shillong, 37, 38
Shimla, 12, 13, 166
Shingbha Rhododendron Sanctuary, 20
Shipra, 213
Shir Omkar Mandhata Siddhnath Temple, 202
Shiv Niwas Palace, 227
Shiva, 93
Shivanand Ashram, 207

Shravanabelagola, 163
Shri Aurobindo Ghosh, 265
Shri Bhagwati Temple, 67
Shri Govindjee Temple, 30
Shri Radhakrishna Temple, 132
Siddhaval, 213
Sidi Bashir mosque(s), 141
Sidi Sayyid mosque, 141
Sikkim Research Institute of Tibetology, 19
Sikkim Time Corportion, 20
Sikkim, 18
Siliguri, 19, 21
Siliserh Lake, 182
Sims' Park, 34
Simtola, 59
Singhik, 20
Sir George Everest, 9
Sisodia Rani ka Bagh, 223
Sobha Singh's, 23
Solapur, 264
Sonamarg, 3
Sphatikshila, 189
Spiti, 165
Spituk Gompa, 40
Srinagar, 3, 4, 5, 28, 41, 46
Srirangam Temple, 144
Se Cathedral, 66
Subhas Chandra Bose, 43
Suchindram, 93
Sudh Mahadev, 47
Sukhna Lake, 125
Sultanpur Lodhi, 187
Sun Temple, 155
Sunderbans, 107, 267
Sunehri Kothi, 178
Suraj Mal, 180, 240
Suraj Sen, 235
Surajpur Baragaon, 134
Surinsar Lake, 139
Suru river, 45
Surya, 158
Suryakund, 28
Swami Vivekananda, 93
Swamimalai, 147

Swarg Dwar, 76
Swarna Bhandar, 152

Tabo, 165, 166
Taj Mahal, 160, 220, 221, 276, 277
Taj-ul Masjid, 237
Tamdil Lake, 52
Tansen's Tomb, 235
Tantya Tope, 132
Taptkund, 28
Tara Devi Temple, 193
Taragarh Fort, 205
Taran Taran, 187
Tawi river, 138
Taxila, 215
Teli ka Mandir, 235
Temi Tea Garden, 19
Temple of Bajreshwari Devi, 23
Thanjavur, 146, 147
Tharangambadi, 146
The Glen, 12
Thirubuvaiyaru, 147
Thiruvaiyaru music festival, 146
Thiruvananthapuram, 93
Thyagaraja, 146
Tibet, 50
Tibetan, 19
Tiger Hill, 6
Tipu's Palace, 118
Tiruchirapalli, 128, 144
Tirumalai Nayak Palace, 128
Tiruvanaik, 144
Tiruvarur, 147
Tlawng, 52
Tomb of Hoshang Shah, 242
Tomb of Itmad-ud-Daula, 221
Tonk, 178
Trichy(s), 144
Trichy, 147
Trikuta Mountains, 199
Trivandrum, 88
Triveni Ghat, 207
Tsomgo Lake, 20
Tuirial, 52
Tulsi Manas Mandir, 149

Tulsidas, 189
Tungabhadra Dam, 261

Udagamandalam, 34
Udaipur, 32, 227, 274, 275, 276, 277
Udayagiri Fort, 93
Ugra Narasimha, 261
Ujjayni (Ujjain), 213
Ulka Devi (Temple), 50
Ulsoor Lake, 118
Umaid Bhawan Palace, 230
Umiam Lake, 37
Urgyan Dzong, 45
Utensils Museum, 141
Uttar Kashi, 28
Uttaraini, 50

Vadodra (Baroda), 141
Vagator, 66
Vaigai River, 128
Vailankanni, 147
Vaishali, 136, 197
Vaishno Devi Temple, 15
Vaishno Devi, 138, 199
Vajrasana, 195
Valiapalli, 81
Valley of Flowers, 27
Van Vihar, 237
Vapi, 91
Varanasi, 149, 211
Vattakottai, 93
Vayaloor, 144
Vedha Shala, 213
Venuvana, 152
Versova, 102
Victoria Memorial, 107
Victoria Terminus, 102
Vidayadhar, 223

Vidhan Sabha, 118
Vijai Mandir Palace, 182
Vijay Stambh, 249
Vijayanagar, 191
Vijayawada, 130
Vinay Vilas Mahal, 182
Vinayaka Temple, 144, 149
Virupaksha Temple, 261
Visapur Fort, 258
Vishnupad, 195
Vishnupur, 107
Vishram Ghat, 215
Vishvakarma Cave, 161
Vishwa Bharti, 193
Vishwanath Temple, 156
Vithala Temple, 261
Vivekananda Rock Memorial, 93
Vrindavan, 216

Wakha Rgyal, 46
Wakha, 45
Wards Lake, 37
Wenlock downs, 34
West Bengal, 18
Western Ghats, 25, 54, 81, 258
Wildflower Hall, 12
Wodeyars, 246
World Wildlife Fund, 169

Yamnotri, 27, 28, 29, 207
Yamuna, 28, 210, 215
Yuksom, 19
Yumthang, 20

Zangsti, 40
Zanskar range, 45
Zoological Gardens, 107